LANDSCAPES OF LOSS

LANDSCAPES OF LOSS

THE NATIONAL PAST IN POSTWAR FRENCH CINEMA

Naomi Greene

PRINCETON UNIVERSITY PRESS   PRINCETON, NEW JERSEY

1999

Library of Congress Cataloging-in-Publication Data
Greene, Naomi, 1942–
Landscapes of loss : the national past in postwar French cinema /
Naomi Greene.
p. cm.
Includes bibliographical references and index.
ISBN 0–691–02959–8 (cloth : alk. paper).—
ISBN 0–691–00475–7
(pbk. : alk. paper)
1. Motion pictures—France—History. 2. Motion pictures—Social
aspects—France. 3. France—In motion pictures. I. Title.
PN1993.5.F7G72 1999
791.43′658—dc21   98–35156 CIP

This book has been composed in Janson

The paper used in this publication meets the minimum
requirements of ANSI/NISO Z39.48-1992 (R1997)
(*Permanence of Paper*)

http://pup.princeton.edu

Printed in the United States of America

10 9 8 7 6 5 4 3 2 1

Contents

Acknowledgments   vii

I. Introduction   3

II. Alain Resnais: The Ghosts of History   31

III. Battles for Memory: Vichy Revisited   64

IV. Bertrand Tavernier: History in the Present Tense   98

V. Memory and Its Losses: Troubled Dreams of Empire   130

VI. *A la recherche du temps perdu*: The Specter of Populism   159

Epilogue   190

Notes   195

Index   227

Acknowledgments _____

A SPECIAL THANKS TO:

The Borchard Foundation for allowing me to begin this book in a place that was not only beautiful but charged with memories of the French past;

Jacqueline Simons for her insightful comments concerning many chapters;

Paul Slater for his meticulous help in preparing the manuscript;

Mary Murrell for her support not only as an editor but also as a friend.

LANDSCAPES OF LOSS

I

Introduction

Myth and Memory

One of the most striking phenomena on the French political and cultural landscape of recent decades is, surely, a preoccupation with the national past and the ways it has been remembered. Not only has this preoccupation found an important echo in French cinema but films have played, and continue to play, a vital role in the way France remembers its past and, consequently, conceives of its present. That role is the subject of this book: through an analysis of selected figures and directions in postwar French cinema, it explores the ways in which films have both reflected and formed national images past and present.

In the introduction to *Les lieux de mémoire*—a work that has done much to shape the current meditation on French history and memory—historian Pierre Nora announces both the preoccupation with a certain tradition of national historical memory and the sense that it is being lost. "We speak so much of memory," laments an eloquent Nora, "only because it is no longer there."[1] This observation leaves no doubt that the current meditation on the national past reflects the attitudes and needs, the uncertainties and fears, of the present. Of course, France is by no means the only country in which history takes on the color of the present. Every nation creates images of its past that respond to contemporary modes of thought and feeling. But the weight of the past, and, consequently, the significance it holds for the present, are particularly heavy in France precisely because history has long provided such a crucial dimension of that country's national identity. A powerful source of collective identity and pride, the glories of the French past embodied, and fueled, what Charles de Gaulle, a man immersed in French history, would call a "certain idea of France." In the celebrated opening passage of his memoirs, de Gaulle described his own intense patriotism even as he underscored the vital continuity between the nation's past glories and what he saw as its inherent *grandeur*. "All my life," confessed the general, "I have had a certain idea of France. It is inspired by sentiment as much as by reason. The emotional side of me imagines France . . . as dedicated to an exalted and exceptional destiny. . . . If, however, mediocrity shows in her acts and deeds, it strikes me as an absurd anomaly, to be imputed to the faults of Frenchmen, not to the genius of the country. . . . In short, to my mind, France cannot be France without *grandeur*."[2]

In light of the historical continuity so central to France's "destiny," it is not surprising that the blows dealt to French *grandeur* in the last half-century have prompted a meditation on the nation's past—on a long tradition of history and memory—as well as its present. In the course of this meditation, long-standing images and perceptions of French history have been challenged and transformed; at the same time, the theme of memory—in particular, that of national historical memory—has come to enjoy an unprecedented resonance. Linking these two phenomena, Pierre Nora suggests that the contemporary preoccupation with memory is prompted by the fear that what has been called the national "substance" or "essence" is fast disappearing. "Few eras in our history," he writes, "have been such prisoners of their memory; but few also have lived in such a problematical way the coherence of the national past and its continuity."[3]

In recent years, questions regarding the "coherence of the national past and its continuity" have made themselves felt throughout French cultural and political life. Novelists and essayists—one thinks, for example, of Marguerite Duras and Patrick Modiano—have created works haunted by the past. Historical biographies and novels, as well as both specialized and popular journals dealing with history, have enjoyed striking success.[4] Television programs, too, have responded to, and furthered, an interest in the national past. "Clio," noted historian François Dosse in 1987, "inspires an ever-growing public that is eager to learn about its past. People rush to hear historians speak. Television and radio studios welcome researchers who would formerly have remained in the anonymity of their archives, confined to a restricted circle of scholars."[5]

Even as an interest in history has spread beyond the confines of the university, the issue of memory has moved to the forefront of historiographical investigations. A prime example of this, of course, is *Les lieux de mémoire* itself. A massive seven-volume collection of essays, *Les lieux de mémoire* explores French history from the perspective of the "sites" or "places"—both physical (monuments, libraries, museums) and symbolic (flags, celebrations)—charged to transmit its memory/memories. Completed over a period of eight years,[6] *Les lieux de mémoire* has enjoyed great critical acclaim as well as widespread influence.[7] Not only were editor Pierre Nora and his colleagues asked to assist on an official government project designed to protect specified "sites of memory," but the very term "lieu de mémoire" has become part of the French language.[8] (The 1993 edition of a major French dictionary, *Le Grand Robert*, defines *lieu de mémoire* as a "significant entity, whether material or nonmaterial in kind, that has become a symbolic element of the memorial heritage of a given community, as a result of human will or of the work of time.")

The interest in French memory that animates the essays in *Les lieux de mémoire* has also inspired works that examine the ways(s) in which particular eras of recent French history have been remembered. This is the case, for example, of two studies to which this present book is much indebted. In *The Vichy Syndrome: History and Memory in France since 1944*, Henry Rousso traces the festering wounds left by the Occupation; Benjamin Stora delves into the bitter legacy of the Algerian War in *La gangrène et l'oubli: La mémoire de la Guerre d'Algérie*.[9] It is, surely, works such as these that American historian James Wilkinson had in mind when, in 1996, he observed that "over the past ten years historians of modern France have become interested in one of the most evanescent forms of evidence: memory. Like so many disciples of Marcel Proust, they have been wrestling with the ways in which memory is preserved, with the transmission and repression of evidence, and with the distortions that befall images of the past."[10]

Historians and novelists are not the only "disciples of Proust" to have ventured into the recesses of French memory in recent years in search of the national past. French filmmakers too—and this, of course, constitutes the crux of the present book—have also displayed a fascination with the nation's history. At times bordering on an obsession, this fascination is, I think, worthy of analysis for a variety of reasons. On the most obvious level, film offers the most visible evidence of a widely shared fascination with national memory and history. But in addition to its visibility, cinema also offers a privileged site, a very special perspective, from which this fascination may be explored. As various commentators have noted over the years, films seem particularly well attuned to the slightest tremors of our collective psyche. They sense changing attitudes and moods more quickly than does the more private realm of literature or the more rarefied world of academe. "For the study of *mentalités*," write the authors of *L'histoire de France au cinéma*, a book that casts an encyclopedic eye over the representation of history in French film, "cinema is, in fact, a more sensitive barometer than literature or school curricula."[11] Using a strikingly similar metaphor, director Bertrand Tavernier declares that "filmmakers are the seismographs of their epoch. They bear witness, even unconsciously, to everything that surrounds them."[12]

Imbued with a particular sensitivity to groundswells of feelings and to changing sensibilities, films also lend themselves to the expression of sentiments that have yet to assume verbal form, or that resist clear articulation. The oft-noted oneiric dimension of film—its power to create moods, to make us suspend belief, to render (to borrow a phrase from Jean Cocteau) the "unreal" real—brings it close, in fact, to the workings of both dream and memory. Film is a perfect medium for the expression of the leitmotifs and repetitions, the ellipses and distortions, that are defining impulses of both these realms. Underscoring the dreamlike dimension of memory itself, as well as the gap that separates it from history, Nora might well be describing techniques and impulses fundamental to cinema. "Insofar as memory is affective and magical," he writes, "it makes use only of details that suit it; it is nourished by recollections [that are] hazy or telescoped, global or free-floating, particular or symbolic—sensitive to every kind of transference, screen, censorship, projection."[13]

As this remark suggests, the "screens" and "censorship" discerned by Freud in the workings of individual memories also characterize shared memories of the national past. Here, too, cinematic memories of the past are of great interest. For if films are especially sensitive to half-hidden moods, or to unacknowledged desires, they also capture and reflect the ways in which such moods and desires may work to "screen," to soften and repress, the most troubling zones of the national past. In so doing, they suggest how "political myths," which tap into the collective psyche even as they make free use of "screens" and "censorship," shape widely accepted assumptions about, and images of, the national past.

I have taken the term "political myth" from a work by French historian Raoul Girardet, *Mythes et mythologies politiques*. In describing what he considers the most potent "myths" or "legendary narratives" of his country,[14] Girardet implicitly suggests their kinship with cinema. In his view, a political myth consists of a "dynamic of images" that cannot be "encompassed, defined, enclosed within precise contours without a necessarily reductive conceptualizing operation that always risks betraying [them] or . . . depriving [them] of richness and complexity."[15] No less than such a myth, of course, a film also consists of a "dynamic of images" that loses its force, its power, when reduced to what might be seen as a "conceptualizing operation." (In the case of a film, such an "operation" might consist, say, of an account of its plot or a discussion of its themes.) This means that just as cinema lends itelf to the expression of dreams, so, too, is it a powerful medium for the transmission of historical and political myths that, frequently, soften or obscure the most brutal or unpalatable of historical truths even as they give rise to compelling visions of the national past.

Clearly, France is not the only country in which reigning political myths are perpetuated—or, more rarely, challenged—by cinematic images. One has only to think of images of the American frontier to feel how powerfully Hollywood has shaped a certain vision of the United States. But it is also true that the respect traditionally accorded cinema in France has contributed to the important role it has played in regard to myths bearing on the national past. Speaking, for example, of the way(s) in which the somber period of the Occupation has been remembered, historian Henry Rousso makes the point that films "seem to have had a decisive impact on the formation of a common, if not a collective, memory."[16] In a still broader sense, it might be said that if, for reasons to be explored later in this chapter, earlier French film did much to create a "certain idea of France," starting in the 1960s filmmakers played an important role in shattering this hegemonic vision of the national past.

This process of "shattering" is one that has consistently called into play two fundamental French political myths: that which Girardet describes as the myth of "French unity" and that of the "golden age." Frequently interrelated—that is, the "golden age" is often perceived as a lost moment of harmony and unity—these myths touch on the deepest layers of national identity and memory. And both reflect the fact that, at least from the Revolution until recent decades, France has been a deeply divided nation. Indeed, one commentator describes the history of France as a series of "actual or cold civil wars punctuated by more or less long periods of national reconciliation."[17] For centuries there was little common ground between those on the Right—for whom the "real" France lay in monarchist, Catholic, and nationalist traditions—and those on the Left, who saw French identity in terms of the universal and secular values of the Enlightenment and the Revolution. For the former, the nation's "golden age" was one of imperial *grandeur*; for the latter, it resided in the Revolution and the Republic. Underscoring the fundamental nature of this divide, Pierre Nora echoes a widely shared sentiment when he suggests that France consists not of one nation but, rather, of two: a monarchy, which stretched back to 987 and achieved its "full maturity" under Louis XIV; and a "revolutionary" nation characterized by the "absolute radicalism of its principles and their suitability for export." Observing that this "duality" is a defining feature of, and unique to, France, Nora proceeds to argue that it is precisely because of this fault line that France has been a nation obsessed with its history, its continuity, and its identity. "It is surely one of the reasons," observes Nora of this duality, "why France enjoys such a unique and central relation with its past, with its memory, or, to put it another way, with its history and with politics, which are forever charged with the mission of patching up the torn robe of the nation's past."[18]

In recent decades, it is true, the traditional lines of this divide seem to be growing fainter. For many reasons—the economic and social transformations that began in the 1960s, the end of the Marxist dream and the decline of the Communist Party, the rise of a "new Right" prepared to accept the legacy of the Revolution—formerly intractable lines are now being breached. The dream of revolution no longer sustains those on the Left; many on the Right are less concerned with French *grandeur* than with the nation's competitiveness in the global marketplace. The extreme Right, which, in an earlier incarnation, embraced the monarchist and religious values of *la vieille France*, now has a distinctly populist dimension. (Approximately three-quarters of those who vote for the far-Right party *Le front national* are workers.) It is now the Communists who, despite earlier inter-

nationalist ambitions, tend to resist the austerities demanded by incorpora-
tion into the European Community.

But despite these fundamental changes, it remains true that discussions
and representations of the past inevitably call forth the specter of earlier
conflicts and of persistent national "myths." And while political and social
lines may be shifting, the nation's long-standing preoccupation with its
"history and its continuity," with its very identity, has never been more
acute. (Indeed, these changes may fuel this preoccupation insofar as
France's duality was a defining feature of its identity.) In the world of film,
this preoccupation has prompted a meditation on the national past without
precedent in the history of French cinema. It is a meditation that, as I plan
to show, does much to explain why a long tradition of memory and history
appears at risk—why, in Nora's words, "memory is no longer there."

Cinematic portrayals of the French past have already attracted the attention of scholars and commentators on both sides of the Atlantic. The authors of *L'histoire de France au cinéma* (1993) provide a valuable overview
of the ways in which films have portrayed various periods of French history;
Images of the Algerian War: French Fiction and Film, 1954–1992 (Oxford:
Clarendon Press, 1994), by Philip Dine, analyzes cinematic and literary
representations of the Algerian War; *New Novel, New Wave, New Politics:
Fiction and the Representation of History in Postwar France* (Lincoln: University of Nebraska Press, 1996), by Lynn A. Higgins, explores the presence
of history in works stemming from what the author refers to as the new
écriture (which is cinematic as well as literary) of the 1960s. Although the
present book bears upon many of the same issues raised in these studies, it
approaches them in a somewhat different manner. Unlike *L'histoire de
France au cinéma*, it is focused on a particular era of French cinema; at the
same time, its scope is at once more limited and more extensive than that
of either Dine or Higgins. More limited, clearly, in that it is principally
concerned with film. More extensive in that it explores representations of
particular eras—such as, say, the Occupation and the Algerian War—as
part of a broader meditation, stretching from the 1960s to the 1990s, on
the national past.

To trace the shifting arc of this meditation, the various chapters of this
book, which bear upon different layers or strands of the past, are arranged
in an order that is roughly chronological. Thus chapter 2 is devoted to a
director who, in some ways, is indelibly associated with the immediate
postwar era: Alain Resnais. While Resnais's career spans nearly a half-century, his name immediately brings to mind several films, made early in his
career, that constitute what philosopher Gilles Deleuze has called a "global
memory" of the horrors—the camps and the bomb—of the 1940s. But even
as films such as *Nuit et brouillard* (*Night and Fog*, 1955) *Hiroshima mon amour*

(1959), and *Muriel ou le temps d'un retour* (*Muriel*, 1963) evoke "global" atrocities and suffering, they also reveal some of the cracks, the fissures, that would eventually envelop and corrode a "certain idea of France." Censorship restrictions in force throughout the 1950s and 1960s ensured that these works could only hint at some of the darkest zones of the French past. But their insistence on the repressions of memory, on the "lies" of consciousness, point to the buried presence of such zones. In this respect, I argue, it is telling that when the social and political climate changed, and the restrictions of censorship eased, Resnais did confront some of the most shame-filled eras of the French past: both *Stavisky* (1974) and *Providence* (1976) concern the deep roots, and the terrible consequences, of French anti-Semitism.

At the time these last two films appeared, in the mid-1970s, Resnais was by no means the only director engaged in a process of painful national soul-searching. Quite the contrary. By then, the cracks sensed in a film like *Muriel* had virtually erupted under the pressure of converging political, social, and cultural impulses. The antiauthoritarian New Left or *gauchiste* climate ushered in by the student rebellion of 1968, the weakening of censorship, the growing influence of the new cultural history or *l'histoire des mentalités*—all these prompted an explosion of films that challenged traditional images of the French past even as they underscored fundamental divisions at work in French society. Chapter 3 explores what was undoubtedly the most dramatic indication of this challenge: the cycle of so-called *rétro* films. Set in the period of the Occupation, works such as *Lacombe Lucien* (Louis Malle, 1974) and *Le dernier métro* (*The Last Metro*, François Truffaut, 1980) were marked by a new willingness to explore the somber realities of the Vichy era. But, at the same time, they also displayed revealing ambiguities that, I argue, reflected the persistence of certain fault lines, the immense difficulty of coming to terms with one of the most divisive and troubling moments of French history. Important players in an intense battle for memory—a battle Americans know full well from controversies that stem back to World War II and to Vietnam[19]—they showed how memory, to borrow a phrase from James Wilkinson, often functions as a "shield in the present rather than as a bond with the past."[20]

The battle for memory waged by the *rétro* films pointed to some of the deepest divisions in French society—divisions frequently obscured, repressed, by the myth of French unity. In so doing, it also revealed the often protean nature of political myths: their ability to change shape in response to changing historical circumstances and imperatives. For in challenging, or questioning, the view of the Occupation that had held sway ever since the end of the war, *rétro* films inevitably confronted what has been called the "myth of the Resistance": the notion that during the Occupation the vast majority of French men and women rallied to the active cadres of the

Resistance in their collective opposition to the foreign invader. And this myth, which had been launched by de Gaulle before the war was over in an effort to calm collective anxiety and to restore the nation's shattered morale, was clearly a latter-day incarnation of the far broader myth of French unity.

In the course of the 1970s, *rétro* films were not alone in challenging this fundamental myth. Reaching further back into the past, still other films demonstrated that what Nora calls the "nation's robe" had been torn long before Vichy—indeed, long before the modern era. Frequently inspired by the *Annales* school of French historians, or by what Anglo-Americans tend to call the "new social history," these films portrayed clashes and conflicts traditionally ignored or repressed by "official" histories. This approach to the past characterizes the director who is the subject of chapter 4: Bertrand Tavernier. In a series of historical melodramas that now spans a period of several decades, Tavernier has consistently aimed at shedding new light on little-known eras or events of the nation's past. But even as his films have sought to strip history of what Tavernier calls its "varnish," they have also testified to the changing political landscape of the present. Sometimes, that testimony could hardly have been clearer or more conscious: for example, Tavernier's historical films of the 1970s viewed the past through the challenging *gauchiste* lens brought to the fore by the student rebellion of May '68. At other times, however, the weight of the present was indistinct, perhaps unconscious. Thus despite their *gauchiste* perspective, these same films also endowed moments of revolt and revolution with a melancholy nostalgia that seemed to foreshadow what is surely the great ideological drama of recent years: the collapse, barely a decade after the events of May '68, of the dream, the "myth," of revolution.

The nostalgia that is felt in Tavernier's cinema, and that imbues the dream of revolution with the glow that clings to spent ideals, is also present in the work of other directors. Indeed, it might not be too much of an exaggeration to say that, by the 1980s, the past was seen less as a battleground for the ideological tensions of the present than as a site of melancholy nostalgia for vanished worlds. As the dream of May grew dim, conflicts bearing on the myth of French "unity" gave way to nostalgic evocations of a lost "golden age." But the nature of this Edenic moment varied greatly. For example, in the case of the films discussed in chapter 5—notably *Le crabe-tambour* (*The Drummer-Crab*, Pierre Schoendoerffer, 1977) and *Outremer* (*Overseas*, Brigette Roüan, 1990)—the "golden age" that glows so brightly in memory's eye is linked to the rise of empire. Recalling an era when the nation still believed in her civilizing mission, in the central role she had been elected to play on the world stage, these films also underscored the power cinema lends to the expression of political myths. That is, in both works, the past is filtered through the experiences of distinct social groups that have long nourished their own versions or "myths" of critical moments of the past. Embodying the splintered memories of distinct groups rather than those of the nation as a whole, these films also demonstrate what Pierre Nora—in an essay discussed at the conclusion of this chapter—views as the shattering of a long tradition of national historical memory.

Memories of a "golden age" also mark the films featured in chapter 6: those belonging to the so-called *cinéma du look*. But this time the vanished world evoked is one associated with cinema itself. Viewing the past through the lens of earlier films, works such as *Diva* (Jean-Jacques Beineix, 1981) and *Les amants du Pont-Neuf* (*The Lovers of Pont-Neuf*, Leos Carax, 1991) constantly allude to remembered images from classics by René Clair, Jean Renoir, and Marcel Carné. But in evoking these populist classics of the 1930s, these contemporary works inevitably call to mind not only earlier films but also the social world in which these remembered classics were embedded. Permeated by an implicit contrast between "then" and "now," they demonstrate how powerfully cinema itself functions as a site of memory; at the same time, they confirm Girardet's observation that the image of a lost "golden age" may well be the most powerful of all French political myths.[21]

Frequently giving life to deeply resonant political myths, postwar historical films come in a dazzling variety of shapes and forms. Encompassing the work of some of France's most respected directors, they range from costume melodramas to modernist experiments, from personal documentaries to naturalist dramas. Sensibilities and approaches, intentions and expectations, vary greatly. For some directors, to borrow a phrase from the eminent French historian Jacques Le Goff, "history is the very matter" of their films.[22] For others, instead, the past is little more than a source of exotic color—a pretext for beautiful costumes and striking sets. Indeed, in 1981 the lack of historical depth that characterizes many films set in the past prompted Marc Ferro, an *Annales* historian with a particular interest in cinema, to lament that French cinema reflected a national reluctance to deal with the most disturbing issues and conflicts of the past. Instead of probing the sources of conflict, French cinema, he charged, turned history into a series of "dreams" and "evasions." "In France," he declared, "history-as-problem [*histoire-problème*] has much less of an audience than history-as-dream [*histoire-rêve*], history-as-escapism [*histoire-évasion*], than History."[23]

In one sense, it is difficult to quarrel with Ferro. To the serious student of history, a good number of the historical films made since the 1960s may be little more than "evasions" or "dreams." But, first, I do not think that the refusal to confront the most disturbing zones of the past is particularly French. Aren't the vast majority of American films dealing with traumatic eras such as Korea and Vietnam also evasions or dreams? Besides, few countries can boast of directors as serious about history as, say, Alain Resnais and Marcel Ophuls, or René Allio and Bertrand Tavernier. Last, and just as important in this context, as Ferro himself argued convincingly in an earlier work, even the "dreams" and "evasions" that cinema creates to mask or repress troubling areas of the past may be as revealing as the most serious of documentaries. "If it is true," said Ferro, "that the not-said and the imaginary have as much historical value as History, then cinema, and especially fictional films, open a royal way to psycho-socio-historical zones that the analysis of 'documents' never reaches."[24]

Informed by Ferro's conviction that films lead us deep into "psycho-social-historical" zones, this book explores not only the work of directors clearly preoccupied by history but also the ways in which what Ferro calls the "imaginary" universe of far less serious films may reflect fundamental attitudes and impulses, or prejudices and needs. Urging historians to examine political myths, Girardet argues that "in terms of knowing a society, the study of its dreams constitutes an analytical instrument whose efficacy should not be ignored."[25] This holds true, surely, for the "dreams" seen on-screen. If cinematic "dreams" sometimes say little about the "real" past, they say a great deal about the way the past is viewed and remembered. Whatever the stance a film takes toward the past—whether it is impelled by hope of future change or by despairing nostalgia, whether it seeks to celebrate or to challenge earlier images and representations—it is a stance that sheds light on the present. The historical films of Alain Resnais reflect Cold War anxieties and the erasures of censorhip just as surely as those of Bertrand Tavernier and René Allio are infused with the changed political perspectives engendered by the events of May '68. Representations of a "golden age" are, implicitly or explicitly, laments for a less than golden present. From a still broader perspective—and this issue is discussed in the concluding part of this chapter—today's preoccupation with memory is itself an indication of contemporary anxieties. "The choices that we make," observed director René Allio in a discussion of film and history, "are never innocent; we always make them at a moment of History and of our own history, keeping in mind the relationship . . . between contemporary History and the way past History is perceived."[26]

What Allio calls the relationship "between contemporary History and the way past History is perceived" is, of course, complex and multidimensional. Even as film reflects contemporary moods, so too does it exert its own influence. Like myths, films spring from, and create, social reality. Cinema is not only a "source" of history, to use a term of Marc Ferro's, but frequently an "agent." It is difficult to imagine, for example, that Louis Malle would have focused on the question of collaboration in *Lacombe Lucien* had France not begun to question the Gaullist view of the Occupation that had held sway since the end of the Occupation. And this interrogation, in turn, owed a great debt to still another film: Marcel Ophuls's *Le chagrin et la pitié* (*The Sorrow and the Pity*, 1970–71). Furthermore, critics and viewers alike reacted to *Lacombe Lucien* in certain ways precisely because of *Le chagrin et la pitié*. Similarly, if many films reflect today's interest in the colonial past, so, too, does their success heighten this interest and inspire still other works on the same subject. In this complex network of influences and relations, "dreams" may be as revealing as the most sober of documentaries; myths may inform the most meticulous of historical reconstructions. It is precisely this network—the meeting-ground of past and present, of dreams and reality, of history and myth—that this book proposes to explore.

"A Certain Idea of France": Images Past and Present

While postwar French cinema has represented the national past in unprecedented ways, the interest it has displayed in French history is hardly a new phenomenon. Quite the contrary: as suggested earlier, virtually from its inception, French cinema served as an important site of national memory. With strikingly few exceptions, from the late 1890s until the mid-1950s, films embodied a certain vision of French history. In large measure, the specific nature of this vision, which was particularly conscious and hegemonic, was formed by, and reflected, a fundamental historical convergence: the period that saw the birth of French cinema also saw French collective memory assume the patriotic and nationalistic contours that would define it for generations.

It is true, of course, that these contours had begun to take shape well before the 1890s. In *Le peuple* (1846), the great French historian Jules Michelet—whom Nora describes as the very "soul" of *Les lieux de mémoire*—spoke of his country in the same patriotic and quasi-reverent tones that, nearly a century later, would reverberate throughout de Gaulle's paean to a "certain idea of France." Michelet's conviction that his country had been chosen to "incarnate a moral ideal of the world"—that France was destined to spread the message of the Enlightenment and the Revolution far and wide—led him to consider the "tradition," the *grandeur* of the French past, as a source of inspiration not only for France but for all of humanity. Deeming France a kind of "religion," a "living fraternity," Michelet lyrically declared that "all other histories are mutilated, only ours is complete . . . the national legend of France is a streak of immense and uninterrupted light, a true Milky Way for the eyes of the world."[27] A just appreciation of this "national legend" was, he felt, an essential ingredient in the education of every child, every future citizen. Thus Michelet maintained that a father's first duty toward his son was to teach him about *la patrie* and its glories past and present. "To have renewed faith in France and to hope in its future," declared the French historian, "one must go back to the past and fathom its natural genius."[28]

In 1870, less than a quarter-century after Michelet wrote his stirring hymn to France in *Le people*, the country suffered a humiliating military defeat at the hands of Bismarck's Germany. Unexpected and decisive, this defeat, which led to the collapse of the Second Empire and the birth of the Third Republic, forced France to concede the provinces of Alsace and Lorraine to Germany. It also signaled a terrible period for Paris, the city that had gleamed so brightly during the Second Empire: first came a winter of seige and near starvation; then, a period of civil warfare when the Commune, the revolutionary government established while the city was still under seige, was suppressed by troops sent in from Versailles. The very enormity of these blows, however, gave rise to renewed currents of patriotic and nationalist sentiment. Infused with a "cult of memory" for the "lost provinces" of Alsace and Lorraine, these currents brought with them an exaltation of the military together with an insistence on the heroic value of sacrifice for, and love of, country.

In this intensely patriotic climate, the very notion and function of history was transformed. That is, for the founders of the Third Republic, history was not merely the study of the nation's past but also a means by which to create a new sense of national unity and purpose. The memory of the nation's past glories, it was hoped, would point the way to a brighter future. This sentiment was at the core of a famous speech that writer and scholar Ernest Renan delivered at the Sorbonne in March of 1882. "Like the individual," declared Renan, "the nation is the end product of a long past of efforts, of sacrifices, of devotion. Of all the cults, that of our ancestors is the most legitimate. Our ancestors have made us what we are. A heroic past, great men, glory . . . this is the social capital on which to build a concept of the nation."[29]

What Renan described in this speech as his country's "social capital," that is, its "heroic past," was considered a vital dimension in the education of every schoolchild. Never had Michelet's admonition, that a "father's first duty" toward his son was to inculcate in him a sense of national pride, been taken so seriously. School textbooks were now designed to create a kind of civic religion, to make every child feel part of a country that was united not only geographically but also spiritually and ideologically. Noting that the founders of the Third Republic used every possible means to "consolidate the national glue" of a country that had been humiliated and defeated, French historian Michel Winock proceeds to observe that their educational program, in particular, was designed to "assure a veritable nationalist pedagogy: history, geography, civics, and morality . . . everything had to help forge the national soul: to keep the memory of the lost provinces alive, to develop the use of the French language at the expense of 'dialects' and 'patois' . . . to animate the cult of national heroes."[30]

By the end of the nineteenth century, of course, there was a new means, one whose power was still in its infancy, to "animate the cult of national heroes" and to "forge the national soul." Beginning in 1895, French cinema—and, in particular, historical films—could be used to perpetuate the patriotic vision of the national past deemed essential to France's very "soul." The "great national *récit*," to borrow a phrase from historian Jean-Claude Bonnet, could now be told not only by historical paintings and plays but also, and in some sense above all, by moving images.[31] Like its schoolrooms, the nation's moviehouses became a place in which a "nationalist pedagogy" could be circulated. Indeed, many historical films were little more than textbook illustrations come to life, *tableaux vivants* of famous characters and scenes from the French past that were already engraved upon the popular imagination. For example, David's famous painting of Marat stabbed in his bath by Charlotte Corday inspired a 1897 film, *L'assassinat de Marat* (*The Assassination of Marat*), by Georges Hatot. The death of Robespierre also gave rise to an early film (*La mort de Robespierre [The Death of Robespierre]*, Georges Hatot, 1897), as did Rouget de Lisle's stirring creation of the Marseillaise (*Rouget de Lisle chantant la Marseillaise [Rouget de Lisle singing the Marseillaise]*, Gaumont film, 1898).[32] Not surprisingly, two of France's greatest patriotic figures—Joan of Arc and Napoleon—were each the subject of several early films. Both Georges Hatot (*Jeanne d'Arc*, 1898) and Georges Méliès (*Jeanne d'Arc*, 1900) portrayed the maiden who embodied, in the eyes of a rapturous Michelet, both the "Virgin and the Country." While the memory of Joan of Arc could not help but evoke essential French fault lines—a nationalist and religious heroine for those on the Right, the Maid of Orleans was a young girl of the people for those on the Left[33]—no similar schisms surrounded that of Napoleon. The historical figure most frequently represented in French cinema, the emperor was almost invariably seen as the very embodiment of French *gloire*.[34]

In the years preceding the First World War, at a time when French cinema itself achieved an international dominance never to be realized again, historical films became at once more complex and more prestigious. In large measure, this was due to a new production company, the *Film d'Art*, that was determined to render the art of cinema as serious and respected as that of the stage, to make people feel that going to a film "was another way of going to the theater." For its first ambitious production—which featured stage actors from the *Comédie-Française*, an original score by Camille Saint-Saëns, and a script by a member of the French Academy—the *Film d'Art* chose, significantly, a major historical event that had already inspired two earlier films: *L'assassinat du Duc de Guise* (*The Assassination of the Duke of Guise*, 1908) portrays the assassination, at the hands of Henri III, of one of the principal instigators of the St. Bartholomew's Day Massacre of French Protestants in 1572.[35] This highly literary and theatrical production was soon followed by a wave of historical films that, like *L'assassinat du Duc de Guise*, approached the French past with great solemnity. Their mood of veneration seemed in perfect accord with a moment that saw French nationalism entering what historian Michel Winock calls a "new phase." Sparked by fears of German aggression, this phase was one in which nationalists on both sides of the ideological divide, who had been bitterly polarized a decade earlier by the Dreyfus Affair, began the move toward reconciliation that would end in the "Sacred Union" of 1914. Underscoring the pedagogical nature of the historical films made during this period, Marcel Oms makes it clear that their exalted vision of the national past appealed to those at both ends of the ideological spectrum: to Republicans (who were committed to the cause of secular education) as well as to traditionalist Catholics. The productions of the *Film d'Art*, writes Oms, "simply perpetuated images [*une imagerie*] that helped render credible the vision of national History desired by various ministers of Public Instruction since 1880. . . . Comparing secular and Catholic visions of the History of France, one sees the [same] persistence of crucial episodes; the representation of the same exemplary characters made familiar through images; a climate of identical historical spirituality—all of which helped create a national consensus bathed in a certain religiosity indispensable to the Sacred Union."[36]

The wave of patriotism that led to the "Sacred Union" of 1914 receded after World War I, calmed, no doubt, by the return of the "lost" provinces of Alsace and Lorraine and the all-too-transitory sense that the world had entered an era of peace. But the exaltation of the French past seen in earlier historical films, the climate of "historical spirituality" and "religiosity" they exuded, continued unabated.[37] In fact, the 1920s saw the rise of lavish and costly historical spectacles that frequently lasted several hours. Noting that these films were the most "prestigious of the decade"—in fact, many enjoyed grandiose premieres at the Paris Opera—film historian and critic Richard Abel theorizes that they responded to a twofold impetus. On the economic front, he suggests, it was hoped that these large-scale epics could compete with American superproductions. But ideology, says Abel, also played a role: in the postwar era "the historical reconstruction film contributed to the process of national restoration and redefinition . . . by resurrecting past historical moments of French glory and tragedy."[38]

Moments of "French glory" clearly dominate what are probably the two best-known historical epics of the period: Raymond Bernard's *Le miracle des loups* (*The Miracle of the Wolves*, 1924) and Abel Gance's *Napoléon* (1927). Both feature intensely patriotic figures. The legendary heroine of *Le miracle des loups*, Jean de Hachette, played a military role not unlike that of Joan of Arc in defending her native town of Beauvais against a seige launched by Charles the Bold in 1472. (Indeed, in the film, Jean is given the aura of sanctity that often surrounds the Maid of Orleans: for example, when she encounters a pack of savage wolves in the mountains, they miraculously spare her life—hence the title of the film.) As for *Napoléon*, which is probably the best-known French film of the silent era, Gance's epic is virtually a hymn to the glory of imperial France and to the *grandeur* of its hero. Whether braving a tempest at sea as he sails his small boat from Corsica to France, or communing with the dead heros of the Revolution, or leading his conquering armies to victory throughout Europe, Gance's Bonaparte is a man of destiny, a gigantic figure who embodies one of the most heroic moments of French history.

It is telling that the exaltation of imperial power and the sense of *grandeur* permeating *Napoléon* also characterize the historical films of a director who, in certain respects, could hardly be more different from Gance: Sacha Guitry. A consummate man of the theater who was also a great personality, Guitry directed and starred in his own productions. Although he began making films in the silent era—his 1914 documentary in praise of French culture, *Ceux de chez nous*, introduces viewers to luminaries such as Monet, Rodin, and Renoir—it was years later, in 1937, with *Les perles de la couronne* (*Pearls of the Crown*) that he began a series of hugely popular and highly imaginative historical epics in which, it has been said, he created "guitrizations" of history.[39] In *Remontons les Champs-Elysées* (1938) Guitry plays a Parisian schoolteacher who leads his students backward in time through centuries of French history as they walk along the Champs-Elysées; *Si Versailles m'était conté* (*Royal Affairs of Versailles*, 1954) also spans the centuries as a succession of the aristocratic figures who inhabited, or visited, the great château of Versailles parade before us. Although Guitry's mastery of cinematic style (Resnais and Truffaut number among his admirers) has always won more praise than has his quirky view of history, in which bedroom antics loom larger than military victories, there can be little doubt about his love for the magnificence of royal power or his patriotic fervor. In this respect, it is noteworthy that Guitry not only included Napoleon in at least five films but also lent his own features to the emperor on at least two occasions. "Was he a royalist?" asks Pierre Guibbert of this polished performer, "it's never been clearly established. . . . But he was animated by

an undeniable national sentiment. Like de Gaulle—although this compari-
son might seem sacrilegious—he had a certain idea of France that was
linked to the sense of a dynastic continuity of great men: in particular, great
monarchs."[40]

The consistency of Guitry's historical films—the fact that the same spirit
animated both those of the 1930s and those of the 1950s—underscores, of
course, the powerful hold exerted by a "certain idea of France." Indeed,
despite the trauma of the war and Occupation, this idea would not really
be challenged, at least not directly or openly, until the upheavals of May
'68. In the course of *les événements*, as they would come to be known, student protesters, joined by striking workers, managed to paralyze the country for over a month.[41] Although important economic and social changes,
as well as the experience of the Algerian War, had begun to transform
France at least a decade earlier, the events of May seemed to mark the
beginning of a new moment in French history. "May 1968," writes Arthur
Hirsh, "represents the end of one era and the beginning of a new one. It
was the crucial turning point in the transition from the new left criticism
of traditional marxism to a new vision of an egalitarian and libertarian society that begins to emerge in the 1970s."[42] Ushering in a new political and
social climate, *les événements* also prompted the departure of de Gaulle from
the political arena. Although the general did not actually step down from
power until the following year, the events of May made it clear that he had
outlived his time. For the young radicals of '68, and for many of their
generation, the man who had saved the national "honor," and who embodied a "certain idea of France," was now lost in "anachronistic dreams of
national *grandeur*"; he had become the very symbol "of the hierarchical,
military-industrial, techno-structural, bureaucratic State" that the mili-
tants of '68 wanted to destroy.[43]

   The institutions and structures of the present were not, of course, the
only ones that found themselves hotly contested in the wake of May. As if
to demonstrate the tremendous weight exerted by French history in the
nation's political consciousness, images of the national past also came
under intense interrogation. This interrogation was largely nourished by
three principal converging impulses: the challenging political spirit born
of *les événments*; what might be described as the *gauchiste* preoccupation
with power and marginality (issues often associated with the work of philosopher Michel Foucault); and *l'histoire des mentalités*. Giving rise to new
conceptions and representations of the past, these impulses merged even
as they drew strength from one another. As they did so, the very notion of
history underwent a seismic change. It became clear that history was not an
impartial and immutable given to be enshrined in textbooks and reverently
handed down from one generation to the next. Rather, like all social arti-

facts or constructs, it was a product of culture and ideology that was inevitably subject to the pull and tug, the ideological biases and social constraints, of the present. As historian Jacques Le Goff, who served as an editor of *Annales* in the course of the 1970s, would later write: "The past is reconstructed as a function of the present just as much as the present is explained by the past."[44]

As if to illustrate the ways in which prevailing attitudes determine our view of the past, historical works began to reflect a distinctly post-'68 concern with power and, consequently, with the very nature of the state. (The task of ascertaining the "techniques and tactics" of power, declared philosopher Michel Foucault, could only begin "after 1968, that is to say on the bases of daily struggles at a grass-roots level, among those whose fight was located in the fine meshes of the web of power. This was where the concrete nature of power became visible.")[45] Resurrecting moments and events ignored by, repressed from, "official" versions of the French past, historical works began to explore both the "centers" of power and its "margins." Thus they evinced a new interest in regional movements and in popular revolts that challenged the authority of the central state as well as the presumed "unity" of the nation. So, too, were they drawn to "marginalized" groups—lepers and Jews, witches and sorcerers, prisoners and the insane—whose harsh treatment often said much about the societies in which they lived. Only by rereading the "margins," argued historian Jean-Claude Schmitt, could one avoid the "unanimous," and, by implication, false or self-serving, discourse of the "center." "Today," wrote Schmitt in 1978, "a kind of 'Copernican Revolution' affects the writing of history. It has been perceptible for fifteen years or so even if it has been in the making for longer. Traditional perspectives have not necessarily been abandoned but they appear insufficient. . . . From the center, it is impossible to perceive, to write, the history of the whole of society without reproducing the unanimous discourses of those in power."[46]

What an enthusiastic Schmitt described as a "Copernican Revolution" in the writing of history clearly owed a debt not only to the *gauchiste* spirit born of May '68 but to the way(s) in which that spirit both reflected and influenced the new cultural and social history associated with the *Annales* school. By now, this approach has become so widespread that it is easy to forget that it began, in France, with the group of dissident historians who founded the review *Annales* as long ago as 1929. From the first, *Annales* historians embraced an approach that was in sharp contrast with the "official" history promulgated by French schools and textbooks since the time of the Third Republic. Focused on *la longue durée*, they were not concerned with the history of nation-states, much less the French past per se. The great characters of history known to every French schoolchild were noticeably absent from their works. Viewing history from "below"—from the perspective of ordinary people—they drew upon various disciplines (economics and geography, sociology and psychology) in order to trace a "total picture of past societies." Their aim, as Jacques Le Goff would later write, was to "rethink events and crises in terms of the slow and deep movements of history, to be interested in, and to feature, men and social groups rather than individuals, to prefer the history of the concrete realities of daily life (material and mental) to isolated events." In so doing, he continued, they sought nothing less than to "metamorphose the collective memory of men."[47]

As the years went by, this search for "collective memory" entered the historical mainstream even as its focus began to shift. By the 1960s and 1970s, explorations of, say, migration flows or agricultural cycles were eclipsed by the study of *mentalités*: the patterns of thought and behavior that had characterized the daily lives of ordinary people in the past. In their search for clues to past *mentalités*, *Annales* historians turned to data formerly disdained or ignored: to superstitions and folklore, to religious beliefs and artistic representations, and to scientific and medical practices. Legal documents and court records were prized as particularly valuable sources of information. Although such documents usually concerned the fate of individuals, that fate was clearly linked to collective mores, to social practices and religious beliefs, that had held sway in the past. Suggesting that the *histoire des mentalités* has enjoyed tremendous cultural resonance precisely because it is at the meeting point of "the conscious and the unconscious . . . the marginal and the general," Jacques Le Goff hardly seemed to exaggerate when he deemed it one of the most important "phenomena of the scientific and intellectual life and of the collective psychology of the latter half of the twentieth century."[48]

Nowhere was the resonance of the new social history, together with the *gauchiste* spirit born of '68, more visible, or more dramatic, than in cinema. As French film historian René Prédal remarks, one of the defining characteristics of French cinema of the 1970s—and one that distinguished it sharply from the New Wave of the 1960s—was a preoccupation with "social reality" understood as "politics, sociology, and history."[49] As Prédal points out, the mid-1970s, years in which a newly discovered interest in the past was at its peak, saw the appearance of at least twelve films dealing with French history. Indeed, the year 1974 alone witnessed works as diverse as *Lacombe Lucien*, Louis Malle's enigmatic psychological portrait of a young collaborator; *Les violons du bal*, Michel Drach's semiautobiographical reminiscences of the odyssey of a Jewish family during the Occupation; *Section spéciale*, Costa-Gavras's investigation of the sinister workings of Vichy bureaucracy; *Stavisky*, Alain Resnais's stylized re-creation of a famous scandal of the 1930s; *Que la fête commence* (*Let Joy Reign Supreme*), Bertrand Tavernier's fresco of the period of the Regency; and *Lancelot du*

Lac, Robert Bresson's disquieting portrait of the violent underside of the Middle Ages.[50]

As an increasing number of films turned toward the past, the "certain idea of France," the very embodiment of "official history" so carefully nourished by a long tradition of historical films, found itself under constant attack. The veneration and solemnity that marked earlier cinematic representations of the past, both in historical epics and in adaptations of literary classics, virtually disappeared. Indeed, these traditional genres themselves faded from view as other kinds of films—documentaries, realistic dramas, meticulous reconstructions of former eras—explored the past. Instead of portraying the glories and triumphs of the national past, many of these works began to analyze its most unpalatable episodes, to resurrect its most divisive eras. The great historical figures who had dominated earlier films were eclipsed by ordinary people even as the focus shifted from the "centers" of power to the "margins" of society. Thus Versailles and Paris gave way to the provinces; obscure assassins and oppressed peasants replaced heroes and heroines like Napoleon and Joan of Arc; the Revolution itself—and here the weight of May was particularly strong—seemed of less interest than popular revolts.

Virtually all these impulses could be seen, for example, in what was probably the first film clearly inspired by the convergence of the new history and the *gauchiste* spirit sparked by '68: René Allio's *Les Camisards* (1970). A highly politicized rereading of the French past, *Les Camisards* underscores the repressive nature of the French state even as it challenges the myth of national unity. Its very subject, the eighteenth-century revolt of a band of persecuted Protestants dubbed "les Camisards" after an article of dress, evokes the memory of the religious divisions and wars that plagued France for centuries. Imbued with the specter of fundamental French fault lines, *Les Camisards* also eschews the traditional iconography, culled from textbooks and paintings, seen in earlier historical films. Instead, to trace the doomed uprising of this religious minority, these *marginaux* of an earlier era, the director returns to original texts: much of the voice-over narrative heard throughout the film consists of extracts from actual Protestant diaries. (These documents had recently been discovered and published by *Annales* historian Philippe Joutard.)[51] This perspective allows Allio both to seize history from "below"—through the eyes of the Protestant rebels rather than through those of individuals in the seat of power—and to re-create the material realities and social practices that governed the lives of the persecuted Camisards.

Unlike earlier historical films, in which characters speak in decidedly contemporary tones, *Les Camisards* leaves no doubt that the past is, indeed, a foreign territory. Marked by a mentality radically different from our own, members of the Protestant sect actually communicate in tongues during one intensely mystical ceremony. But even as Allio's film insists on what he called the "shock," the "strangeness," of the past,[52] it also acknowledges the weight, the bias, that the lens of the present inevitably imposes upon it. Infused with the passions of May '68,[53] the Protestants' rebellion hints not only at the students' revolt of that year but at other, far more deadly, struggles. What Allio called the "schema" of the Camisard rebellion, in which the rebels' guerrilla tactics were met with escalating violence on the part of the state, could not help but remind audiences of the wars in Vietnam and Algeria. Referring to the long shadow cast by the Algerian War in *Les Camisards*, Allio noted that when he read actual Protestant diaries concerning this event, they spoke to him "more of the present than of the past. . . . The whole Algerian War seemed to have been reproduced in the schema of the war of the Camisards."[54]

Les Camisards was, certainly, more militant and uncompromising not only politically but also aesthetically than most subsequent works devoted to the French past; marked by a very loose narrative structure, the film also featured nonprofessional actors. But, to varying degrees, the impulses animating *Les Camisards*—that is, its determination to reread the past and to challenge a "certain idea of France," its focus on ordinary people rather than on famous characters of history, its rejection of traditional iconography in favor of a return to original sources—were visible in later historical films. Like *Les Camisards*, many explored little-known moments of the French past that had never before been seen on-screen. Still others challenged not only long-standing images of well-known periods or events but also the way(s) in which such images had been perpetuated by an earlier cinematic tradition. This was the case, for example, of two films, both by leading directors, about the Middle Ages. In different ways, both Robert Bresson's *Lancelot du Lac* and Eric Rohmer's *Perceval le Gallois* (1978) put into question the portrait of medieval spirituality and courtly love featured in a long tradition of films ranging from early works about Joan of Arc (and Jean de Hachette) down to Marcel Carné and Jacques Prévert's wartime classic, *Les visiteurs du soir* (*The Devil's Envoy*, 1942). Despite its title, *Lancelot du Lac* is not a romantic tale about the legendary knight Lancelot and his love for Queen Guinevere but, rather, a grim and intensely realistic fresco of medieval warfare and savagery. (Permeated by the sound of sword striking sword and the thuds of falling horses and men, this unsettling drama reminded one critic of the massacres portrayed by Sergei Eisenstein in his 1924 silent classic, *Strike*.)[55] In a very different way, *Perceval le Gallois* also subverts conventional images of medieval chivalry and love. In Rohmer's stylized rereading of a *roman courtois*, heroism disappears beneath the shadow of irony as King Arthur's legendary knights are made to seem inflexible, misguided, naive.

By the 1980s, it is true, films seem to grow both less confrontational and less experimental in their approach to the past. Even as the *gauchiste* spirit of the 1970s disappeared from view, French cinema began to witness a resurgence of conventional historical genres like lavish spectacle films and literary adaptations of French classics.[56] But although such films clearly harked back to earlier traditions, they also suggested just how much attitudes toward the past had changed. For one thing, they showed that the *Annales* approach to history, its concern with the unknown corners of the past, its focus on the lives of ordinary people, remained strong. In this respect, two lavish spectacles by director Jean-Paul Rappenau are exemplary. Based on the famous play by Edmond Rostand, *Cyrano* (1990)—produced, it is said, with the biggest budget ever in French film—tells a melodramatic tale of love and adventure set in the seventeenth century. But, significantly, the film also attempts to capture the *mentalité* of a specific era: the unease of a moment in which religious faith was beginning to crumble before the onslaught of rationalism and libertarianism.[57] Like *Cyrano*, *Le hussard sur le toit* (*The Horseman on the Roof*, 1995), which is based on a novel by Jean Giono, is also a romantic melodrama: set at the time of the Risorgimento, it depicts the growing passion between an Italian patriot and a French woman as they flee through a Southern French countryside that has been ravaged by a cholera epidemic. But, once again, meticulous attention is paid to the historical context: in particular, to the social and medical practices surrounding the epidemic. One of the film's most striking scenes, in fact, shows how those who have come into contact with the disease are virtually imprisoned to prevent its spread.

Along with this concern for past *mentalités*, films have continued to reveal a transformed vision of the national past. Punctuated by remembered scenes of the devastation and death endured by Napoleon's conquering armies, *Le colonel Chabert* (Yves Angelo, 1994) suggests the dark underside of French *grandeur* and the terrible cost of imperial glory; focused on the court of *le roi soleil*, *Ridicule* (Patrice Leconte, 1996) does not depict the glories that defined the reign of the Sun King but, rather, the highly refined verbal viciousness, the meanness of spirit, that prevailed at court. Nor have the nation's deep fault lines, the source of repression and strife throughout long centuries, been forgotten. The religious divisions and conflicts portrayed by Allio in *Les Camisards* have been repeatedly addressed by subsequent films: *Tous les matins du monde* (*All the Mornings of the World*, Alain Corneau, 1991) portrays the beliefs and behavior of those ascetic souls who embraced Jansenist teachings in the seventeenth century; Patrice Chéreau's *La reine Margot* (1994) spares us none of the horrors—in one scene a street is literally filled with corpses—of the slaughter of French Protestants during the the St. Bartholomew's Day Massacre. If the "shock" of the past, to borrow Allio's phrase, continues to reverberate in such films, it is a shock that owes as much to their darkened vision of the national past as it does to their portrayal of distant *mentalités*.

Present Anxieties

What impulses, then, fuel the somber view of the national past that marks French cinema of the last quarter-century? and that gives rise to the current obsession with French history and memory? These questions clearly bring us back to the presence of contemporary fears and uncertainties concerning French identity. For it is hardly coincidental that today's preoccupation with the national past began in an era, the mid-1960s, when a "certain idea of France" was beginning to crumble. It was at this period of tremendous change and dislocations that people first began to speak of the importance of conserving the nation's *patrimoine*: that is, its heritage of cultural, historic, and artistic riches. (Within less than a decade this need would seem so compelling that 1978 would be declared the year of Patrimony.) And, as suggested earlier, the publication of *Les lieux de mémoire* in 1984 saw the creation of still another term—"site of memory"—that, like *patrimoine*, both reflected and fueled a growing preoccupation with the national past and with the ways it has been remembered. This preoccupation is currently so strong that, some fear, it eclipses all thoughts of the future;[58] others, like Pierre Nora, are convinced that now it is only memory that gives the idea of the "Nation . . . its pertinence and its legitimacy."[59]

The preoccupation with memory and history that characterizes contemporary France is, certainly, part of a broader phenomenon. As Saul Friedlander observes, liberal Western countries in general seem to be experiencing a kind of historical discontinuity together with an obsession with the past. "There seems to be," writes Friedlander, "a pervasive reference to the past and, simultaneously, a growing detachment from it as relevant for the present and the future."[60] In the view of certain commentators, the phenomenal success enjoyed by the new social history itself can be attributed to an acute sense of contemporary rootlessness and insecurity. Some, like historian Jacques Le Goff, hope that the *l'histoire des mentalités* can allay such feelings. Suggesting that the "acceleration" of history has prompted the masses of industrialized nations to cling nostalgically to their roots, in an eloquent passage Le Goff writes:

> In our world where collective memory changes, where man, confronted with the acceleration of history . . . wants to escape from the anguish of becoming an orphan of the past, without roots, where men are passionately in search of their identity, where people everywhere try to inventory their heritage and to preserve

it . . . where bewildered people seek to master a history that seems to escape them, what could be better [suited] to bring them information and answers than the new history?[61]

Others, however, like Stanley Hoffmann and Pierre Nora, appear to regard the *Annales* approach itself as one more symptom of the discontinuities, the sense of bewilderment, we feel in regard to the past. Observing that the French, in particular, are experiencing a "gradually growing sense of radical discontinuity" from their history, Hoffmann asks whether the fascination they feel for the stranger aspects of the distant past masks a reluctance to come to terms with traumatic episodes of more recent French history. Clearly alluding, in part, to the *Annales* school, Hoffmann sadly observes that most contemporary historians use an approach that is "ethnographic rather than political; it is the investigation of worlds we have lost, a sampling of vanished riches, not a celebration of how every stone fits into the national monument and every jewel into the nation's crown . . . today we indulge either in the nostalgia of past peoples or in curiosity about individuals."[62] And Pierre Nora seems to take Hoffmann's reasoning one step further still. Pointing to "striking parallels" between key dates in French history and "methodological advances of French historiography," Nora suggests that historians turned away from the study of the "nation" just when France was entering a period of decline. "The depression of 1930," observes Nora, "coincides with the creation of *Annales* . . . the years following the end of the Algerian War [saw] the advance of *l'histoire des mentalités*."[63]

Clearly, opinions vary concerning the role and the nature of the new social history. But there *is* a shared sense that today's obsession with the past, with memory and its sites, owes a great deal to the "acceleration of history"—to rapid and profound changes that have destroyed long-standing traditions and historical continuities. In this respect, it is significant, surely, that such changes have occurred with breathtaking speed in postwar France. In the course of two generations, a traditional and largely rural society, marked by sharp class distinctions and based on values associated with family and church, has been transformed into an increasingly urbanized and multicultural country on the leading edge of the technological revolution. "France," writes sociologist Gérard Mermet, "is witnessing the end of an era, if not a civilization."[64] In an equally dramatic vein, still another French sociologist, Henri Mendras, argues that the period from 1965 to 1984 saw France undergo nothing less than a "second Revolution." It was a "revolution" that affected not only the country's class structure and its economy but also traditional ideological divisions as well as social values and customs—particularly those concerning women and sexuality. Summarizing these overwhelming changes, Mendras writes:

Does the end of this Revolution mean that we are entering a new world? We can clearly see that the great social structures of the nineteenth century are collapsing: four massive and antagonistic classes are splintering into a multitude of groups. . . . Major institutions—the Church, the Army, the Republic, the Schools, the Communist Party and the unions—are losing their symbolic aura . . . because the French are [now] in general agreement concerning the public sphere. The great national debates are calming down.[65]

There seems little doubt that, as Mendras writes, France (no less than the United States and other Western countries) is entering what is often called "a new world order." But a host of problems make it clear that it is a far more dangerous and unsettling world than that envisioned by the relatively optimistic Mendras even as recently as 1988. France must confront economic stagnation, the difficulty of conforming to standards established by the European Union, escalating violence, the influx of immigrants and the rise of the far Right, unemployment, and homelessness.[66] Given this array of problems, it is perhaps not surprising that the word "fear" appears in the titles of at least two books about contemporary France: Alain Duhamel's *Les peurs françaises* (Paris: Flammarion, 1993) and Sonia Combe's *Archives interdites: Les peurs françaises face à l'histoire contemporaine* (Paris: Albin Michel, 1994). Underscoring the sense of crisis that is felt in a wide variety of domains—education, law enforcement, spirituality, the family—in a book entitled *La France raciste* Michel Wieviorka analyzes the current French mood of fear, insecurity, and nostalgia in the following terms. "Massive urbanization is perceived as having destroyed everything; consumer society and television have done the rest. A deep sentiment of decadence and degeneration is mixed with fear and the theme of insecurity. The past is perceived as a golden age, and discourses feed upon the image of a multifaceted crisis."[67]

Not unexpectedly, anxieties about the present began to make themselves felt with particular intensity as the postwar period of economic growth and expansion ground to a halt with the recession of 1974. While prosperity tends to create optimism about the future, difficult economic times, as historian Philippe Joutard notes, make people eager to return to the "golden age" of the past, to "take refuge in family, community, and tradition." Indeed, Joutard argues that even the events of May '68—usually interpreted as the beginning of a new era—were permeated by a deep nostalgia for the past. From that time on, he writes, "students returned to the soil, regional movements developed, and minority cultures took hold."[68]

Along with the nostalgia for the reassuring contours of a traditional world has come increased resistance to, and suspicion of, immigrants. One of the legacies of the colonial past is that the largest immigrant group in

France consists of North Africans Muslims (who number about five million) from former French colonies. Their presence fuels debates about what it means to be "French" in a multiethnic and multireligious society. Right and Left remain bitterly divided on whether French-born children of immigrants should be automatically granted citizenship. "Will we still be French in thirty years?" asked an issue of *Figaro-Magazine* in 1985. No longer, as in the past, is one culture, one religion, automatically equated with "Frenchness." (In this respect, of course, France has always been different from the United States, which sees itself as a country of immigrants with different traditions, cultures, and religions.) And Islam, which is often perceived not only as an "alien" religion but as a powerful culture and a "way of life," poses particular problems. It is feared that Muslims (especially those who are deeply religious) either will be "unassimilable" or will be assimilated at the cost of a transformation of French identity. Such fears have given rise to a new incarnation of the xenophobic nationalism that asserted itself toward the end of the last century. Qualifying this xenophobic and fearful nationalism as "closed," as opposed to the "open" nationalism of de Gaulle that proudly saw France take a leading role among the nations of the world, Michel Winock links it to a widespread sense of crisis and decline. "The demographic decline of France and Europe," he writes, "the constraints exerted on the job market by economic mutations, the end of the great movements of secularization and urbanization that began at the end of the nineteenth century—all these factors create anxiety in a population which has been struck by unemployment (or the fear of unemployment), stripped of protective structures (the village community, the church, the patriarchal family), and which lacks a collective agenda."[69]

As Winock suggests, debates about "Frenchness" and "national identity" may crystallize around immigrants, but they obviously reflect still other fears: in particular, that France is losing the important political, social, and cultural role it has long played in Europe and the world. On the cultural scene, it is clear that Paris is no longer the artistic mecca that it was for centuries. Nor can contemporary French thought and culture match the influence exerted by existentialism in the immediate postwar years or by French "theory" in more recent decades. From a broader political and historical perspective, France is now, it is generally acknowledged, an "average power" that is fast losing even the preeminent role it long enjoyed in respect to its former colonies in Africa. Tracing the nation's decline back to the First World War, Pierre Nora writes that before that time France was able to pride itself "in having been the historical laboratory for all the great European experiences—from feudalism to the Republic . . . from the Crusades to colonialism." Now, instead, France can only react to "great phenomena that come from elsewhere."[70] Or, as an American commentator puts it succinctly, France is no longer the place where "history" happens but "just the place where history happened."[71]

In light of this sense of diminished power and prestige, even seemingly apolitical phenomena can fuel nationalist preoccupations. In a 1997 debate over smoking, for example, it was suggested that enforcement of a ban on cigarettes would make France resemble "puritan" America.[72] In this context, it is not difficult to see a preoccupation with the "purity" of the French language as a sign of distress that English has replaced French as an international language; so, too, is it tempting to attribute economic measures designed to protect the French film industry (measures that led to tortured GATT negotiations) to fears that the collapse of a national cinema implies a loss of French culture and identity. Such fears can only be exacerbated by the looming presence of the European Union with its threat of a diminished political identity for France. As Stanley Hoffmann points out, in France the erosion of political autonomy has important cultural ramifications. Noting that French cultural identity has always been linked to centralized political institutions and programs, Hoffmann argues that the "French state's abandonment of many of its powers over the French economy, the 'Europeanization' or 'globalization' of that economy, cannot fail to affect French cultural identity."[73]

Nor can anxieties about the present be alleviated by the promise of a brighter future. Marxism may still be used as a tool to analyze the present; but it no longer offers utopian hopes for the years to come. In France, as elsewhere, the decline of left-wing messianism has been prompted by converging social, political, and economic developments. In the course of the 1970s, left-wing dreams were shattered both by the relatively belated awareness of the horrors of the Gulag (Solzhenitsyn was translated into French in 1974) and by the revelation of the atrocities and brutalities that accompanied "revolutionary" struggles in places such as Cuba, China, and Cambodia.[74] At the same time, many young leftists, nourished in the antiauthoritarian climate of May '68, began to move away from a French Communist Party perceived as monolithic, old-fashioned, and hierarchical.[75] In addition to these ideological blows coming from within and without, the Left was also faced with the decline of the traditional working class as well as a rapidly changing economic and social environment in which some of its most firmly held beliefs were called into question.[76] On the one hand, it was becoming clear that national economies had to think, above all, in terms of international competition; on the other, as Americans have been made so acutely aware in recent years, the ambitious social programs of "big government" and the welfare state ("l'état-Providence") had begun to seem a luxury that few nations could afford.[77] The difficulty, if not impossibility, of realizing traditional leftist goals became painfully apparent when the Socialists came to power under Mitterand and tried to pass from theory to practice. "The left," as Stanley Hoffmann wrote in 1984, "which during its long opposition nurtured old myths and new illusions, has been forced, by Mitterand and necessity, to endorse *Realpolitik* abroad, austerity at home, and to subordinate its dreams of social justice to the imperatives of economic growth and private profits."[78]

The decline of Marxism did far more, however, than force the Socialists to change course or provoke a realignment of French political parties. Undermining a revolutionary tradition that stretched back to 1789, it touched upon a vital dimension of the nation's identity. At the same time, by signaling the demise of the "ideologies of progress" nourished by Enlightenment thought, it put an end to the very notion of what Jacques Le Goff calls "a linear, continuous, irreversible progress that follows the same path in all societies."[79] The sense of decline this engendered has been fueled still further by global economic realities. Like other countries of the West, France must confront the inescapable fact that the centers of world power, along with money and markets, are steadily moving eastward. It must compete both with advanced economies like those of the United States and Japan and with the cheap goods of developing nations like China. If exhaustion is not yet total, there can no longer be any doubt that the long centuries when Europe dominated the world are coming to an end. As a new millennium dawns, it brings with it the twilight sense that an old world order is collapsing—a world order in which France, and Europe, played a vital role. "A particular phase in the history of Europe," writes Václav Havel, "appears to be drawing to a close . . . Europe has ceased to be the center of colonial power or the control room of the world, and it no longer decides the world's fate."[80] As uncertainties cloud the future of France and Europe, the past assumes a dramatic intensity.

Virtually all of these critical issues—the loss of French *grandeur* and of a certain world order, the "acceleration" of history and the advent of a society based on global competition and high-technology consumer capitalism, the crisis of ideology and the debates over French identity—set their stamp on cinematic representations of the past. Sometimes, the presence of these issues could hardly be clearer: the elegiac portrait of revolution seen in Tavernier's historical films of the 1970s leaves no doubt about the terrible void many experienced as left-wing utopian hopes crumbled in the course of that decade. More often, though, anxieties are felt indirectly: the dreamlike haze that surrounds memories of the colonial past in works such as *Outremer* and *Le crabe-tambour* suggests the dark shadow of contemporary racism; the aestheticized "falseness" of *Les amants du Pont-Neuf* contains echoes of a beloved populist world that seems to have vanished forever. But whether the traces of these impulses are implicit or explicit, taken together they bear witness to a period of deep and widespread crisis. "We are in the midst of living the crisis of our political representations," writes Michel Winock, "a crisis of the Nation-state about to merge in a larger European unity; a crisis of national memory that can be seen in the historical revisions of our founding myth of Revolution; a crisis of working-class leadership with the erosion of unions and the Communist Party; a crisis of Socialist ideology. . . . On what shared beliefs can we found a new concept of citizenship?"[81]

It is, certainly, this sense of deep national crisis that gives rise not only to the obsession with the past which is reflected in French cinema but also to films that are permeated, albeit in different ways, by a profound melancholy. The mournful weight of the past is, certainly, most intense in the cinema of Alain Resnais: in his films, repressed and shifting memories seem to hold thought and action captive. But, to varying extents, a similar sense of paralysis affects the protagonists of other films. If the numbness that afflicts the characters in *Le crabe-tambour* and *Outremer* can be explained by the trauma of decolonization, no similar explanation comes to mind for the aimlessness of the homeless young people who roam about contemporary Paris in *Les amants du Pont-Neuf*. The preoccupation with memory seen in these films may recall the search for lost time undertaken by the narrator of Proust's masterpiece. But the joy that awaits Proust's narrator when he retrieves the past is nowhere to be found in these recent works. Here, instead, the past takes on the somber colors of the present even as it becomes entombed in what might be seen as cinematic "sites of memory." It is the various shapes of these haunted and often funereal sites that will be examined in the following chapters.

II

Alain Resnais: The Ghosts of History

The Shape(s) of Memory

Although the cinema of Alain Resnais spans a period of half a century—his first film, *Van Gogh*, was made in 1948—the director's name invariably calls to mind a series of deeply historical films he made relatively early in his career in the 1950s and early 1960s. Focused on the worst horrors of our time, these works echo with the roll call of the dead: with the untold millions who died in the Spanish Civil War (*Guernica*, 1950), in the camps (*Night and Fog*), and in the ashes of Hiroshima (*Hiroshima mon amour*). Deeply embedded in a Cold War climate of fear and anguish, these films bear the ineradicable mark of an era still stunned by revelations of Nazi atrocities and traumatized by the specter of annihilation that accompanied the bomb. As Hendrik Hertzberg, borrowing a phrase from essayist E. B. White, observes: "It is difficult to overestimate—and before long it will be difficult to remember—the degree to which 'the stubborn fact of annihilation' darkened the imagination of the world during the decades after Hiroshima and Nagasaki."[1]

Commentator after commentator has paid tribute to the power with which Resnais's early films evoke "this stubborn fact." Noting that then minister of culture Jack Lang asked French television channels to show *Night and Fog* during one of the many controversies of the 1970s and 1980s rooted in the Vichy period, historian Michael Roth describes Resnais's film as one of the "most startling, powerful films made about the Nazi period."[2] In the eyes of French critic Serge Daney, *Night and Fog*, *Hiroshima mon amour*, and *Muriel ou le temps d'un retour* (*Muriel*), a 1963 film that deals with the practice of torture during the Algerian War, are nothing less than "unimpeachable witnesses of our modernity." In the postwar period, says Daney, Resnais was the only one to understand that cinema "had to deal with an extra person: the human species. And that person had just been denied (in the concentration camps), blown up (by the bomb) and diminished (by torture). Traditional cinema was incapable of 'portraying' that. A way had to be found. And thus Resnais."[3] And Gilles Deleuze goes even further. Endorsing René Prédal's suggestion that virtually all of Resnais's characters resemble camp survivors, Deleuze declares that it is not only Resnais's early films but his entire oeuvre that testifies to the wave of death and destruction that enveloped the world in the 1940s. "Resnais," observes the philosopher, "has only one cinematographic subject, body, or actor: he who returns from the dead."[4]

If, as Deleuze suggests, this single "subject" dominates Resnais's cinema, it is a subject that makes itself felt not only through the characters of his films but also—and in some sense, above all—through their mood. With scripts written by many different collaborators, the subjects of Resnais's films vary greatly. (One of the few modern *auteurs* to rely heavily on literary scripts, Resnais has collaborated with eminent men and women of letters including Jean Cayrol, Marguerite Duras, and Alain Robbe-Grillet.) Some, like *Night and Fog* and *Hiroshima*, deal explicitly with the horrors of our time: others, like Resnais's second feature, *Last Year at Marienbad* (*L'année dernière à Marienbad*, 1961), seem to turn their back on history. But virtually all exhibit the same mood of mourning and melancholia that, in a work like *Hiroshima*, was so clearly linked to the suffering endured by the "human species." Peopled by men and women for whom time has stopped—numbed survivors chained to the past by remembered trauma—his films are infused with the "malady of death," to use a term associated with Marguerite Duras, that came in the wake of the camps and the bomb. They bear witness to what an eloquent Julia Kristeva describes as the altered modes of thought and behavior, the "psychic disorders," prompted by the "monstrous historical spectacles" of our time. Such spectacles, writes Kristeva, "have brutalized consciousness by an explosion of death and madness that no dam, ideological or aesthetic, seems able to contain. That pressure had intimate and inevitable repercussions in psychic disorders."[5]

Characterized by a collapse of individual identity, by feelings of paralysis and alienation, these "psychic disorders" are, clearly, at the core of Resnais's cinema.[6] Resnais's women, in particular, display what Kai Erickson describes as the classic symptom of trauma—that is, the "continual reliving of some wounding experience."[7] Sometimes, as in *Hiroshima*, the nature of that "wounding experience" is known, comprehensible; at others, as in *Marienbad*, it remains ambiguous, uncertain. But whether imaginary or real, it has left an indelible mark on its victims. Wounded and numb, they remain incapable of choosing, of taking action. Lacking not only a sense of identity but, often, even a name—in *Hiroshima*, the female protagonist is called by the name of her birthplace; in *Marienbad*, she is simply the "wife"—they inhabit a prisonlike world of *temps morts*, of endless waiting. Although they appear to crave love, they flee from human contact, from passion. The female protagonist of *Marienbad* is constantly pleading to be left alone: "laissez-moi," she keeps exclaiming.[8] That of *Muriel* invites an old lover to her home only to constantly reject him. Often prey to madness and suicide, they are given to cries and moments of hysteria, to the obsessive litanies and fragmented phrases of those in the grip of boundless depression. Reliving a past trauma, the protagonist of *Hiroshima* aimlessly wanders the streets until her pain erupts in a hysterical cry; in *Stavisky*, the protagonist's neurasthenic wife suffers from premonitory nightmares; unable to choose between husband and lover, the hypersensitive protagonist of *Mélo* (1986) finally takes her own life.

The anxiety that besets the characters is, moreover, echoed, intensified, by the world around them. One of the most striking characteristics of Resnais's films, in fact, is their deeply psychological nature. Here, thoughts and feelings seem to come alive, to embed themselves in shapes and shadows, in movements and mise-en-scène. Around the time he made *Marienbad*, in fact, Resnais spoke of his wish to capture and create thoughts and feelings. Expressing a desire to actually film "what goes on in someone's head," in an oft-cited interview he remarked that he saw film as a way of approaching "the complexity of thought, its mechanism. . . . When I see a film I am more interested in the play of feelings than in characters. I think that we can achieve a cinema without psychologically defined characters, a cinema where the play of feelings would circulate just as, in a contemporary painting, the play of forms manages to be stronger than the story."[9]

Transcending any particular character or characters, this "play of feelings" transforms the world itself into a melancholy mental space where everything speaks of anxiety and imprisonment, of uncertainty and anguish. The endless, tracking movements of the camera in *Hiroshima*, the repeated falling shots of *Je t'aime je t'aime* (1968), the dreams of falling in *Stavisky*—all suggest a boundless anxiety, a futile desire to find the buried layers of a traumatic past.[10] As the world becomes a huge mental space, the line between the human and the inhuman is erased: rooms, cities, and objects convey the "play of feelings," the death-haunted anguish and impotence, that the spectral characters are often unwilling or unable to voice. "Landscapes," says Deleuze, "are mental states no less than mental states are maps, the two crystallized into one another."[11] Stone, the very embodiment of a universe set under the sign of petrification, is everywhere. The frozen statues and mirrors of *Marienbad*, the strange pyramidal formations of *Stavisky*, the moss-covered rocks of *Providence* (1976), all evoke the glacial aspect of cemeteries, the cold of a universe under the mortal sway of the inorganic. The empty rooms and stone walls of the prison camp in *Night and Fog*—an emptiness haunted by the ghosts of millions—appear, displaced, in film after film: in the endless corridors of the national library in *Toute la mémoire du monde* (1956); in the deserted streets of Hiroshima; in the lifeless garden and frozen statues of *Last Year at Marienbad*.

In the end, though, these ghosts may not be the only ones that haunt Resnais's cinema. The psychic pain that afflicts his characters, and that is embodied in the icy world they inhabit, may have still another dimension. For if, as commentators have suggested, works such as *Hiroshima* and *Muriel* reveal a profound "engagement" with the "human species," they also suggest historical memories rooted in realities that are particularly French. This brings me to the crux of this chapter. For I would argue that Resnais's cinema bears witness not only to the long reach of "global" memories but also to those stemming from some of the darkest and most repressed zones of the national past. It is not only the "monstrous historical spectacles" of the camps and the bomb that provoke the pain and melancholy felt in Resnais's cinema. It is also the bitter memory of the Algerian War and, especially, that of the Occupation.

In general, this aspect of Resnais's cinema has been relatively ignored. It may well be that his meditation on the national past, on the specific contours of French history and memory, has been eclipsed by the sheer power of his engagement with the "human species." And it is also true that his indictment—for such, I think, it can be called—of French attitudes and behavior *was* muted. It was implicit rather than explicit, indirect rather than direct. To a large degree, of course, this holds true of Resnais's approach to the past in general: even the horrors recalled in *Night and Fog* and *Hiroshima* are evoked indirectly rather than directly. That is, instead of re-creating or representing the past directly—in the manner, say, of a film like *Schindler's List*—Resnais almost invariably seizes it through "traces." Sometimes, as in his early works, these traces are physical: hence the newsreels and photographs documenting the destruction wrought by the bomb in *Hiroshima*. More often, though, and especially in later films, these physical reminders of the past give way to ones that are solely mental: i.e., to the haunted memories and psychic scars that torment virtually all of Resnais's characters. And even when Resnais uses palpable traces of the past, he takes care to remind viewers of the chasm that separates such traces from the lived experience. For example, the voice-over text of *Night and Fog*, which was written by novelist and former deportee Jean Cayrol, constantly points to this chasm by reminding us of the limits faced by knowledge and representation. Voicing the dilemma central to those who would commemorate the Holocaust,[12] Cayrol's text expresses both the need and the impossibility of remembering an experience that cannot be understood or imagined by those who were not there. As the camera tracks through the dormitories of a now-empty concentration camp, the text insists that "no description, no picture" can restore the "true dimension" of the camps. "What remains of the reality of these camps," it asks, "despised by those who made them, incomprehensible to those who suffered here. . . ? No description, no picture can restore their true dimension: endless, uninterrupted fear. . . . Of this brick dormitory, of these threatened sleepers, we can only show you the shell, the shadow."[13]

The fact that it is impossible to capture more than the "shell, the shadow" of history is, surely, one of the reasons that Resnais did not confront certain aspects of the French past more directly or explicitly. Still, it seems to me that other factors, deeply rooted in French history and politics, were almost certainly at work. On the most obvious level, censorship restrictions ensured that, for decades, the director could not portray or address, at least in a direct or unequivocal manner, the most disturbing zones of recent French history. In this context, it is important to remember that for a quarter of a century after the end of World War II, French films remained subject to mechanisms of censorship put into place in July of 1945.[14] Moreover, French censorship, unlike its American counterpart, was concerned not only with morality but also, and perhaps above all, with politics. Indeed, on more than one occasion, Resnais's films, with their distinctly left-wing stamp, encountered difficulties for political reasons. A 1953 documentary made in collaboration with Chris Marker, *Les statues meurent aussi* (*Statues Also Die*) was banned because its discussion of African art seemed to cast a jaundiced eye on French cultural imperialism. Even *Night and Fog*, which is now hailed as a powerful document about the Holocaust, met with problems. Resnais was forced to mask a scene depicting a camp guard who was wearing a French cap or *képi*; this telltale detail, it was feared, suggested French complicity in the Final Solution.

Nor were these overt instances of censorship the only ones to create difficulties for the director. Several of his films were also suppressed in less draconian ways. Even though Resnais altered the offending scene in *Night and Fog*, the film was withdrawn from the 1956 Cannes festival; the official explanation for this was that it "wounded the national sentiment of a participating nation"—namely, Germany.[15] So, too, was *Hiroshima mon amour* denied a place among the "official" French selections at the Cannes festival of 1959.[16] Once again, the ostensible reason was that it risked upsetting a foreign country: in this case, the United States. Still, there may well have been unacknowledged pressures closer to home. As Lynn Higgins observes, "it was not the Americans that the film would offend, but the French. According to Edgar Morin, Resnais was told that his film was incompatible with the ideals of the Fifth Republic."[17]

Whether overt or subtle, the restrictions of censorship were, moreover—and this is, perhaps, the most telling point—both the product and the reflection of a historical moment in which the darkest zones of recent French history were consistently repressed and erased. For more than two decades after World War II came to an end, French memories of that somber time were subject to amnesia, both conscious and unconscious, and to a constant process of revision. It is the smothered unease of this era that gives Resnais's cinema, I think, its special cast. Marking a particular moment in the evolution of French memory of the Vichy past, his films are rooted in, and yet implicitly denounce, the climate of "unfinished mourning" and "repression" that, in the eyes of historian Henry Rousso, characterized Vichy memory from the end of World War II until the early 1970s.

Rousso makes these observations in a book explicitly devoted to the "history of the memory of Vichy": *The Vichy Syndrome: History and Memory in France since 1944*. It is Rousso's thesis that the trauma of the Occupation has been so long-lasting and powerful precisely because, from the very first, the most bitter zones of the Vichy past—the internal divisions and ideological conflicts that saw French men and women pitted against one another, the presence of collaboration, the deportations of Jews—were deliberately obscured, repressed, denied. The terrible weight of these zones meant that, unlike what occurred in the aftermath of World War I, the end of the Occupation did not see a united nation joined in mourning for those fallen in battle. No such collective mourning was possible after World War II. How could France commemorate a period not only of defeat and Occupation but of virtual civil war? And whom was the nation to mourn? deportees? Frenchmen sent to labor camps? people killed in bombardments or at the hands of other Frenchmen? "Of the 600,000 French dead," writes Rousso, "only a third had died weapon in hand. The rest had vanished in bombardments, executions, massacres, and deportations or had fallen victim to internal combat in France or its colonies. Traditional forms of commemoration were inappropriate to such circumstances. Hence the authorities maintained a discreet silence about the war and its enemies."[18]

The "discreet silence" about the worst realities of the Vichy past went hand in hand with the creation of what Rousso calls the "myth of resistancialism." Launched by de Gaulle even before the war came to an end, this myth obliterated the dark zones of the Vichy past even as it suggested that the French had been united in their resistance to a foreign invader. In a famous speech made immediately after Paris was liberated in 1944, de Gaulle set forth the main outlines of this "myth" as he rallied the French by extolling their courage and their unity. "Paris!" he declared, "Paris outraged! Paris broken! Paris martyred! But Paris liberated! Liberated by itself! Liberated by its people with the help of the armies of France, with the support and help of all of France, of the France which fought, of the only France, of the true France, of eternal France!"[19]

The image of a France that had been "outraged" and "martyred," but not defeated and divided, was calculated, of course, to restore the unity and morale of a nation that had been shaken to the core. It demonstrated, in fact, the vital role that political myths often play at moments of great social crisis.[20] But it also bore little resemblance to the terrible truths, the worst traumas, of those years. "The exculpatory lie," writes William Pfaff, "told to the French by General de Gaulle in 1944, with the cynicism of great statesmanship—that the Resistance was the Nation—is today understood by nearly everyone to have been a lie, and, indeed, was so understood at the time."[21] Not only did de Gaulle ignore the role of the Allies in France's liberation but he was careful to avoid any mention of the bitter ideological struggles of the Occupation and its aftermath. Acting as if the anti-Republican, anti-Semitic, and collaborationist government of Vichy had never existed, de Gaulle described his country as one in which a united people, confronted only by a foreign invader, had rallied behind the active cadres of the Resistance to liberate "eternal France."

Originally designed to restore national morale at a moment of terrible crisis, this myth grew stronger in the course of the 1950s. As the Cold War settled over Europe, the perceived threat of Communism in France encouraged the reemergeance of the traditional Right; discredited and silenced by the taint of collaboration after the war, it was only too eager to forget its behavior during the war and to see former *résistants*, many of whom were Communists, eclipsed by the idea of an abstract and mythical national Resistance. Moreover, de Gaulle himself, who was recalled to power in 1958 to avert a crisis at the time of the Algerian War, had every reason to further consecrate the myth he had launched fourteen years earlier. As the man who, from exile in London, had saved the "honor" of France by urging his countrymen to resist the invader, he himself was the very embodiment not only of national *grandeur* and unity but also of national resistance. Since he saw himself as both the incarnation of France and a symbol of the Resistance, it was but a short step to the equation of France itself with the Resistance. Heightening the general's own *gloire*, this equation was welcomed by most of the French, who wanted nothing better than to put the past behind them. "As early as the mid-1950s," comments Rousso, "many French people clearly wished to lay controversy about the past to rest, and the invented honor of the Gaullists seemed perfectly tailored to fill the bill. . . . A generation undeniably embraced the Gaullist image and ignored what few discordant voices remained."[22]

As suggested earlier, it is precisely the historical and political climate that Rousso describes here—one in which history was "manipulated" and "rewritten" by those in power even as the larger public willingly embraced an "exculpatory lie"—that reverberates throughout Resnais's cinema. If his films bear witness to the "monstrous historical spectacles" of our time, so, too, do they reflect, I would argue, the pervasive climate of bad faith, of amnesia and repression, that governed French memories of the Vichy past throughout the 1950s and 1960s. In a sense, of course, it is impossible to distinguish between two such closely intertwined strands of historical memory. How is one to disentangle the melancholy prompted by the spectacle of human barbarity from the climate of "unfinished mourning" that bathed French memory of the Vichy years? or distinguish between horrors that defy imagination and representation and those that have been repressed by the weight of censorship both conscious and unconscious? Still, one need not deny that the memory of the "global" horrors evoked in *Night and Fog* and *Hiroshima* resonates throughout Resnais's cinema to affirm that there *are* aspects of his films—the particular shapes taken by "psychic disorders," the specific contours of melancholy and repressed memories, the presence of illusions and mysteries—which point to the weight of guilt and denial that characterized Vichy memories until the early 1970s.

In this context, it is significant, for example, that Resnais's characters are not only chained to the past; they are also given to lies and deceptions, both conscious and unconscious, concerning that very past. Similarly, it is not only that they forget the past; it is also that they deliberately (re)invent and rewrite it. Resnais's paralyzed protagonists may resemble camp survivors; but, unlike the latter, they are constantly editing their tales of what really happened. Moreover, as if to quell inner uncertainties and unwelcome truths, they display a strange determination to convince others—and themselves?—of their version of events.[23] This phenomenon is, in fact, at the very core of Resnais's second feature, *Last Year at Marienbad*. Set in a ghostly hotel whose precise location is never made clear, *Marienbad* features an eternal triangle—husband, wife, and handsome stranger—engaged in desperate attempts at "persuasion." The stranger repeatedly tries to convince the woman that they had an affair the previous year; she denies it. There is no way to know if he is telling the truth, or she, or if everything is imaginary. Faced with conflicting versions of the past, we are drawn into a world of ambiguity and illusion. We can no more trust what the characters say about their own lives than we can believe the stories, the "fictions," they weave about the stone statues that line the hotel's formal garden. Although the film elicited varying interpretations—one critic felt the hotel was really a clinic and the wife a patient; another maintained that the man was describing future events—the essence of the film lay, as Resnais himself remarked, in its very ambiguity.[24] Deeming it a work "that takes place entirely at the level of appearances," the director observed that everything in this film "is equivocal. We cannot say if a scene takes place today, yesterday, or a year ago; or if a thought belongs to one character or to another. Everything—reality and feelings, what is dreamed and what is not—is put into question."[25]

Moreover, it is not only the characters in Resnais's films, and their desperate attempts at persuasion, that seem to reflect a historical moment in which the past was denied and "rewritten." Everything in his cinema speaks of ambiguity and illusion, of uncertainty and doubt. *Marienbad* may well be, to borrow Resnais's term, the most "equivocal" of his films. Still, to varying degrees, all his films frustrate our attempts to determine "truth," to arrive at "reality." Indeed, Resnais deliberately breaks with a variety of long-standing cinematic conventions in order to underscore the illusory nature of all that is seen and heard—to subvert what André Bazin saw as the ontological realism of the very medium of film. A good example of this is his use of sound and image. Instead of using synchronous sound, which tends to reinforce the believability of what is seen, Resnais constantly splits sound and image. For instance, in *Marienbad* the whispering voices of unseen hotel guests fill the sound track, while the thoughts of the protagonists are conveyed through mysterious images that may or may not be "true." In *Muriel*, we hear about something *after* it happens: while seeing the images of a new sequence, we hear, in voice-off, the sound track that presumably belongs to the preceding one. In both cases, this technique means that attention is divided—are we to believe what we hear? what we see? neither?—even as belief is undermined. Unable to trust either eye or ear, the spectator is never allowed to forget the unreal nature of the world that unfolds on-screen.

Even as reality is drained of weight and substance, mysteries and ambiguities come to the fore. Even the parameters of space and time become as uncertain, as unstable, as the tales told by the characters. Treating us like the time traveler of *Je t'aime je t'aime*, films whirl us from past to present, from real to imaginary, while the present—devoured by memory, by mental images both real and imagined—constantly eludes us.[26] Like temporal divisions, spatial boundaries also dissolve. Resnais carefully avoids conventional establishing shots that would allow us to fix ourselves in recognizable spaces. Instead, he favors oblique angle shots, dizzying vertical pans, and, above all, insistent travelings that constantly propel us forward and direct our attention to the unknown universe that lies outside the frame. This persistent sense of mystery—of things unknown and unknowable, of truths unseen and untold—is further accentuated by camera work. At times, close-ups are so extreme that images remain unclear and mysterious; at others, the camera lingers so long on objects or people that it creates what critic Pascal Bonitzer deems a kind of nonnarrative suspense. Noting that the "meaning" implicitly promised by such long-held shots is never forthcoming, Bonitzer asks: "What do these tableaux mean, why are they there? . . . the whole representation becomes problematic."[27]

To suggest a link between the "problematical" or "equivocal" nature of Resnais's cinema and the lies and evasions that marked French memory in the postwar period is not to deny, of course, that the unreal and stylized illusions brought to life in his films may well reflect a variety of other impulses. On a personal level, one must keep in mind Resnais's avowed love of the stage: "I like real places," the director once confessed, "when they look like decor!"[28] (Originally attracted to theater rather than film, he was also drawn to the melodramatic excesses of silent film.)[29] And this personal attraction to the "illusions" of stage and screen dovetailed with a cinematic moment in which filmmakers, exemplified in France by the New Wave, deliberately eschewed, questioned, traditional cinematic realism. From a still broader perspective, this very questioning might be seen as one more indication of the postwar legacy of historical anguish. Divorcing humankind from a universe rendered alien and absurd, the "monstrous historical spectacles" of the 1940s also prompted the acute awareness, which is explicitly voiced in *Night and Fog*, of the impossibility of seizing and representing the "real." "As if overcome or destroyed by an all too powerful wave," writes Julia Kristeva of this awareness, "our symbolic modes have been emptied, almost annihilated, petrified. At the edge of silence the word 'nothing' emerges—a modest defense in the face of incommensurable internal and external disorder."[30]

There is no doubt that all these impulses—which are at once personal, cultural, and historical—inform Resnais's embrace of stylized illusion and intense theatricality. But above all, I would argue, the "equivocal" nature of Resnais's cinema points to the climate of "lies" and "illusions" that governed French historical memory in the decades following the war. To demonstrate further why I think this to be the case, I would like to turn to several films in particular. For not only do these works touch on some of the most troubled zones of the French past; they also indict—with varying degrees of explicitness—a world in which historical truths were manipulated and repressed. In the earliest of these films, it is true, the outlines of these zones remain indistinct: the dark secrets of French history cast but the vaguest of shadows in *Toute la mémoire du monde*; the internal conflicts of the Occupation remain in the background in *Hiroshima mon amour*. But in later films, these secrets—and the accusations they elicit—come into sharper focus. *Muriel* confronts the legacy of Vichy as well as that of the Algerian War; *Stavisky* explores the political and moral climate that paved the way for Vichy. Taken together, these films constitute nothing less than a mournful meditation on the national past.

Buried Secrets: *Hiroshima mon amour*, *Muriel*

Although Resnais first achieved international recognition with *Hiroshima*, he had been making documentary shorts for over a decade before the release of his first feature. And, as commentators have frequently observed, these shorts—which are, unfortunately, relatively little known and difficult to see on either side of the Atlantic—announce, often in a masterful way, themes and stylistic features that would later be orchestrated and amplified in the director's feature works. Deeming these early films "preludes" to a future work, critic Robert Benayoun points out that "for almost each short by Resnais there is a feature that complements it . . . *Toute la mémoire du monde* naturally accompanies *Marienbad*, *Night and Fog* calls forth *Hiroshima* . . . from *Les statues meurent aussi* to *Stavisky* it is but a short step."[31]

In the context of such continuities, one short in particular might be seen as a "prelude" to the meditation on the national past that Resnais pursues in later films. I am speaking now of a documentary about the French national library, or *Bibliothèque nationale*: *Toute la mémoire du monde*, commissioned by a government agency concerned with cultural affairs. Although the subject of this short might seem far removed from the historical convulsions evoked in works such as *Guernica* and *Night and Fog*, *Toute la mémoire du monde* assumes an undeniable interest in terms of French history. For the *Bibliothèque nationale*, which stems from collections that originally belonged to French monarchs, constitutes an archtypal site of French memory. In fact, the imposing building seen in *Toute la mémoire du monde* is generally counted among the great "institutions of memory" constructed in the course of the last century.[32]

In a sense, of course, this may be stretching a point. That is, Resnais's decision to make a film about the national library was fortuitous insofar as *Toute la mémoire du monde* was a commissioned work.[33] But what was certainly not fortuitous is the way in which Resnais transformed the *Bibliothèque nationale*—this monument to the national past—into a place of secrets and mystery, of claustrophobia and unease. Revealing his ability to create a distinct "play of feelings" without the presence of "psychologically defined characters," Resnais turns the library into a vast mental space in which memories are jealously guarded and carefully locked away. Comparing the library seen in *Toute la mémoire du monde* to a "gigantic memory," Gilles Deleuze remarks that its "carts, shelves, stairways, elevators and corridors constitute the elements and the levels of a gigantic memory where men themselves are no longer anything but mental functions or neuronic messengers."[34]

A "gigantic memory" as well as a monument to the national past, as seen in *Toute la mémoire du monde* the library is also, significantly, a place that refuses to lay bare its secrets, or even its layout, to the viewer. This refusal is clear from the outset: eschewing establishing shots that would enable us to get our bearings, Resnais plunges us into the library's cavernous and forbidding subterranean vaults where gleams of light can barely dissipate the surrounding darkness or penetrate the secrets that seem to lurk in hidden corners. As the film progresses, sharply angled shots, incessant travelings down endless corridors, and high-contrast lighting create a persistent sense of mystery and unease even as they turn the library into a kind of Piranesian prison. A sense of confinement lingers even when we reach the roof: the eye is greeted not by shots of the sky and the surrounding neighborhood but, instead, by the iron grillwork that encloses the library's dome.

Deemed a "fortress" and a "citadel" by the voice-over text, the monumental library resembles nothing other, in fact, than a huge prison in which books, rather than people, are inventoried, stamped, locked away. Here, low-angle shots turn marching guards into ominous jailers, while impassive stone busts gaze sternly as uniformed guards go about their tasks. Struck by the sense of imprisonment that clings to the library, critic Noel Burch described Resnais's portrayal of the *Bibliothèque nationale* thus: "Finally, having got past all the barriers separating the 'prisoners' from the outside world, we reach the 'cell-blocks': the stacks, with their long dark aisles filled by the echoing footsteps of invisible guards."[35] For Canadian critic Peter Harcourt, too, the library seemed a "great prison in which one can wander endlessly along extended corridors."[36] Of course, as Harcourt went on to remark, the "prisoners" of the *Bibliothèque nationale* differ from conventional inmates in that they are locked away not as punishment but, rather, "to guarantee their continued life." True enough. Yet one shivers for the fate of these volumes guarded so carefully behind iron grates. Even the allusion, at the end of the film, to the "happiness" of the reader who finds an ardently desired book or shred of knowledge, seems misplaced here. How is such "happiness" possible within these cavernous walls and forbidding halls? Designed as a "place of memory" to keep the past alive, the funereal library seems, instead, to have assumed the form of its tomb. Is it too much to imagine that it is a tomb enclosing some of the darkest, and most carefully guarded, secrets of the national past?

It is with Resnais's first feature, *Hiroshima mon amour*, that these secrets begin to take shape. They are still overshadowed, it is true, by remembered traumas both global and personal. The memory of global horror, of the "monstrous historical spectacles" of our time, is embodied, of course, in the city where the film takes place: set in Hiroshima, Resnais's film unfolds in a place that has come to incarnate, and to symbolize, the wave of suffering and destruction that swept over the world in the 1940s. The personal trauma evoked in the film is that suffered by its female protagonist: a young French actress whose lover was killed during the Occupation. But behind these collective and individual dramas, one can glimpse, I think, the indistinct and uneasy shape of national conflicts: behind the repressed memories of the female protagonist lie those of a country given to amnesia.

As the film opens, it is the memory of global horror that prevails. For *Hiroshima* begins with a powerful, almost unbearable, evocation of the fate suffered by the hapless inhabitants of Hiroshima. A mysterious opening image, an extreme close-up of what appear to be human bodies covered by particles that resemble ashes from a nuclear explosion, is followed by a long sequence that juxtaposes shots of present-day, rebuilt, Hiroshima with "traces"—that is, archival evidence (newsreels, photos, museum exhibits)— of the destruction wrought by the atomic bomb. As images and reconstructions of burned flesh and deformed bodies pass before us, a conversation is heard between two voices, male and female, that presumbably belong to the bodies glimpsed in the opening shot.

In this conversation, Resnais underscores the dilemma that, as suggested earlier, was explicitly voiced in *Night and Fog*: the tension between the need and the impossibility of discussing or representing the horror of the Holocaust or that of Hiroshima. In the words of Marguerite Duras, who wrote the script for *Hiroshima*, the conversation is an "operatic exchange" showing that it is "impossible to talk about Hiroshima. All that one can do is talk about the impossibility of talking about Hiroshima."[37] And, indeed, the words spoken, and repeated, between the two voices demonstrate nothing other than this "impossibility." Again and again, the woman insists that she has "seen" everything that happened at Hiroshima. "I saw everything," she intones. "Everything." Again and again, and just as insistently, the man counters: "You saw nothing at Hiroshima. Nothing." Finally, as if acknowledging that he is right, that she saw "nothing" because she was not there that fateful day, she is moved to defend the traces she did see. "The reconstructions," she insists, "were done as seriously as possible. The films were made as seriously as possible. . . . The illusion . . . is so perfect that tourists cry." But even then he is implacable. When she insists that she, too, was moved to tears by the fate of Hiroshima, he responds: "No. What would you have cried about?"

As this long sequence comes to an end, it becomes clear that the voices do indeed belong to the lovers whose bodies, gripped in a passionate embrace, were glimpsed in the opening shot. She is a French actress who has come to Hiroshima to make a film about peace; he is a Japanese architect. As the film progresses, it gradually emerges that the "impossibility" of talking about the collective tragedy that befell Hiroshima finds a personal echo in the life of the French woman. The doomed and intense passion she presently experiences for the Japanese man, and the presence of Hiroshima itself, revive long buried and deeply traumatic memories of her first love. Scattered flashbacks, which begin to form a narrative as the film progresses, reveal that during the Occupation, as a young woman in the provincial French city of Nevers, she loved a young German soldier who was killed toward the end of the war. In the course of the purges that accompanied Liberation, like other women accused of "fraternization" with the enemy, she was forced to have her head shaved for her "crime." Nearly mad with grief and pain, she was confined to the basement of her parents' home until the crisis of suffering passed and her hair grew back. Then, with the help of her mother, she fled to Paris to begin life anew. There, she married, had children, and began a career as an actress. Never, however, in all the intervening years, has she told anyone, even her husband, about the trauma of grief and shame suffered in Nevers. Now, however, relentlessly questioned by her Japanese lover, she slowly, brokenly, tells him everything.

Her confession, though, brings not catharsis but more suffering still. Unable to forget the past, she finds herself paralyzed in the present: she can neither remain with her new lover nor decide to leave him. As she wanders the streets of Hiroshima in a daze, she is tormented by the knowledge that by telling the Japanese man of her past, she has betrayed her first love. Despite herself, she knows, she is forgetting the intensity of that earlier passion. In desperation, she tells the Japanese man that he, too, will be forgotten in his turn. "I'll think of this adventure as of the horror of oblivion," she laments. "I already know it."

A film about trauma both collective and individual, *Hiroshima* is also, of course, a work about remembering—and about forgetting. In a sense, Resnais shares the dilemma that confronts both the city of Hiroshima, which seeks simultaneously to remember its past and to reconstruct itself anew, and his melancholy heroine. Like her, he feels both the need to forget the past and the anguish that comes in doing so: the "horror of oblivion."[38] On the one hand, as Resnais himself acknowledged, one must forget the past in order to live and act. "The problem came up for me," he said, "when I made *Night and Fog*. It was not a question of creating one more monument to the dead but of thinking of the present and of the future. Forgetting must be constructive. . . . Despair is inaction."[39] But on the other, even the most "constructive" act of forgetting brings with it the sense of betrayal and loss experienced by the desperate protagonist of *Hiroshima mon amour*. As long as her earlier love and pain were buried within her, they remained alive. They were part of a trauma that, as Lawrence Langer observes in connection with Holocaust survivors, "stops the chronological clock and fixes the moment permanently in memory and imagination, immune to the vicissitudes of time."[40] But once these memories move to the forefront of consciousness—once they are *told*—they lose their "aliveness," their immunity to the "vicissitudes of time." As the protagonist knows only too well, in remembering and relating her past, she turns it into a shadow of what she actually experienced. Like the image of a film, it becomes a trace, a husk, of what once existed. She discovers what historian Michael Roth calls the "scandal" of *Hiroshima mon amour*: the realization that "nothing is unforgettable and that, on the level of both collective memory and personal memory, to make the past into a narrative is to bring it into confrontation with the forces of forgetting. . . . Narrative memory, which is at the core of historical representation both on paper and on film, *transforms* the past as a condition of retaining the past. *Hiroshima mon amour* examines the costs of this transformation."[41]

But this "scandal" is not, I would argue, the only one in *Hiroshima*. Behind the heroine's personal trauma one discerns the indistinct shape of still another scandal, at once individual and collective, that also involves forgetting, betraying, the past. Bearing on the national past, this second scandal is not fully explored, not fully "remembered," in the film just as it was not fully "remembered" in France in the late 1950s. In other words, the public humiliation inflicted upon the protagonist in Nevers invokes a moment of the French past that, in 1959, was still confined to the buried recesses of collective memory. Her punishment evokes the specter of all the hatred and the abuses unleashed by the purges that erupted as the Occupation came to a convulsive end. The period of *l'épuration* reenacted the terrible divisions of the Vichy years even as it set the stage for new conflicts that, growing more bitter with time, would make it even more difficult for French men and women to confront the realities of the Occupation. As Henry Rousso reminds us, no one was satisfied that the demands of justice were met during the purges. Not only did the sentences meted out by the courts vary widely—much depended on the nature of the court, the social status of the defendant, the date of the trial—but the "reasons" for collaboration were ignored. In some cases, obviously, these "reasons" stemmed from ideological conviction or even patriotic passion. "How were the courts to judge men," asks Rousso, "who laid claim to a 'certain vision of France' though obviously not the same as de Gaulle's?"[42]

And what of the women who, like the heroine of *Hiroshima*, were punished for "fraternization" with the enemy? Weren't many of them victims of the sexual hypocrisy, the puritanical bad faith, that had characterized Vichy morality itself? Weren't they, as Lynn Higgins writes in a discussion of *Hiroshima*, little more than sacrificial victims? "The French woman of *Hiroshima mon amour*," observes Higgins, "serves . . . as a substitute victim: she is a member of the community but at the same time marginal to it because of her sex and her age; she is also innocent of any real military or political crimes and deflects attention from them in the town. . . . She is thus a substitute for all the members of the community."[43]

Hiroshima does not, as suggested earlier, confront such issues directly. And I am not sure that the woman is seen as a "substitute" for the members of the community. But Resnais certainly underscores her total moral innocence: the youthful passion she feels for the German soldier contains no trace of the self-interest, the calculated motives, that might have led others to turn to Germans as lovers or protectors. And he also makes clear the extent of the suffering she has repressed for fifteen years: the remembered sequences of her in the basement—head-shaven, half-mad with grief, fingernails scratching at the stone walls—are among the most powerful in the film. (Some commentators felt these sequences were *too* powerful, that Resnais was drawing an implicit equation between the individual sufferings of his heroine and the collective tragedy that befell the city of Hiroshima.) By emphasizing the disproportion between the heroine's "crime" and her "punishment," the film indirectly condemns that punishment as cruel, unjust, inhuman. In so doing, it implicitly questions the "justice" of the purges even as it points to memories, both individual and collective, which, like that of the protagonist, have been buried since the end of the war.

The traumatic national memories glimpsed in *Hiroshima* assume a far more distinct cast in *Muriel*. Written by Jean Cayrol, who had collaborated with Resnais on *Night and Fog*, *Muriel* is the first film in which the director portrays a French milieu, that of the provincial bourgeoisie, populated by characters whose behavior patterns and attitudes stamp them as unmistakably French. Through them, he evokes not only the historical moments and events (the defeat of 1940, the Occupation, the Algerian War) that dealt mortal blows to a "certain idea of France" but also the ways in which the painful memories of these events were suppressed and erased. "More than any other film," wrote the editors of *Les cahiers de la cinémathèque* a decade after the film was first released, "*Muriel* [asked] French spectators to situate themselves in relationship to their own past . . . at a moment when the certainties of the French Empire and of the Sacred Union— memories transmitted by previous generations and bolstered by cinema— were collapsing. *Muriel* bears valuable testimony to the moment when bad memories, buried for too long, [were] finally exposed to the light."[44]

In *Muriel*, the lingering weight of "bad memories" is filtered through traces both physical and mental. As in *Hiroshima*, the physical traces of the past are once again embodied in a city: in this case, in Boulogne. In this windswept northern port, modern buildings and new neighborhoods, as well as half-glimpsed ruins, serve as constant reminders of the extensive damage inflicted by bombing raids of World War II. As for the psychic traces left by the past, they are found, as always, in the haunted memories, the fears and uncertainties, of the protagonists. The film's opening scene introduces us to two of these hapless creatures: Hélène, a middle-aged antique dealer in Boulogne, and her stepson, Bernard, a young veteran of the Algerian War. Before long, Hélène and Bernard are joined by Alphonse (an ex-lover of Hélène's) and his companion, Françoise (a young actress), when the latter arrive for what will turn out to be an extended visit.

Essentially a psychological portrait of these four characters, like all of Resnais's films *Muriel* features protagonists who are prey to anguish, solitude, uncertainty. But, significantly, of the four protagonists, it is the members of the older generation, Alphonse and Hélène, who consistently attempt to contain this anguish by indulging in lies and deceptions about themselves and others. And it is principally through them that Resnais evokes not only the "collapse of certainties" transmitted by previous generations but also the climate of self-serving half-truths, of deliberate amnesia, that, in the early 1960s, characterized French memories of the Vichy era.

In this respect, it is telling that both Hélène and Alphonse are given to desperate "persuasions" about the past. Each makes repeated attempts to convince the other of what "really" happened when their romance was shattered at the outbreak of World War II. But, even more than in *Hiroshima*, everything remains unclear: we never know if one, or both, are lying. Have they created a "false" past? And if so, has it been done consciously and deliberately?

The climate of uncertainty and deception that suffuses their versions of the past extends, moreover, well into their present lives. An enormous gap separates the personas they present to the world and their innermost selves. Although, for example, Hélène is a staunch upholder of middle-class values and social proprieties, she is secretly a compulsive gambler who has incurred enormous debts. Refusing to acknowledge this addiction either to herself or to others, she is blind to her own feelings and motives in still other ways. She has invited Alphonse for a visit, yet on the eve of his arrival, she abandons him in order to keep an appointment with another man; and while she encourages his attentions, she withdraws from him whenever they are alone. Neither she nor the viewer seems to know why, in fact, she sought this strange reunion. Did she hope for a renewal of their relationship? Does she need to feel youthful and desirable once again? Is she upset, as she claims, about what happened twenty years earlier? Or is she really distressed about the presence of Alphonse's companion, Françoise? These questions remain unanswered because Hélène is so clearly unable or unwilling to probe her deepest feelings, to confront her real self.

Hélène's pattern of self-deception, of lies and evasions, is even more dramatic in the case of Alphonse. His conduct, too, generates a series of unanswered questions: why, for example, has he brought his current girl-friend on a visit to a former lover? And why does this "aging Romeo" (as Françoise calls him) insist that Françoise is his "niece" when it is clear to everyone that she is his mistress? Given to lies about the present, Alphonse is, significantly, even more deceitful when it comes to the past. The extent of this deceit is revealed at the end of the film in a sequence that functions as a kind of psychological climax. It begins with the unexpected arrival of Alphonse's brother-in-law, Ernest. Determined to bring the errant and immature Alphonse back to his long-suffering wife, Ernest is only too happy to reveal the "truth" about the "aging Romeo." And it turns out that all the claims Alphonse has made about his life, past and present, were untrue. Contrary to what he said, he is not a widower. More important, though, throughout the film Alphonse has regaled anyone who would listen with nostalgic tales about his former life in Algeria, a life cut short, presumably, by the outbreak of war. Now, it is revealed that the past Alphonse painted in such glowing colors never existed. The pitiful owner of a bankrupt restaurant on the mainland, Alphonse never possessed a thriving café in Algeria. In fact, he never set foot outside France.

If Alphonse is haunted by images of an Algeria that never existed, Bernard is held captive by Algerian memories that are all too real. Like Hélène and Alphonse, Bernard, too, is given to ambiguous and deceptive behavior. But in contrast with his elders, the lies he tells are both conscious and comprehensible. Traumatized by his experiences as a soldier in Algeria, he is obsessed, in particular, by the memory of a young woman, Muriel—hence the title of the film—who was tortured and savagely beaten to death by his military unit in the course of the war. (Bernard has made the terrible discovery, said Resnais, that "we are all capable of frequenting horror without realizing it. We are all capable of behaving in a way that later appears incomprehensible and inexplicable to us.")[45] Bernard feels even more alone, and more anguished, because in France—indeed, in the bosom of his family—he must confront people who refuse to acknowledge the realities of the war, the atrocities he witnessed and in which he took part. "You can't talk about Muriel," a former army comrade, Robert, counsels him. "Every Frenchman feels alone. He is dying of fear. He'll put the barbed wires around his little world. He doesn't want trouble." Faced with these "barbed wires," Bernard becomes increasingly estranged and hostile. Unable to talk about the "real" Muriel, he has invented, seemingly for the benefit of his stepmother, a "false" Muriel, a young woman who is, he says, his fiancée. But in the end his repressed emotions—a combination of rage, anger, and guilt—erupt in an act of violence: seizing a gun, he kills Robert who, unlike him, has shown no remorse for what happened in Algeria.

The impossibility of "talking about" Muriel, an impossibility that prompts Bernard's act of violence, is underscored still further in *Muriel* by a device that is relatively rare in Resnais's cinema: the use of a film-within-a-film. Shot by Bernard during his service in Algeria, this footage, we are led to assume for much of the film, documents the incident of torture that continues to obsess the young man. But when, toward the end of *Muriel*, we finally see Bernard's film, it contains no trace of the critical incident. The voice-over recounts the episode blow by blow, but the scene itself is never witnessed. Instead of Muriel's agony and her death, the images of Bernard's film depict only soldiers who exchange laughter and banter as they go about their daily tasks.

A black hole at the center of *Muriel*, the "missing" scenes of Bernard's film have multiple reverberations. To begin with, they clearly serve as a reminder of Resnais's persistent refusal to represent or re-create the past, to evoke historical trauma other than through its traces. Just as it was "impossible" to show the reality of the camps in *Night and Fog*, or to talk about Hiroshima, so, too, suggests the film-within-a-film of *Muriel*, is it impossible to directly record the terrible fact of torture. But these "missing" scenes can also be interpreted in a somewhat narrower context: as a reflection, an indictment, of the harsh restrictions imposed by French censorship at the time of the Algerian War. And no issue related to that bitter struggle was more divisive, or more politically sensitive, than the practice of torture on the part of French authorities. (Indeed, a 1960 film dealing with this subject, Godard's *Le petit soldat*, was banned until 1963— that is, until the war ended.) In this context, the "missing" sequences of Bernard's film might well refer to the kind of images Resnais would have been unable to put into *his* film about the Algerian War, into *Muriel* itself.

An implicit indictment of French censorship, the "missing" scenes of Bernard's film may well have a still broader social resonance. That is, they may allude not only to overt censorship but to the climate of repression, the uneasy silence, that surrounded memories of the Algerian War. Once that humiliating and controversial struggle came to an end, most French people wanted to forget it as soon, and as totally, as possible. No one wanted to hear about the experiences, the memories, of veterans like Bernard. It is surely this attitude that, in the film, contributes to the terrible frustration and impotence experienced by the young man. If it is "impossible" to talk about Muriel, it is not only because of censorship but also, and perhaps above all, because of people like Hélène and Alphonse who continually erect "barbed wires" to avoid disturbing truths. If Hélène holds any possible unpleasantness at bay with a strict attention to social conventions, Alphone paints a portrait of an imaginary Algeria—sunny, open, welcoming—that masks and replaces the image of a nation ravaged by war. Their attitudes ensure that, as Marie-Claire Ropars-Wuilleumier notes, "Algeria will belong to the past without having known the glare of the present."[46]

And there is still another dimension to the silence that surrounded memories of Algeria. Pushed into the uneasy recesses of repressed memory, the experience of Algeria seemed to communicate with, to prolong, that of the national trauma preceding it: the defeat of 1940 and the German Occupation. It is not only that people were eager to forget both these devastating defeats. It is also that these national disasters, which shattered France's self-image, were deeply interconnected. Signaling the end of France's reign as an imperial power, her defeat in Algeria did more than echo the country's earlier humiliation; it also awakened some of the internal divisions, the bitter fault lines, that made memories of Vichy so difficult to acknowledge. Both supporters and opponents of the Algerian War often called upon the memory of 1940 to justify the stance they had chosen. On the Left, among many who opposed the war, the struggle to retain Algeria marked a resurgence of fascism; in their eyes, de Gaulle's assumption of power in 1958, when it was feared that the country was on the verge of civil war, recalled the way in which Pétain had been drafted to lead a faltering nation in July of 1940. On the Right—especially the extreme Right, which harbored a certain nostalgia for Vichy—the struggle to keep Algeria "French" was seen as nothing less than a defense of Western civilization.

If the Algerian War inevitably brought back memories of Vichy, as suggested earlier, it also prompted de Gaulle to enhance the myth of resistancialism, to incorporate it into what Pierre Nora calls a "rhetoric of *grandeur*." Just as he had first launched the resistancialist myth to restore the nation's shattered morale in 1944, so, too, in the aftermath of Algeria, did he have recourse to a "rhetoric," an "invented honor," designed to soften, to obscure, the humiliations of that struggle. The general, writes Nora, "magically transformed the most crushing of French defeats into a form of victory. He made [France] forget that it had lowered its flag in Algeria by ushering it almost simultaneously into the club of nuclear powers. He lulled the new constraints of Atlantic dependency behind a mystique of independence and an exploitation of populist anti-Americanism. He compensated for the abrupt arrival of the third industrial revolution by an emotional appeal to eternal France."[47]

It is precisely this political and social climate, in which the past was "magically" rewritten to compensate for the difficult realities and uncertainties of the present, that is reflected in *Muriel*. Behind the pathetic lies told by Hélène and, especially, by Alphonse, one glimpses the official lies, the "rhetoric of grandeur," promulgated by those in power. Behind the individual anxieties and neuroses of the characters, one senses a nation gripped by paralysis and uncertainty. Boulogne itself, a bewildering maze of bleak and sterile modern buildings in which nothing distinguishes one street, one neighborhood, from another, is the perfect geographical expression of a nation that, as one pedestrian complains of the city, has lost its "center." If, confronted with this essential lack, members of the older generation seek refuge in lies and deceptions, their behavior inevitably affects those whose lives would normally stretch into the future. Thus the tragedy that befalls Bernard occurs not only because of what happened in Algeria but also because those closest to him—and, implicitly, France itself—refuse to acknowledge the past.

Grand Guignol: *Stavisky, Providence*

Eleven years after making *Muriel*, in 1974, Resnais returned to the French past. He did so with a highly stylized re-creation of a famous French political scandal of the 1930s, *Stavisky*. As in the case of *Toute la mémoire du monde*, the choice of subject for this film was, in a sense, fortuitous—the result of chance and expediency. Apparently Jorge Semprun, who had written the script for *La guerre est finie* (*The War Is Over*, 1966) and who had since become very successful, approached the director with the idea of *Stavisky* during a decided lull in the latter's career. And the fact that French star Jean-Paul Belmondo was interested in playing the title role made raising money for the film relatively easy. But, once again, if the choice of subject did not originate with Resnais, the resulting film could hardly have been more personal. Infusing his lifelong love of theater into *Stavisky*, in this work Resnais explicitly links the climate of lies and illusions evoked in preceding films to a critical decade of modern French history.

By the time Resnais made *Stavisky*, of course, the social and political climate in France had changed dramatically. By the mid-1970s, Resnais's obsession with history and memory—an obsession that had set him apart from his New Wave contemporaries in the preceding decade[48]—had become a widely shared phenomenon. While it had been impossible to openly explore the darker zones of the French past in the early 1960s, a decade later a host of films, as well as historical and literary works, were intent on doing just that. And, indeed, in evoking the Stavisky Affair of 1934, Resnais explicitly confronted two of the most troubled and long-repressed zones of the national past. Imbued with the specter of French anti-Semitism, the Stavisky Affair both reflected and prompted the political and ideological divisions that set the stage for France's defeat in 1940 and for the *guerre franco-française* that raged during the Occupation.

The figure at the center of the Stavisky Affair was a French-Jewish financier of Russian or Eastern European origin: Serge Alexandre Stavisky. To this day, some of the details of the scandal—most notably, the manner of Stavisky's death—remain murky. What is clear, however, is that Stavisky was both a gifted speculator who amassed a fortune through shady dealings, and a man who knew how to cultivate political allies among members of the reigning Radical Party. He was also an obvious target for those on the Right and extreme Right: a rich and foreign-born Jew who courted those in power, he corresponded to, and fueled, xenophobic passions and anti-Semitic stereotypes. Not surprisingly, then, when Stavisky was implicated in a fradulent bond scheme toward the end of 1933, the affair had profound political and ideological ramifications. His enemies were quick to denounce his political allies on the Left who, in fact, may well have profited from his schemes and thus been eager to protect him. As a result, when Stavisky was found dead in mysterious circumstances, despite the fact that he appeared to have committed suicide, it was widely suspected that he had been silenced by the police to stifle potentially embarrassing revelations.

The consequences of the Stavisky Affair were dramatic: not only did public outrage at official corruption bring down the cabinet of Camille Chautemps, but the extreme Right sensed an opportunity to deal a mortal blow to the Republic itself. On February 6, 1934, an attempted coup was in the making when Royalists, protofascist leagues, and disgruntled veterans converged on the Place de la Concorde and prepared to cross the Seine and break into the National Assembly. There, they were met by left-wing demonstrators. Describing the ensuing riots and battles, historian Eugen Weber writes: "That Tuesday evening and long into the night, as one rioting wave after another broke on the Concorde bridge, as kiosks and overturned buses flared on the square and near it, as the 'Internationale' of participating Communists mingled with the 'Marseillaise,' fifteen people died and fifteen hundred were wounded."[49]

The riots were suppressed; the Republic survived. But the events—and the fear of fascism raised by the behavior of the Right—had an important political legacy. Frightened groups and parties on the Left put their differences aside to join in a new unity that would spawn the Popular Front. (The leader of the Popular Front, Léon Blum, would become a target for the kind of rabid anti-Semitism that had been directed at Stavisky.)[50] At the same time, the ideological clash between Right and Left prompted by Stavisky's fall both prefigured and encouraged a period of dizzying political swings and bitter ideological warfare in which France seemed to slide helplessly toward Vichy. Indeed, the late 1930s witnessed a political polarization that was probably as intense as that spurred by the passions of the Dreyfus Affair. Evoking the parallels, and the lines of continuity, between these two strife-torn eras, Michel Winock observes that in the late 1930s only the "trial" itself—i.e., like that of Dreyfus—was lacking.[51]

Although the specter of the Stavisky Affair and its disastrous consequences hovers over *Stavisky*, Resnais does not portray the scandal per se. Nor does he seek to trace a realistic portrait of the man and his era. Instead, this intensely stylized and theatrical film consists of a series of almost Brechtian tableaux that deliberately fragment the chronology of events leading up to, and following, Stavisky's fall. Although, for once, Resnais reconstructs historical events in *Stavisky*, this reconstruction itself is built around the "traces" of the past like those seen in previous works. But this time even the "traces" are rendered unreal. Instead of using actual photographs and newsreels as he did, say, in *Night and Fog* and *Hiroshima*, Resnais re-creates photographs and photo-essays of the period by having his actors assume the poses once taken by historical figures.[52] This technique serves at least a twofold function: underscoring the important role played by the press in creating the aura of celebrity (and, later, of notoriety) that surrounded the figure of Stavisky, it also suggests the ways in which the media shapes perceptions and representations of history.

In general, the extremely complex and intellectual nature of Resnais's films had not provoked the wrath of critics before *Stavisky*. But the fact that *Stavisky* portrayed real people and events in a distanced and unreal manner seemed to give critics pause. Some, moreover, may well have expected a more partisan, or overtly political, film from the left-wing Resnais.

They may have hoped that Resnais would take advantage of his subject to shed new light on Stavisky's fate or to denounce the political schemes and manipulations of the Right. (Such expectations could only have been heightened by the fact that the script for *Stavisky* was written by Jorge Semprun, who was known for committed works like the 1969 *Z*.) Then, too, the look and setting of the film may have led others to expect a realistic *rétro* drama in the manner of, say, *Lacombe Lucien*. But Resnais's film, as it turned out, fulfilled none of these hopes. "Resnais was charged," comments James Monaco, "with 'at the same time saying too much and too little' about his subject, for ignoring the social and political complications that surrounded the Stavisky scandal, for being too academic, and for paying 'too little attention to historical fact.' "[53] Not surprisingly, critics on the Left were often the harshest. For example, writing in the left-wing film journal *Positif*, Paul-Louis Thirard went so far as to reproach Resnais for rendering the political film "ridiculous."[54]

In retrospect, the mixed reception accorded *Stavisky* was probably due as much to Resnais's persistent iconoclasm as to prevailing political winds. It is clear that *Stavisky* did not fit the mold of the "political" film as it was conceived at the time. But it is also clear that *Stavisky* did not ignore the historical context or render the "political film ridiculous." Quite the contrary. Indeed, I would argue that, far more than many overtly left-wing films of the 1970s, *Stavisky* prompts a meditation not only on a critical era of the national past but on fundamental political and historical issues that stretch into the present. Focused on long-standing divisions and fault lines in French society, it points to persistent strains of French xenophobia; in exploring the role played by the press in fanning the flames of the Stavisky scandal, it also raises questions, which could hardly be more contemporary, concerning the power of the media. In these and other respects, it is as relevant to the France of the 1990s as, in the eyes of two enthusiastic critics, it was to the France of the 1970s. Resnais's film, wrote Youssef Ishaghpour and Pierre Samson in 1974, "does not explain history or describe great events. It does not deliver a message about the famous [Stavisky] affair in line with the preconceived ideas of the public. It is a film about our present: about the meaning of inflation and the constant change of policies, about a society in crisis."[55]

The broad sweep of Resnais's historical concerns, as well as the sense of social and political "crisis" that informs *Stavisky*, is evident in the film's opening sequence. For *Stavisky* begins with a scene that depicts one of the towering figures of twentieth-century history: Leon Trotsky. As the film opens, the former Russian leader is seen arriving in France where he has come to seek political asylum. In the following scene, Trotsky is ushered, quickly and secretly, into a kind of courtroom; as the stone bust of Marianne, the symbol of the Republic, looks on impassively, Trotsky is cautioned that he must refrain from political activity if he wishes to remain in France. As the exiled leader drives away, an onlooker, who later seems to act as Trotsky's secretary, comments on the symbolic dimension and the historical importance of this scene. "A page of history has been turned," he says; "one of the great leaders of the October Revolution has begun the life of an exile."

Throughout the film, as in the opening sequence, Trotsky is never on-screen for very long. Yet, in some ways, he is at the epicenter of the themes and issues informing this extraordinarily complex film. Recurring shots of the car taking Trotsky into lonely exile create a leitmotif that insistently reminds the viewer of the broad historical context surrounding the Stavisky Affair: his presence connects the upheavals of the Russian Revolution to the coming battle between the Soviet Union and Hitler's Germany. At the same time, as a man who was twice forced into exile—first by political developments in his native land and then by those in France—the figure of Trotsky also points to the hordes of refugees, of displaced persons, who teemed across Europe's borders in the 1930s and 1940s.

An instigator and a victim of global upheaval, Trotsky was also linked, both directly and indirectly, to the Stavisky Affair. Expelled from France by the right-wing government that came to power in the wake of the scandal, Trotsky left for Mexico—where, of course, he would be assassinated. But if his fate was indirectly sealed by the Stavisky Affair, his expulsion from France, like the scandal itself, also foreshadowed the downward path that French political life and ideals would take in the late 1930s. In the course of these turbulent years, the Republican ideals that welcomed Trotsky upon his arrival in France, ideals embodied in the stone bust of Marianne glimpsed in the film's opening scene, seemed increasingly threatened by the nation's rising fear and hatred of foreigners. Seen from this perspective, Trotsky's expulsion from his adopted country prefigured one of the blackest episodes of the Occupation: the mass deportations of foreign Jews who, like the Russian leader, had taken refuge in France.

As portrayed by Resnais, moreover, Trotsky is not only a man whose fate was indirectly linked to that of Stavisky; he is also, in some ways, both the twin and the opposite of the French financier himself. Both were "foreigners" who corresponded to, embodied, Jewish stereotypes—the Jew as revolutionary, as rich and crafty businessman—long central to anti-Semitic mythologies. Indeed, as a leading French sociologist, Pierre Birnbaum, notes, in the depths of the French political imagination these two stereotypes frequently merged not only with one another but also with still more deeply rooted images of Jews. Both the revolutionary and the rich Jew, writes Birnbaum, "are modern figures of the image of the wandering Jew that, buried in the depths of collective memory, fuels the fear of a foreign plot designed to destroy the very identity of French society."[56] As if to further identify themselves with the image of the "wandering Jew," this rootless cosmopolitan who changes identity as easily as he does home or country, both Trotsky and Stavisky changed their names even as they created new personas for themselves. Both men, as James Monaco observes, "recreated themselves: Stavisky invented Alexandre, while Bronstein invented Trotsky."[57]

In the end, though, the similarities between Trotsky and Stavisky pale beside a critical difference. For if the two were exiled and reviled Jews who "recreated themselves," their dreams—that is, the "images" they sought to create—could hardly have been more different. Their opposing dreams, in fact, corresponded to the great clash of ideologies that set the stage for the Stavisky Affair and, beyond that, for the wave of global destruction of the 1940s. While Trotsky is the archrevolutionist, Stavisky, who floats fraudulent bonds and believes that everything and everyone can be bought, is the quintessential capitalist.[58] Stavisky is as eager to finance the reactionaries in Spain who will launch the Spanish Civil War as he is to cooperate with leftists in France who happen to be in power. "I don't frequent the Socialist-Radicals," he says, as if to underscore his total indifference to politics and ideology; "I frequent Power."

Throughout *Stavisky*, Resnais makes it clear that the gulf between Stavisky and Trotsky extends to the world that surrounds his title character. There is never any doubt that Stavisky is the product, and the epitome, of a corrupt world in which the beliefs and principles held dear by Trotsky have been totally eclipsed by expendiency and opportunism, by greed and cynicism. It is here, of course, that *Stavisky* paints a damning portrait of the nation at a critical moment of its history. This portrait is sketched, rapidly but tellingly, in one of the film's earliest sequences. In this scene, Stavisky is seated in the lobby of his hotel, the elegant Claridge, with his friend the Baron Raoul, an aristocrat who has squandered a fortune. As the Baron glances over the morning papers, his eye is caught by a story about an English lord who, out of sympathy with mistreated Jews in Germany, has renounced the Christian faith to embrace his Jewish origins. "That shows stupidity," says the cynical Baron, "not nobility." As for Stavisky himself, while he complains about the "lies" that are directed against him in the rabidly anti-Semitic and often corrupt right-wing press,[59] he sees nothing wrong with corrupting others when the occasion arises. As he speaks with the Baron, it becomes clear that he finds it as easy, as normal, to buy a diamond necklace for a pittance from a woman he casually seduces as to bribe a cabinet minister or a police inspector.

In the corrupt and artifical world inhabited by Stavisky and his friend, everything is for sale and everyone has assumed a "role." Stavisky himself is a consummate showman: a chameleon figure who has erased his shady beginnings, and who has made a fortune by bringing illusions to life for others, he is always onstage. Unlike the remote and shadowy figure of Trotsky—always seen in extreme longshot, the Russian leader seems somehow inaccessible to the camera—Stavisky constantly demands our attention. Played by the exuberant Jean-Paul Belmondo, he holds center stage whether he is talking, gesticulating, or even, as on rare occasions, lying still. When first seen, for example, he makes a star's entrance as he strides into the luxurious lobby of the hotel and effusively greets friends and acquaintances.

To emphasize the unreal and theatrical nature of Stavisky and the world that surrounds him, Resnais fills his film with echoes of stage and screen. While the Baron Raoul is played by a real star of early film, Charles Boyer, Stavisky's beautiful wife, Arlette, is made up to resemble a diva in a 1920s melodrama. Indeed, Arlette first appears in a silent sequence, reminiscent of early newsreels, in which she is seen parading before admiring fans in Deauville.[60] And the theatrical nature of the characters is reinforced by that of the film itself. Using shooting techniques of the 1930s,[61] *Stavisky* pays particular homage to the elegant comedies—often marked by the presence of charming con artists like Stavisky—of Ernst Lubitsch and of Sacha Guitry. (The protagonist of one of Guitry's best-known films, *The Story of a Cheat* [1936], bears more than a passing resemblance to Stavisky.) Even the fact that the imperial Stavisky answers to the name of "Sacha" might well allude to Sacha Guitry's famous, almost campy, portrayals of various French kings. For his title character, said Resnais, "I thought of the way in which Sacha Guitry played Louis XV or Louis XIV. He always kept the viewer aware that it was he, Sacha Guitry, playing the king."[62]

Some of the most important scenes of *Stavisky* take place, moreover, in a theater that Stavisky has bought and grandiloquently named "L'Empire." It is here, for example, that Stavisky has a long discussion with a young Jewish actress about his own Jewish origins. His attitude is very different from that of the young woman: whereas she is forthright about her Jewishness—"they will never let us forget who we are," she tells Stavisky—he takes refuge in masks and disguises. And it is also here that he rehearses the role of the "specter" in Jean Giraudoux's *Intermezzo*, a "role" that foreshadows his death. (Deeming this "role" the most important of Stavisky's life, the Baron explains that it "was a herald of death—not only of the deaths of February 6 but of the death of an era, of an entire period of history.") Discussing the intensely theatrical nature of his title character, Resnais confessed that "there is no doubt that what seduced me in the character of Alexandre is his relation with theater and spectacle in general. Moreover, the memories that I have of this era remain strongly imprinted with theatricality. Stavisky seemed to me a fantastic actor, the hero of a serial novel. He had the gift of making phantasms become concrete through royal gestures. . . . He was someone who continually lived as if onstage. . . . I saw the whole film as a kind of black, menacing, *guignol*, like a *danse macabre*."[63]

Resnais's last remark points, of course, to the core of the film—the dark underside of the theatricality that defined Stavisky and his era. For beneath this world of luxury and display, of theater and illusion, lie the instability and decay that were eroding the Republic itself. A stylized drama infused with echoes of Lubitsch and Guitry, *Stavisky* is also a *danse macabre* about death both individual and collective. Stavisky's death is but the prelude to the death of the Third Republic that would soon collapse in the anguish and chaos of defeat. Throughout the film, stylized funereal images point to the imminence of Stavisky's death and, beyond that, to the crumbling of an era. A weary Stavisky stretches out on a tomb; a strange pyramid keeps coming into view; red stains on a white tablecloth announce the violent end that Stavisky would meet in a Swiss cabin nestled against a snowy mountaintop.

The most significant portents of death, and the most insistent reminders of the links between Stavisky and his era, come in the form of strange scenes that resemble highly original flash-forwards. Initially, these scenes, which punctuate the film and fragment the narrative, are very puzzling: in an early one, for example, the Baron, who has just been speaking with Stavisky, faces us and, without transition, delivers a monologue in which he analyzes his friend's character and motives. As the film progresses, how-ever, and these mysterious sequences grow more frequent and lengthy, it gradually becomes apparent that the Baron and others have emerged from the diegetic time and space of the narrative and are giving testimony at hearings that were held *after* Stavisky's death to determine whether he took his own life. As the "meaning" of these scenes comes into focus, the sense of temporal boundaries grows increasingly uncertain. In one later scene, for example, the Baron, referring to Stavisky, asks: "What is he saying? Arlette seems fascinated." With this question, as Robert Benayoun re-marks, the Baron gives the impression that he has joined us in the present and is watching the film with us.[64] In other words, we are no longer in the future but in the present; the entire film, as well as Stavisky himself, has been pushed into the recesses of the past.

As the boundaries separating past, present, and future dissolve, the living financier seems to melt into the mythic figure—the man at the center of the Stavisky Affair—he will soon become. These strange flash-forwards thus involve the very nature of historical memory: in this case, the process by which a charming con man named Sacha was turned into a key historical figure of the 1930s. In this manner, the hearings serve as a kind of hinge between Stavisky the man and the Stavisky Affair—between the tragedy of an individual and that of a nation. They become a reminder, which becomes increasingly insistent as the film progresses, that the *danse macabre*, the melancholy guignol performed in *Stavisky*, pertains not only to the man himself but to the world that surrounded him.

This critical link between the individual and the collective is underscored, moreover, by several key allusions. For example, Stavisky is afflicted by a strange paralysis that might well be seen as a metaphor for the paralysis that gripped French political institutions of the late 1930s. And two important references to Shakespeare also suggest the death that awaits both Stavisky and his era. One occurs when we first meet Arlette: awakened from sleep by Stavisky, she tells her husband of a recurring nightmare in which an animal rolls down a snowy slope after it has been killed. Obviously allusions to Stavisky's death, these disturbing images also suggest the prophetic dream recounted by Caesar's wife in *Julius Caesar*—a play in which the assassination of a ruler is linked to political maneuvering and upheaval. And toward the end of the film, shortly before Arlette's prophetic dream is realized, she and her husband attend a performance of *Corialanus*. Marked by a scene in which a would-be dictator denigrates democracy, Shakespeare's play almost seemed to be alluding to the right-wing riots that would follow Stavisky's fall. (This allusion to *Coriolanus* was no mere invention on Resnais's part. As historian Eugen Weber observes, at the time, an actual production of Shakespeare's drama at the *Comédie-Française* became "the focus of opposition to parliament, to democracy, to the corruption that had taken on—so demonstrators alleged—a national dimension.")[65]

Commenting on the theatrical allusions in *Stavisky*, Youssef Ishaghpour links them squarely to the historical period portrayed in the film. *Stavisky*, he writes, "oscillates between Guitry and Shakespeare, between the cowardice of a bourgeoisie in crisis and the shadow of advancing fascism. Between them Giradoux's specter is sinking into . . . death."[66] In portraying this era, *Stavisky* depicts a world in which personal and national destiny meet even as theater and illusions, both individual and collective, prove fatal. The social and political climate depicted here is as empty, as illusory, as Stavisky's fraudulent bonds. The recurring image of a strange pyramid may well suggest, as James Monaco writes, the pyramidal scheme, the fraudulent bonds, used by Stavisky to cover his debts. ("Stavisky," writes Monaco, "was the peak of a structure of fraud that reached deep into the bowels of French society.")[67] But it also evokes, of course, the tombs of a defunct civilization. The very symbol of a decaying and corrupt civilization, Stavisky was also its product and its victim. He represented, and manipulated, a world in disarray in which, to borrow a phrase from a French economist, "makers of miracles . . . proposed magic remedies."[68] Stavisky's ability to manipulate these "remedies"—remedies as theatrical and illusory as the plays he produced at "L'Empire"—led to his own death even as they paved the way for one of the most traumatic eras of French history.

In Resnais's next film, *Providence*—which was made in English, in 1976, and written by David Mercer—the *danse macabre* performed in *Stavisky* becomes at once more frenetic and more funereal. Often considered one of Resnais's finest films, *Providence* is also one of his most "equivocal." For here the "lies" of *Muriel*, the performances of *Stavisky*, have mushroomed and enveloped the entire world. That is, virtually the whole film consists of a series of stylized theatrical scenes that emerge from the fertile imagination of the film's principal protagonist, Clive Langham. Masterfully played by John Gielgud, Clive is a dying writer who turns to theater (and to alcohol) to distract himself from the pain that wracks his body and the fears that assail his mind. (He is prey, for example, to gruesome images of his own corpse being crudely cut open in an autopsy.) As if to keep death itself at bay, he spends his sleepless nights endlessly writing and rewriting the dramatic scenes that constitute the body of *Providence* itself.[69]

In many respects, Clive is undoubtedly Resnais's most autobiographical character. A writer who echoes Resnais's disdain for critics who separate form and content,[70] Clive is a self-described "sentimental Bolshevik" who seems to share the director's political sympathies. He also resembles the director in that he, too, turns to "spectacle" to calm existential fears—to find the "reassurance" that is lacking in life. ("There is something reassuring in a painting," remarked Resnais in the course of a 1980 interview; "it is a closed and completed object; whereas existence goes in every direction, every which way. Reassuring like every spectacle! One likes spectacle when one is anguished.")[71] Drawn to spectacle precisely because it is *not* life, like Resnais, Clive invents imaginary worlds that proclaim their "unreal" nature by means of melodramatic excess and intense stylization. Thus it is not surprising that the principal drama of his imaginary sketches is made of the very stuff of melodrama: it concerns the marital tribulations of an unhappy couple: Claud, an arrogant lawyer played by Dirk Bogarde, and his long-suffering wife, Sonia (Ellen Burstyn). In the course of the scenes imagined by Clive, Claud takes a mistress (who turns out to be dying of cancer); Sonia is drawn to a young man (who does not return her affections); Clive himself bemoans the loss of his wife Molly, who probably committed suicide. As if to remind us that we are literally within someone's brain, a place where nothing is "real," the mood, tone, and sets of these imaginary scenes change with disorienting speed. Nightmarish scenes of werewolves alternate with melodramatic sequences of domestic discord; people step in and out of character or refuse to utter the lines they have been assigned; mysterious characters, who may have figured in another draft or even another play, stubbornly refuse to leave or disappear. In the blink of an eye the decor changes from a realistic room to the obvious trompe l'oeil of a painted ocean.

But the similarities between Clive and Resnais go beyond their taste for melodrama and spectacle, for "fictions" and "illusions." For no less than his creator, Clive, too, is haunted by the melancholy ghosts of history. The private dramas he loves to imagine are constantly interrupted by unwanted scenes of terrifying historical events that rise up, unbidden, to torment him. At first, these scenes, unlike those evoked in *Muriel* or in *Stavisky*, do not seem to bear on specific events. Rather, it is as if all the horror of the 1940s had been distilled into atrocious nightmares of human savagery. (The film begins, in fact, in a kind of primordial forest where strange, not-quite-human creatures appear to be at war with one another.) Before long, however, as the historical memories tighten their grip on Clive's imagination, these scenes of almost abstract savagery give way to tableaux filled with more recognizable horrors. For example, the growing presence of bombs and explosions suggests episodes of contemporary terrorism as well as scenes of World War II.

Significantly, though, the most distinct and important historical echo in *Providence* is one that points to what is generally seen as the darkest zone of the recent French past: the roundup and deportations of Jews during the Occupation. Recurring images of men and women forced into a large stadium call to mind the notorious deportations of 1942, when Jewish families were assembled in the so-called Vel d'Hiv stadium on the outskirts of Paris before beginning the journey east. (Given the fact that Clive is English, it is all the more telling, if improbable, that these scenes should be such haunting ones.) As the film progresses, moreover, these images begin to form a narrative of their own that weaves itself into the scenes of private domestic warfare taking place between Claud and Sonia.

At the beginning, the image of the stadium is fleeting; it is not clear where this terrifying place is located. Later, however, it appears to be on the outskirts of a city that is increasingly filled with the sounds of bombs and guns. Before long, armed guards or militiamen, whose presence suggests that the city portrayed is occupied or under siege, make an appearance. At the same time, acts of violence increase: as Claud is driving to a rendezvous with his mistress, he sees men in uniform pushing a man into the river; later still he mounts the steps of a courthouse emblazoned with what appear to be fascist slogans. Now the stadium reappears: at first, it is empty and huge; then, suddenly, it is littered with corpses. All these suggestions of growing civil war—suggestions imbued, I think, with memories of the Occupation—reach a crescendo in the melodramatic conclusion of Clive's imaginary narratives. Here, Claud shoots the young man who attracted Sonia; as soon as he does so, guards come running and bear the lifeless body to the stadium. From a position outside (inside?) the barbed wires of the camp, Sonia and Claud can do nothing but watch in horror.

Just as historical violence appears to envelop Sonia and Claud, the scene suddenly shifts. In an abrupt change of scene and mood, the melancholy ghosts of history vanish. The dark forests and enclosed rooms that have dominated the film thus far give way to a sunlit scene set on a green lawn. The striking visual contrast between this scene and the preceding ones suggests that, finally, we have left the slippery slopes of the imagination for the firm ground of the real. And, indeed, before long the characters who have figured in Clive's scenarios appear: they are, it turns out, members of Clive's family who have come to celebrate his seventy-eighth birthday. Claud and Sonia are Clive's son and daughter-in-law; the young man who attracted Sonia, Kevin, is Clive's illegitimate son. In the course of the birthday luncheon, it becomes clear that Clive's imaginary scenarios could hardly have been more "false." For example, in sharp contrast with the arrogant monster of Clive's jaundiced imaginings, Claud is a gentle and solicitous son and a happily married man who has never betrayed his wife. It is not Claud but Clive himself, we suddenly realize, who is harsh and judgmental. Suddenly, any credence we had placed in Clive's preceding narratives crumbles as, says Resnais, "the accuser finds himself accused."[72]

This sequence, of course, forces the viewer to reassess the "truth" of everything that has been seen thus far. Questions abound: did Clive's scenarios reflect his deepest fantasies and fears? was his unflattering portrait of his son inspired by an old man's jealousy of youth and fear of death? did he himself harbor an attraction to Sonia? or is the birthday celebration itself simply another play-within-a-play, no more true than anything else? But even as Resnais underscores the "falseness" of Clive's scenarios—and, consequently, of the film itself—*Providence* takes another startling turn. The accusatory ghosts of the past, the dark recesses of the imagination, cannot be dismissed, it seems, quite so easily. For as the family members depart, Clive prepares to enter the house in which all his imaginings, and his nightmares, took place. As he does so, the disturbing music that accompanied his somber scenarios begins. Once again, it is clear, we are about to enter the world of Clive's imagination, a world where even spectacle offers little protection against the obsessions of the present and the ghosts of the past.

As in the case of *Marienbad*, the profoundly "equivocal" nature of *Providence*, the way in which the line between the "real" and the "unreal" wavers and dissolves, has given rise to many interpretations. In an attempt to unravel the many mysteries of the film, critics have gone so far as to seek clues in the proper names of the characters and in obscure biographical allusions.[73] For some, the birthday scene is "real"; for others, the "truth"—

at least the profound psychological truth of the film—lies in Clive's many scenarios. But it seems to me that, as Resnais himself observed of *Marienbad*, if there is a real "meaning" in *Providence*, it resides in the film's unrelenting "falseness": in what Youssef Ishaghpour deems the "absence of reality." Commenting on the way in which the specter of this "absence" haunts the birthday sequence of *Providence*, Ishaghpour declares that "horror tracks each glance, each word, until the departure at the end when the characters disappear as if at the theater; once again what had seemed to be serene reality for a moment is rendered unreal. . . . The nostalgia for nature, for a lost paradise, haunts all those whose films continue to show the absence of reality in cinema: a world of appearances that *Providence* calls by its name."[74]

Expanding upon the nature of this "horror," this "nostalgia for a lost paradise," Ishaghpour explicitly links it to the terrifying historical memories evoked in Resnais's early films. "*Guernica, Night and Fog, Hiroshima*, and the accumulated horror of recent history," he writes, "reduce to a lie any work that does not speak of them."[75] In this, I think, he is doubtless correct. For even as spectacle, whether imagined by Clive or Resnais himself, "reassures," it also reminds us of the void, the darkness, that lies outside its circle of light. Proclaiming our inability to reach and represent the real, the spectacles brought to life by Resnais's cinema—the "fictions" and illusions of *Muriel*, the performances of *Stavisky*, the ghostly simulacrum that so boldly declares itself as such at the end of *Providence*—bear the imprint of historical anguish. Indeed, they are infused with the self-mocking irony and postmodernist pastiche that, in the eyes of Julia Kristeva, represent the most recent incarnation of the "emptying of symbolic modes" prompted by the atrocities of the 1940s. "Today's desire for comedy," she writes, "comes to cover over—without ignoring it—the obsession with this truth without tragedy. . . . After the winter of obsession comes the artifice of appearance; after the whiteness of spleen, the lacerating amusements of parody."[76]

Stretching from the the "winter of obsession" seen in *Night and Fog* and *Hiroshima* to the "artifice of appearance" marking *Stavisky* and *Providence*, Resnais's films appear to bridge the stages of memory described by Kristeva. But at the same time, as I have argued throughout this chapter, they bear witness to the legacy of historical anguish in a twofold manner. If the "lacerating amusements" imagined by Clive and his creator reflect the nihilist thrust of postmodernism, they also constitute a dramatic embodiment of the "lies" and "illusions" that characterized French attitudes and memories in the postwar years. Implicitly denouncing these "lies," Resnais's films also suggest their ultimate impotence. As Clive and Stavisky know all too well, the world of illusion offers but a frail and momentary dam against the insistences of memory and the demands of history. The "lies" told by the characters in *Muriel* result in alienation and violence; Stavisky's "illusions" lead not only to his own collapse but to that of his era; try as he might, Clive cannot completely repress the historical images, with their echoes of national shame, that ultimately engulf his imaginary worlds. "We might have expected," writes Ishaghpour of these last images, "that imagination could make the barbed wires . . . vanish. [But] it reinstalls them one after another until they surround the whole world."[77] Reinstalling these "barbed wires," *Providence* tells us explicitly that it is the most repressed zones of history which figure most powerfully in our nightmares.

Bearing upon memories at once global and national, Resnais's films are thus not only the most important cinematic embodiment of the crisis of thought and feeling, of perception and representation, triggered by the worst horrors of our century. They were also the first to reveal deep cracks and fissures in the national past—to breach the wall of silence that surrounded the most shame-filled zones of modern French history. It took at least a quarter-century for films, reflecting broader social impulses, to address the haunted memories that give rise to the "missing" scenes in *Muriel*. In that film, as in the others discussed in these pages, Resnais confronted, with varying degrees of explicitness, the most controversial and disturbing moments of the recent French past: the abuses and injustices of the purges, the practice of torture in Algeria, the nature and consequences of French anti-Semitism. In suggesting the ways in which these moments were enveloped in lies and deceptions, these works implicitly attacked the smothering weight of censorship and "taboos" even as they announced the battle for memory that would be waged by subsequent films. It is the contours of this battle, seen in terms of several *rétro* films of the 1970s and 1980s, that are addressed in the following chapter.

III

Battles for Memory: Vichy Revisited

IN OCTOBER of 1997, more than a half-century since the end of the Occupation, France was riveted by the start of a trial that harked back to those dark days. The accused was Maurice Papon: now eighty-seven, Papon, who had held high positions in several postwar governments, had served in the Vichy government as secretary-general of the Gironde *département*. It was in that capacity, the prosecution charged, that Papon had committed crimes against humanity in supervising the deportation of nearly sixteen hundred Jews (including over two hundred children) who, from 1942 to 1944, were sent first to the French camp of Drancy and then to Auschwitz.

Often referred to as "the trial of the century," Papon's trial plunged the country into a period of collective introspection concerning the Vichy years. Night after night, television news commentators raised questions that had never before been posed with such insistence or in such a vast public forum. What, they asked, was Papon's role in the deportations? was he only following German orders, as he maintained, or could he have saved hundreds from their death? should he have resigned his post in protest? Moreover, the nature of Papon's role as a Vichy official inevitably opened onto larger, more troubling, questions. What was the extent of Vichy complicity in the Final Solution? And, more troubling still, was the Vichy government itself, as had long been maintained, a historical aberration? or was it, instead, a continuation of the Republic itself? In other words, was France itself responsible for betraying foreign Jews who had sought refuge within its borders as well as many of her own citizens?

In finally confronting these issues, the French may well be entering the final stages of what historian Henry Rousso, in his influential study, *The Vichy Syndrome: History and Memory in France since 1944*, deems the "Vichy syndrome": the "diverse set of symptoms whereby the trauma of the Occupation, and particularly that trauma resulting from internal divisions within France, reveals itself in political, social and cultural life."[1] In the half-century since the end of the war, this syndrome has gone through a variety of phases. As suggested in connection with the films of Alain Resnais, for years after the war, the so-called myth of resistancialism—the notion that the Occupation saw the vast majority of the French people joined in common struggle against a foreign invader[2]—governed memories of the Occupation years. It was not until the early 1970s that this myth was finally challenged. In the wake of May '68, the traumatic events of the 1940s, which had shattered a national self-image cherished for centuries, became the subject of anxious debate in newspapers and journals even as films and novels displayed a fascination with *les années noires*. Toward the end of the 1970s, this period of "obsession," to use Rousso's term, was amplified by the reawakening of Jewish memory as French Jews became convinced that their memories of the Vichy years were sometimes very different from those of their fellow citizens. In more recent years, a series of impassioned political debates and controversies with roots in the Occupation have borne witness to the continuing strength of the Vichy syndrome.

Ever since the early 1970s, films have played a critical role in the unfolding saga of Vichy memory. Indeed, at the beginning of the 1970s, it was a film, Marcel Ophuls's massive documentary, *Le chagrin et la pitié*, that first challenged images and myths concerning the Occupation that had reigned since the end of the war. Creating what was often seen as a "counterlegend" of the Occupation, *Le chagrin et la pitié* also stimulated the nation's growing obsession with *les années noires*. This obsession, in turn, gave rise to what came to be known as *la mode rétro*: that is, a forties revival visible in worlds as diverse as fashion, historical scholarship, journalism, and, most visibly, cinema.[3] Between 1974 and 1978 some forty-five films dealing with World War II were shot—more than in the course of the entire previous decade. In 1976 alone, *la mode rétro* set its stamp on eleven films, 7 percent of France's total output.[4]

It is not only the number of films dealing with the Vichy past that is striking. It is also their political and social resonance. Throughout at least two decades French cinema was the site of a dramatic struggle for memory. It was a struggle between those who wanted to ignore the wounds of the past and those who insisted that such wounds had to be cleansed before they could be forgotten. As an important "vector" of memory, to borrow still another term from Rousso, French films variously challenged, crystallized, and perpetuated many of the "symptoms" resulting from the trauma of the Occupation. Veering between the need to "know" and the wish to "deny," they suggest why it has proved so difficult to confront, and to exorcise, the Vichy past.

This chapter explores some of the best-known and most successful of these films in the context of the changing shape of French history and memory. Bearing witness to deeply rooted and often unacknowledged ambivalences, and to a shifting political and social landscape, these films allow us to trace, I argue, a psychological profile of the various moments composing the long and often tortured evolution of the Vichy syndrome. This profile begins with a discussion of three films belonging to the period that, in Rousso's terms, first saw the "return of the repressed." Marked by very different views of the French past, *Le chagrin et la pitie*, Louis Malle's *La-*

combe Lucien, and François Truffaut's *Le dernier métro* reveal not only the dramatic contours and tensions of the battle for memory that emerged at this time but also the lingering power of the myth of resistancialism. For despite the challenge posed to this myth in *Le chagrin et la pitié*, in subtle ways its presence continues to inform the representation of the Occupation years set forth in both *Lacombe Lucien* and *Le dernier métro*.

The "reawakening" of Jewish memories provides the context for an analysis of several later films. Against the background of such memories, the portrayal of French attitudes toward Jews in several fictional films—notably Louis Malle's *Au revoir les enfants* (1987) and Claude Chabrol's *Histoire des femmes* (*Story of Women*, 1988)—is compared with that seen in several contemporaneous documentaries. Pointing to a dramatic fault line between documentaries and works of fiction in regard to the Vichy past, the differences between these two groups of films also suggest how difficult it has been for French men and women to acknowledge the strength of French anti-Semitism and the role it played in what are surely the most shame-filled episodes of the Vichy years. This difficulty was further underscored by several political controversies of the 1990s in which those accused of complicity with Vichy crimes resolutely maintained both their ignorance and their innocence. But, as the trial of Maurice Papon and other events of 1996 and 1997 suggest, the time for such denials may finally be over. As France confronts the abyss of recent history, the long battle for Vichy memory seems to be drawing to a close.

The Return of the Repressed

The virtual explosion of Vichy memory that occurred in the early 1970s—the force with which, as Rousso has it, the "mirror" of the past was broken—indicates, certainly, the strength of long-buried memories as well as the weight of repression that had smothered them for nearly a quarter of a century. But here two interrelated questions, which have been touched on in the preceding chapter, immediately come to mind. First, why did it take so long before people were willing to confront the past? before they were ready to examine, to question, the resistancialist myth first proposed by de Gaulle in 1944? And, second, what factors converged toward the end of the 1960s to render possible an explosion of Vichy memory at this particular historical juncture?

In considering the first of these questions—why Vichy memory was repressed for so long—historians inevitably underscore both the deep-rooted nature and the deadly complexion of the internal struggles of the Occupation. Masked by the comforting myth of French unity in the aftermath of the war, the divisions of the Occupation were so bitter, it has often been observed, precisely because they occurred along deep national fault lines that had been put in place generations earlier. Stretching back to the Dreyfus Affair, and, in some sense, to the Revolution itself, these fault lines had manifested themselves earlier at the time of the Stavisky Affair and at that of the Popular Front. Not only did the ideological battles of the Occupation recall these earlier conflicts, but, to some extent, they drew fuel from them.[5] For example, at least to some degree, the measures taken against Jews in Vichy France, particularly at the beginning of the Occupation, can be attributed not only to Nazi ideology and demands but to the native strains of xenophobia and French anti-Semitism that had erupted so virulently in the course of the 1930s. So, too, were the right-wing anti-Republican policies of Vichy rooted in a continuing *French* battle between Right and Left—a battle, in a sense, for the soul of the nation—that had been particularly intense at the time of the Popular Front. Indeed, in a groundbreaking study of the Vichy years that generated a storm of controversy when it was translated into French in 1973, American historian Robert Paxton, who was called to testify in the course of Papon's trial, makes the following important, and by now generally accepted, point. "Vichy's internal project of replacing the cosmopolitan and libertarian Republic by an authoritarian, homogeneous, corporatist state," he writes, "was revenge against the Popular Front more than accommodation to some Nazi blueprint."[6]

The deep national divisions and conflicts that had broken out at the time of the Popular Front assumed, moreover, a far deadlier complexion during the Occupation. In the eyes of Henry Rousso, the internal conflicts of the Vichy era—conflicts he likens to "fratricidal struggles"—constituted not merely a "cold" civil war or one that was purely verbal but, instead, "a civil war *tout court*, at least when seen within the context of French history." And, as Americans themselves have good reason to know, it is civil wars that leave the most intractable scars, the deepest traumas. Indeed, it is usually felt that, even more than the humiliations of foreign occupation and defeat, the internal battles of the Occupation account for the enormous difficulty the French have experienced in confronting this somber period of their past.[7] So, too, do they explain why some of the French can forgive the Germans more readily than they can certain of their compatriots.

The "civil war" that tore France apart during the Occupation is one of the reasons, certainly, that the resistancialist myth exerted such a powerful hold when the war finally came to an end. Masking the realities of *la guerre franco-française*, this myth gave rise to comforting images of collective struggle and unity. But it is also true, as suggested in the preceding chapter, that the power of this myth owed a great deal to politics and to political figures, chief among them, of course, de Gaulle himself. As the man who dominated French politics in the aftermath of the war, and who was recalled to power in 1958, de Gaulle had every reason to perpetuate the stirring myth that he had set forth to bolster national morale and unity in the dark days of 1944. The heroic role that he had indeed played on June 18, 1940—when, from exile in London, he urged his countrymen to join him in resisting the invader—gave him a leading role in the resistancialist version of the past. As he embellished this myth, his own *gloire* was conferred upon the nation: it was not only he who resisted, but all of France; he, in turn, became the very embodiment of the French *grandeur* he so cherished. "Gaullist rhetoric," as Philippe Burrin writes in a reappraisal of Vichy memory, "lent authority to an image of France as 'Free France,' a France from which a handful of traitors had excluded themselves before receiving their just deserts upon Liberation. France, Resistance, de Gaulle: these three words replaced a complex, shifting and divided historical past with one that was glorious and mythic."[8]

But if de Gaulle had every reason to foster the myth of this "glorious" past, so, too, did other politicians and men of state. Or, more precisely, few had reason to question the reassuring version of the past so closely associated with the general. Political leaders and parties on both the Right and the Left had ample motives to keep a somber page of history shrouded in ambiguities and denials. "No major political grouping had any interest," writes Robert Paxton, "in exploring the internal roots of Pétain's policies. The Resisters who controlled the Fourth and early Fifth Republics cherished the image of massive support for de Gaulle from the first hour; the Communist Left wanted to divert attention from its neutralism from 1939 to 1941; conservatives saw Pétain's noble passivity as sabotaged by his prime minister Laval; technocrats rejected any suggestion of Vichy legacy in post-war economic planning and social corporatism."[9] Like politicians, intellectuals, too, may have had their own reasons for not questioning reigning versions of the past. Indeed, Tony Judt suggests that if no leading intellectual—such as, say, Jean-Paul Sartre or Michel Foucault—looked too closely at what had happened during the Occupation, it may have been because "very few intellectuals of any political stripe could claim to have had a 'good' war, as Albert Camus did."[10]

Clearly, the silence that surrounded the Vichy past from the late 1940s to the late 1960s stemmed from a complex web of factors. Traumatic memories that challenged the nation's sense of pride and self-respect, political exigencies, de Gaulle's insistence on French *grandeur*—all these conspired to repress, to erase, disturbing truths and memories about the Occupation. By the late 1960s, however, change was in the air. For by that time, a new generation, which had no firsthand experience of *les années noires*, and which had grown up in a France very different from that of their parents, had come of age. In sharp contrast with their parents' generation, which wanted nothing better than to forget the bleak and divisive years of the

Occupation, many of these young people wanted to know what had really happened in the 1940s. What lay behind their parents' unease, silence, bitterness? More important, perhaps, this was the generation of May '68. Its suspicion of all certainties, all orthodoxies, had helped fuel the events of May '68; now, *les événements*, in turn, opened the floodgates to a period of national soul-searching in which past and present alike came under re-newed scrutiny.

Ushering in a new political and social climate, May '68 also brought about, albeit belatedly, an important change in the political landscape: in April of 1969 de Gaulle stepped down as president. Although the general had won a referendum in the immediate wake of May, the months of up-heaval had made it clear that he had lost touch with the rapidly changing moods of the nation. (He died the following year—on November 9, 1970.) His departure was obviously critical. The very embodiment of French *grandeur*, of a "certain idea of France,"[11] he was, of course, the man most closely associated with the resistancialist myth of the Occupation. His de-parture thus eased the way not only for a new political era but for a sea change in the way Vichy was remembered. "With de Gaulle," writes Jean-Pierre Jeancolas, "a whole *vieille garde* disappears in 1969 and 1970: people who had created for themselves a certain idea of France—and a certain Manichaean and petrified idea of the Resistance (or of Vichy). Between 1970 and 1975, a generation came to power (from Pompidou to Giscard and Chirac) that did not have the same reasons to whitewash the past."[12]

These vital political and generational changes are felt throughout the film that so decisively challenged reigning myths and images of the past: *Le chagrin et la pitié*. Juxtaposing archival footage with interviews with wit-nesses and survivors, this four and one-half hour documentary called into question the version of the Occupation that had prevailed since the end of the war. As Claude Lanzmann would do years later in *Shoah*, a 1985 work about the Holocaust, *Le chagrin et la pitié* accorded a critical role to oral testimony. In so doing, it became a major historical document in its own right; it revealed, as French Academy member Bertrand Poirot-Delpech writes, the "irreplaceable nature of witnesses [*témoignage*] in establishing and transmitting truth."[13]

Concerned with the issue of historical "truth," *Le chagrin et la pitié* was permeated by the spirit of skepticism, the rejection of accepted dogma, that flourished in the wake of '68. In this respect, it is hardly surprising that it was the work of men who had taken part in *les événements*: as employees of the state-owned network of French television, Ophuls and his collaborators had participated in a paralyzing strike against the network and were among those dismissed as a consequence.[14] Ophuls himself acknowledged that the film could not have been made before those watershed events. The genera-tional challenge of that year, he remarked, paved the way for the spirit of national introspection critical to the project of *Le chagrin et la pitié*. "The protest of their daughters and sons," he noted, "helped upset their parents; [it] sowed doubt in their minds and overcame for a time the self-satisfaction that is so characteristic of the French bourgeoisie and which, in the end, is the subject of the film."[15] Imbued with a profound post-'68 skepticism, the film is wary of received dogma whether it comes from the Right or from the Left. (Commenting on this aspect of *Le chagrin et la pitié*, Jean-Pierre Jeancolas writes that it is a film that "no longer believes in de Gaulle or Stalin [or] in the history of monuments, of tombs, and of textbooks.")[16] Not content merely to question long-standing versions of the past, *Le chagrin et la pitié* also investigated how those versions had been created by the media and by propaganda. Animated by a desire to see and judge for itself, the film sought out those who had witnessed, experienced—and, at times, created—the traumatic dramas and struggles of the Occupation.

Shot in 1968–1969 as a film designed for television, *Le chagrin et la pitié* was surrounded by controversy from the very first. Although it was bought by the television networks of twenty-seven countries, and broadcast in Germany itself, in France the state-owned network refused to buy or show the film: "it destroys myths," declared network director Jean-Jacques de Bresson, "that are still needed by the French people."[17] Banned from French homes by what Ophuls calls "censorship by inertia," *Le chagrin et la pitié* finally opened, in 1971, in a small theater in the Latin Quarter before moving to a larger house on the Champs-Elysées. There, in the course of an eighty-seven-week run, it evoked critical reactions that could hardly have been more highly charged or more divergent. While the Communist press hailed it as "gigantic"—a "film that hits you in the gut, in the heart, and in the mind"—the critic for *Le Monde*, Alfred Fabre-Luce, criticized it bitterly for its use of "gimmicks, omissions, and deliberate falsifications." Reserving particular condemnation for its portrait of French anti-Semitism, Fabre-Luce declared that it "is always embarrassing to see survivors [the Jews] heaping scorn on the very man [Pétain] to whom they owe their lives."[18] And what Ophuls described as a film about "courage and cowardice at a time of crisis" was apparently deemed too disturbing to be shown on French television for the rest of the decade. It was only in 1981, when the Socialists came to power under Mitterand, that it was finally seen by a French television audience of fifteen million.

The controversial nature of *Le chagrin et la pitié* stemmed, of course, from the fact that it focused on the most unpalatable and most repressed aspects of the Vichy years: the extent and the consequences of French anti-Semitism and collaboration. Its view of the past was so different from that generally accepted after the war that, in the eyes of historians like Henry Rousso and Stanley Hoffmann, it established nothing less than a "counterlegend" of the Vichy years. This "counterlegend" was one in which the principal player in the resistancialist myth, that is, de Gaulle, is virtually absent.[19] It is also one in which all that the general had erased from the ledger of history—the bitter civil warfare of the 1940s; the brutalities of the *Milice*; the heroic and vital role played by the British; French anti-Semitic legislation and deportations of Jews; widespread enthusiasm for Pétain; divisions within the Resistance—is brought vividly to life.

To create its "counterlegend," to explore the dark underside of life during the Occupation, *Le chagrin et la pitié* presents a huge mound of documentary evidence in which eyewitness testimony and archival material commingle. History is seen both from "below" and from "above" as interviews with ordinary men and women are juxtaposed with those carried out with public figures such as Anthony Eden and Pierre Mendès-France. Constantly moving between contemporary interviews and visual material of the era (newsreel footage, newspaper clippings, and Vichy propaganda films), *Le chagrin et la pitié* concerns the very process of memory as much as it does the facts of the Vichy era itself. The national portrait emerging from this process is that of an occupied people characterized not by resistance and unity but, instead, by widespread indifference and pettiness, by daily fears and small acts of cowardice, by active and passive collaboration. We begin to see the deep-seated attitudes that encouraged collaboration— attitudes that made France, as we are reminded several times, the only European country to actively collaborate. Witnesses may deny the widespread enthusiasm that was felt for Pétain, but newsreel clips repeatedly show us the cheering crowds that hailed the *Maréchal* wherever he went.

The ideological passions that so often fueled the fratricidal struggles of the Vichy years emerge in one of the most compelling interviews seen in the film: an aristocratic figure, Christian de la Mazière, reveals the motives that prompted him to side with the Nazis. Raised in a traditional right-wing milieu, which harbored deep feelings of anti-Semitism as well as a tremendous fear of Bolshevism, de la Mazière had no doubt that, as the slogan had it, Hitler was preferable to Stalin. This conviction propelled him, he recalls, to join a special division of the German army composed of French volunteers. Underscoring the often determining role played by ideology in those years, his reminiscences also demonstrate that, contrary to the popular conception, in many cases collaboration stemmed not from moral turpitude or greed but, indeed, from political passion and even (as in his case) idealism.

Not surprisingly, the interview with de la Mazière, this lucid and moving collaborator, was among the most controversial in the film. Some commentators, like Henry Rousso, felt that it suggested both Ophuls's evenhanded approach and the profound moral ambiguities surrounding the Vichy past. In his view, the interview raised essential questions: should a man like de la Mazière be judged and condemned for actions motivated, in some sense, by patriotism? by his willingness to die for a certain "idea of France"?[20] For other critics, instead, the interview with de la Mazière was all *too* compelling. This was the position taken, for example, by French historian Marc Ferro. Noting that it is not only what interviewees say (or the moral and ideological position they represent) that counts, but also the *energy* that they radiate, Ferro observed, "It should be noted that while the 'collaborator' had ample space, a strong personality, culture, and self-control—all of which are positive qualities—the same was not true of the members of the Resistance."[21]

The very different reactions sparked by the interview with the complex figure of de la Mazière vanish when it comes to many other witnesses who, like him, were sympathetic to Pétain's National Revolution. Indeed, the film frequently seems driven by the need to force certain witnesses—and, implicitly, many of their countrymen—to face buried truths and unpalatable realities. To do so, it plays witnesses off against one another; so, too, does it confront their recollections with objective evidence that contradicts what they have just asserted or denied. "The dramatic power of the film," as Rousso observes, "depends on the distance between the objective image of the event, of the news, and the subjective vision of the actors. Each person's testimony is thus punctuated by a kind of call to order, a constantly repeated: 'Remember.' "[22] The exhortation to "remember" may be most insistent, and the amnesia of many witnesses most profound, when it comes to the deep-rooted currents of French anti-Semitism that played into Nazi hands. Here, denials are particularly shrill; objective evidence, particularly damning. For example, in one revealing sequence, a shopkeeper by the name of Klein in the town of Clermont-Ferrand, which serves Ophuls as a microcosm of the Unoccupied Zone, is asked about the fate met by Jewish merchants during the Occupation. At first, Klein's recollections are vague; the issue, it seems, never concerned him. But then he is shown a notice that he placed in a 1941 newspaper declaring that, despite his name, he was not Jewish. Confronted with this piece of evidence from the past, he is startled and exclaims, "Oh, you know that"—thus revealing all the cowardice, the dissimulation, that he (and how many others?) displayed during the Occupation. Attempting to explain, to justify, his behavior, he makes things worse when he adds that he simply wanted people to know that he was "French," not "Jewish."

The merchant's attitude, his insistent and terrible distinction between "Frenchmen" and "Jews," a distinction at the very heart of French anti-Semitism and xenophobia, is echoed, against a far broader canvas, by Comte René de Chambrun, son-in-law of archcollaborationist Pierre Laval. Ardent in his defense of Laval, Chambrun extravagantly describes him as a "resistance" fighter who did his utmost to save French Jews. Ophuls, citing the terrible numbers of those deported, is forced to "remind" Chambrun that even if Laval defended *French* Jews, he willingly traded foreign Jewish refugees for French workers detained in Germany.[23] And this "reminder" is followed by a sequence that undermines all of Chambrun's strident denials: chilling newsreel clips show Jewish men, women, and children being herded into the stadium of the Vel d'Hiv in July of 1942 while a voice-off tells us of the fate that almost all would meet in Germany. Nor does Ophuls rest his case for French anti-Semitism there: after returning to Chambrun, whose position never wavers, and to news-reels of the era in praise of Laval, he interviews a group of young French men and women who admit to continuing prejudice against Jews in the Auvergne region.

If *Le chagrin et la pitié* began the era marked by a "return of the repressed," *Lacombe Lucien*, made in 1974, marks still another shift in Vichy memories. Like Ophuls's documentary, Malle's film also focuses on somber aspects of the national past that were shrouded in silence for decades after the war ended. In particular, *Lacombe Lucien* addresses the issue of collaboration and the nature of the "civil war" that raged in France during the Occupation. But even as Malle's film probes these lingering wounds, it also softens, sometimes in almost imperceptible ways, the "counterlegend" of the Occupation that assumed such dramatic form in *Le chagrin et la pitié*.

When *Lacombe Lucien* was first released, for the most part it was the film's resemblances to *Le chagrin et la pitié*—rather that what are, I think, the more essential differences—that caught the attention of the majority of critics. And, indeed, the similarities between the two films were striking. Despite its fictional nature, for example, *Lacombe Lucien* had a distinctly documentary cast reminiscent of *Le chagrin et la pitié*. (Shot on location in the remote countryside of southern France, it featured nonprofessional actors who spoke with thick regional accents.) And it also resembled Ophuls's film in that it too approached history "from below," that is, from the perspective of ordinary people. Most important, of course—and it was this, above all, that prompted comparisons with *Le chagrin et la pitié*—*Lacombe Lucien* was the first fictional film to focus on one of the most guilt-ridden zones of the past. Here, as Pascal Ory notes in more general terms of the *rétro* phenomenon, collaborators and Vichyites were finally given "a voice and a face."[24]

Not unexpectedly, like *Le chagrin et la pitié*, *Lacombe Lucien* generated both widespread interest and intense controversy. Ranked sixth at the box office in 1974, it was seen by over a quarter of a million people within three weeks of its Paris release. Critical reaction was as deeply divided as it was impassioned. Hostile criticism came from both ends of the ideological spectrum. "It was accused," writes David Pryce-Jones, "of being histori-cally inaccurate and ideologically suspect. . . . It provoked . . . a violent debate on the nature and causes of the movement that had already been nick-named 'rétro.' "[25] But the film was also the subject of marked enthusiasm and generous praise. Writing in the influential weekly *Le nouvel observateur*, Jean-Louis Bory, for example, declared that it was nothing less than "the first real film—and the first true film—about the Occupation. . . . I know. I was there."[26] On this side of the Atlantic, the film found a staunch admirer in Pauline Kael. *Lacombe Lucien* was, she remarked, a "long, close look at the banality of evil. . . . Without ever mentioning the subject of innocence and guilt, *Lacombe Lucien*, in its calm, leisurely, dispassionate way, addresses it on a deeper level than any other movie I know."[27]

The problem of "evil," as Kael has it, is embodied in the film's protagonist, a young peasant named Lucien. As the film opens—it is 1944—Lucien is seen performing distasteful menial tasks in a hospital ward. In hopes that he can escape from his oppressive job, Lucien returns to the farm where he was raised. But his mother, yielding to the demands of a new boyfriend, sends him on his way. Still determined to avoid returning to the hospital, Lucien now attempts to join a cadre of the Resistance headed by the local schoolteacher. Here, too, however, he is thwarted and rejected: the teacher brusquely dismisses him on the grounds that he is both too young and too ignorant to be a *résistant*. At this point, the course his life will take is determined by sheer happenstance. In the wake of a bicycle accident that causes him to violate the curfew, Lucien is apprehended by French members of the German police. Far more psychologically astute or cunning than the Resistance leader, they ply the young man with drink and press him for information. Naively, drunkenly, he tells them about the Resistance leader; as a result, the schoolteacher is captured and tortured before the eyes of a seemingly indifferent Lucien. Soon, Lucien himself becomes a member of the police unit: for the first time in his life, he is filled with a sense of power and importance.

Undisturbed by his act of betrayal, Lucien is not reluctant to participate in the odious tasks performed by his unit. Like the others, he, too, can be brutal and amoral; and he is happy, it would seem, to bully those he formerly resented as his social betters. But there is also, we soon discover, another side to the ignorant young peasant. When he meets a young Jewish woman named France, who has fled from Paris to the south of France with her father and grandmother, he displays a childlike simplicity and vulnerability. Smitten by France herself, whom he awkwardly showers with gifts, he seems to crave approval from her cultivated father, M. Horn. And it is, finally, this "good" side of Lucien that triumphs at the end of the film. At this point, M. Horn has given himself up to the police, and the young couple has escaped to the countryside. In this bucolic setting, Lucien uses his peasant skills to care for and protect the young woman and her grandmother. But after idyllic scenes of pastoral life, the film comes to a sudden, jolting, halt: a freeze-frame of Lucien is followed by subtitles telling us of his eventual capture and execution at the end of the war.

It is not difficult to see why Malle's portrayal of a young collaborator prompted comparisons between this film and Ophuls's documentary. The mixture of brutality and innocence in Lucien suggested to many the moral ambiguities, the "banality of evil," evoked in *Le chagrin et la pitié*. But it seems to me—and this, I think, has become increasingly clear with the passage of time—that the differences between the two films are, in the end, far more telling than the resemblances. For despite its somber subject matter and dark focus, Malle's film clouds the very issues it seems to address so directly.

To begin with, while Ophuls examines ordinary people caught up in the meshes of history, the characters in *Lacombe Lucien* are, despite the director's repeated insistences that they were rooted in fact, far from typical.[28] This is not to say that no one joined the collaborationist camp for motives similar to Lucien's. Or that no one in the *Milice*—the paramilitary police force established in 1943 to "maintain order" (that is, to combat the growing Resistance) and to further the National Revolution promulgated by Vichy—displayed Lucien's blend of childlike naïveté and unthinking brutality. Some lower-class youths like Lucien might well have been lured into the *Milice* or into certain units of the French police by the promise of gain or the chance to enjoy a certain social status. But it *is* safe to say that few marginalized peasants joined such units; safer still to say that few made this fateful choice because of a combined desire for social status and the sheerest of accidents. Moreover, in sharp contrast with Lucien, the vast majority of *miliciens were*, in fact, motivated by ideological beliefs and convictions. Noting that the bulk of *miliciens* were traditionalists and strict Catholics, historian Jean-Pierre Azéma, author of an important 1975 study of French collaboration, *La collaboration, 1940–1944*, writes that they joined the ranks of the extreme Right because of their "hatred of liberal democracy and of the Popular Front."[29]

It is precisely these motives—rooted in ideological, political, and religious traditions—that are lacking in Lucien's case. Unable to make any real distinction between Resistance and collaboration, Lucien is virtually defined by his ignorance of politics, by what Malle called his "opaqueness." Indeed, the extent of his ignorance, his resistance to any ideological position, consistently strains the imagination even as it indicates some of the fundamental ambiguities of the film. Is it possible that, after four years of propaganda and Occupation, anyone could still ask, as Lucien does, "What is a Jew?" And, when he finally does make an ideological pronouncement of sorts, it is, significantly, attributed to someone else. "M. Tonin," he repeats mechanically, "says that the Jews are the enemies of France." His persistent refusal to take sides is underscored in one critical scene involving a captured Resistance fighter he is guarding. When the young man demands to know what side he, a young Frenchman, is really on, Lucien's only response is to gag the prisoner and paint a mouth on the gag—as if, by this childish gesture, he could make the question, and all of ideology, vanish. Commenting on this gesture, critic Pascal Bonitzer, who discussed the film at length in the pages of *Les cahiers du cinéma*, was moved to make the following observation: "What the prisoner asks of Lucien," he writes, "is to choose one camp or the other, to take a position. But the character of Lucien has no other function than to disappoint such a demand."[30] For Bonitzer, Lucien's fundamental ambiguity, an ambiguity that the French critic perceives at the heart of the film itself, means that, in the end, *Lacombe Lucien* "says nothing about collaboration, except that one could be involved in it by accident and without knowing anything about it."[31]

Bonitzer's conviction that Lucien's ambiguity represents that of the film is buttressed, I think, by the fact that the entire film appears to take place in an ideological vacuum. Although we are made aware of ambushes and arrests, of escalating violence, the characters themselves display few of the passions that fueled the fratricidal struggles of the Occupation. No one, certainly, is as "opaque" as Lucien himself. Still, virtually no one in this film appears to choose sides for moral, political, or ideological reasons. With the single exception of a policeman who nurses a grudge against the Popular Front, even those in Lucien's unit harbor few ideological convictions. In addition to being curiously apolitical, those in the collaborationist camp also constitute a strange collection of individuals. Embittered souls and social misfits, their ranks include a nihilistic, aristocratic dandy and his hysterical would-be actress girlfriend, a brutal ex-policeman, a repressed schoolteacher, and even a slightly sadistic African. Although they might seem to embody a diverse spectrum of French society, closer examination suggests that it is indeed a highly selected and even bizarre cross section of the French populace. Pathological and repressed, indifferent to ideology, they are in sharp contrast to the ordinary people in *Le chagrin et la pitié* who collaborated, or were indifferent to collaboration, for a host of ordinary, banal reasons, including greed, fear, and apathy, as well as ideological conviction.

The subtle yet telling improbabilities that mark those in the collaborationist camp extend, moreover, to the Jewish family. It seems likely that Malle's portrait of three generations of the Horn family was designed to represent the progressive assimilation of Jews in France. Thus the old-fashioned grandmother speaks no French; M. Horn has become a successful Parisian tailor but still speaks with an accent; his daughter—who is

named, significantly, France—appears totally assimilated: blond and wil-
lowy, she cries out at one point that "she is tired of being Jewish." But it is
less the schematic nature of this family portrait that is disturbing than the
specter of stereotypes, which often mesh awkwardly with one another, that
it raises. As a rich and cultured tailor, M. Horn seems to embody two
stereotypes rarely found in tandem: he combines the image of the Jewish
immigrant (who often worked in the garment trade) with that of the Jew
as wealthy cosmopolitan. Like this particular combination of qualities, his
behavior, too, appears improbable. After all, would such a devoted father
abandon his beloved daughter and, in a crisis of despair, suddenly give
himself up to the German authorities? No less than her father, France also
behaves in a puzzling manner. Is it likely that such a beautiful and talented
young woman could fall in love with someone as boorish as Lucien? Indeed, in the view of René Prédal—who notes that Lucien is consistently
portrayed as "dumb, boorish, cadish, and vulgar"—the inexplicable behavior of both France and her father is such that the viewer has less sympathy
for them than for Lucien, "the poor lover who is executed."[32]

But it is not, of course, only the inexplicable or disconcerting acts of
M. Horn and France that appear calculated to awaken our sympathy for
the young collaborator. Lucien's peasant origins, the social rejection(s) he
has suffered, do much to explain, and go far to exculpate, his more brutish
or vengeful actions. How can this poor peasant not be eager, suggests the
film, to exert power over members of the social classes that have exploited
him? The sympathy we extend to Lucien because of his social oppression
is reinforced, moreover, by the love he feels for France. Indeed, if her love
for him is inexplicable, his passion for her surely ennobles and redeems
him. The redemptive quality of his love is underscored dramatically toward
the end of the film when we are given a hint of what Lucien might have
been like in a world untouched by oppression and war. Here, in a pastoral
setting as yet uncontaminated by the horrors and cruelties of the outside
world, the "goodness" of Lucien shines through as he provides for France
and her grandmother.

The fact that these last scenes are abruptly followed by titles informing
us of Lucien's execution and death also works to heighten our growing
sympathy for him. For, as Italian critic Eduardo Bruno observes, the fact
that we learn of his execution after seeing the young man at his best means
that his death comes as a shock, a cause for "regret." And, as Bruno goes
on to note, this "regret" prevents us from judging Lucien's acts as a collaborationist, acts that have constituted the very "fabric" of the film we have
just witnessed.[33] Exploring this same issue from a slightly different perspective, still another Italian critic, Ciriaco Tiso, notes that the presence of
love—which he considers, along with politics, one of the two "poles" of

the film—tends "to redeem the evil of power" even as it allows Lucien to "automatically shed his Nazism."[34]

Together with the marked absence of ideology in the film, the manner and nature of Lucien's redemption—the way in which he "sheds his Nazism"—point to the troubling historical and political issues raised by the film. After all, if actions, whether Lucien's or those of the other *miliciens*, are always explained in the narrowest of personal terms, cut off from the surrounding political context, what happens to the moral dimension, the concrete historical cast, of choices made during those bleak years? For example, can Lucien really be faulted or held responsible for collaborating if that decision was prompted solely by a combination of happenstance (the bicycle accident, the obtuseness of the Resistance leader) and class oppression? And if, as the last crucial scenes of the film suggest, Lucien is really essentially "good," can he be blamed for actions over which he had little control?

It is true, of course, that the tragedy of Lucien, who is portrayed as a kind of innocent savage martyred by external circumstances, echoes a recurrent theme in Malle's cinema. The director frequently portrayed children and adolescents who are suddenly exposed to the brutal realities and the corruptions of the adult world.[35] But, in this case, this theme reinforces a message with disturbing political implications. Suggesting that we are all good and evil, and led into given paths not by individual choice but by chance and destiny, this message implies that Lucien is not really responsible for the choices he makes. Or else, that he is no more responsible than the society that surrounds him. Historical choices are thus bathed in a kind of moral relativism; history and society become the culprits even as the individual is washed clean of sin.

If the moral relativism that emerges from *Lacombe Lucien* reflected a recurring theme in Malle's work, it also seemed, as several commentators complained at the time, very much in tune with the climate of the early 1970s. It is true that *Lacombe Lucien* was released only a few years after *Le chagrin et la pitié*; still, these were years that witnessed a rapidly changing political landscape. While *Le chagrin et la pitié* was born of the upheavals of May '68, Malle's film, instead, corresponded to a moment marked by the fading of ideology and by important changes on the French political scene. The death of de Gaulle, and the erosion of the French Communist Party, resulted in the loss of the two political forces most committed to a certain view of the Resistance and, indeed, of the nation itself. For de Gaulle, as for the Communists, the struggle between those who collaborated and those who resisted was seen in terms of good and evil—terms calculated to exclude, certainly, the moral ambiguities in which *Lacombe Lucien* is bathed. Committed to French *grandeur*, de Gaulle could hardly have endorsed the vision of the country that emerges from Malle's film. It is a vision marked by an absence not only of villains but, more important, of heroes.

The death of de Gaulle, moreover, had still other important political consequences: even as it made it possible for a new memory of Vichy to emerge, it also encouraged shifting political alliances. It was at this time that the traditional Right, which had been sympathetic to Vichy, slowly began to reemerge. Blackened by the taint of collaboration after the war, this Right could only have welcomed the blurred moral landscape, the implicit message of national reconciliation, of *Lacombe Lucien*. Not only does the film portray an obtuse Resistance leader, but, even more important, it features a somewhat sympathetic collaborator who finally sheds his Nazism. Philosopher Michel Foucault was not the only one who found this aspect of the film deeply disturbing. "The Pétainist Right, the old collaborationist . . . and reactionary Right," charged Foucault, "which disguised itself as best it could behind de Gaulle, now believes that it has the right to rewrite its own history."[36]

Nor was it only the traditional Right that found a welcome message in the film. This period also saw the rise of a new Right that was concerned less with traditional ideological issues than with economic success and competition. And, in the view of certain critics, the cynical values of this new political force, which saw everything in terms of business and the marketplace, also found an echo in *Lacombe Lucien*. This, I think, is what Michel Capdenac has in mind when he suggests that Lucien—amoral, apolitical, and opportunistic—is less a creature of the 1940s than very much "a young man of today."[37] Even more explicitly, Christian Zimmer pointed out that Malle's film reflected the conservative regime of Giscard d'Estaing that, in his view, had abandoned the idealistic visions of the past (including those of Gaullism) for the meager, pragmatic goals of technological capitalism. "The *rétro* mode," wrote Zimmer in a discussion of *Lacombe Lucien*, "is not a morbid attraction for a sinister period of history but the reflection, the manifestation, of a political current. Gone are *great ideals*: the Resistance was one, Gaullism another. . . . Gone are virtuous indignation, intransigence, fidelity. . . . At the level of the individual there are only *personal* problems and, at the level of power, only *technical* ones."[38]

In retrospect, it has become even clearer that, as Foucault and Zimmer argued at the time, *Lacombe Lucien* corresponded to a very particular social and historical moment. But, at the same time, the moral ambiguities seen in the film also indicated the deep roots of the Vichy syndrome, the long and arduous task of coming to terms with a guilt-ridden past. By the time Malle made his film, the darkest zones of the past could no longer be ignored. But it was *still* possible to deny, to soften, degrees of knowledge and/or complicity concerning this past. It is, of course, these denials, this softening, that are felt in Lucien's "opaqueness"—in his ignorance of ideology, his bewilderment concerning Jews, his ultimate "goodness." Both acknowledging the presence of these zones and denying the specific guilt of individuals, Malle's film set forth a pattern that would hold sway in a number of later *rétro* films. The unmistakable outlines of this pattern are, in fact, visible in what was certainly *the* most successful and well-known film of the *rétro* cycle: François Truffaut's *Le dernier métro*.

Like *Lacombe Lucien*, *Le dernier métro* was clearly a deeply personal work. Imbued with themes and issues that run throughout Truffaut's cinema, the film is animated, in fact, by one of the director's enduring beliefs: his conviction that the domain of art and illusion—be it that of books, of cinema, of theater—is not only more magical than any other but, in some ways, more "real." This belief was dramatically illustrated, for example, in a 1973 work, *La nuit américaine* (*Day for Night*), that, in many respects, foreshadowed *Le dernier métro*. Devoted to a cinematic troupe in the process of shooting a film, *La nuit américaine* underscored Truffaut's love for the world of illusion as well as the insistent parallels he perceived between art and life.

Unlike *La nuit américaine*, *Le dernier métro*, which appeared in 1980, is focused on the world of theater rather than that of cinema. More important, though, in the context of this chapter, its setting distinguishes it from the earlier film. *Le dernier métro* takes place during the Occupation—more precisely, in the dark days of 1944. Against this somber background, the film depicts a dramatic troupe that is engaged in mounting a new production in Paris. In addition to normal difficulties, the hardships of the era pose a particular set of problems: to succeed with their new production, the troupe must cope with Nazi regulations, the scarcity of supplies, the restrictions and dangers faced by its Jewish members, the threat posed by a hostile critic who is collaborating with the Nazis. To these problems must be added still another hurdle: the director of the play (Jean Poiret), who is Jewish, has been forced into hiding to evade the Nazis. He has taken refuge, in fact, in the basement of the theater where no one knows of his existence except his wife (Catherine Deneuve), a beautiful actress who plays a leading role in the new production.

In addition to her concerns about her husband, the director's wife must also assume the daily tasks of running the theater. Her problems take on an added twist when she finds herself falling in love with her leading man (Gérard Depardieu). Recalling the parallels between art and life that marked *La nuit américaine*, in *Le dernier métro* the romantic triangle of director/leading lady/leading man is mirrored in the play that is being produced. In fact, the very title of this play, *La disparue*, might well be an allusion to the director's precarious situation: changed from feminine to masculine, it designates a man who has "disappeared."

For the most part, *Le dernier métro* consists of a series of melodramatic incidents: the Nazis arrive to search the theater; the leading lady must go to Nazi headquarters and placate the hostile fascist critic; the leading man wants to abandon the theater to join the Resistance. But one after another, difficult situations are resolved and hurdles overcome: the director is able to monitor the play's progress from the basement and ensure its triumph; the hostile critic is roundly thrashed by the leading man; the play is a success. Even as Paris itself is liberated, the romantic entanglements of the film appear to sort themselves out on the stage of the theater. As the film draws to a conclusion, we witness a staged scene of renunciation and *adieux* between two lovers who are played, of course, by Catherine Deneuve and Gérard Depardieu. As the performers take their bows, the director—who has emerged from his hiding place and is now seated in the theater—joins them onstage. With Deneuve between the two men, holding each by the hand, the three joyfully acknowledge the audience's wild applause.

In general, of course, the celebration of theater/cinema that reaches a dramatic climax at the conclusion of *Le dernier métro* would only add to the charm of Truffaut's film. But just as Malle's portrayal of childhood innocence assumes a certain coloration when seen in the context of the Occupation, so, too, I think, does the theatricality of *Le dernier métro* take on a political dimension not seen in a work like *La nuit américaine*. For in *Le dernier métro* the dramas that take place in the theater, both onstage and off, not only eclipse the harsh realities of the Occupation but render them as theatrical, as illusory, as the performances that unfold onstage. The constraints and dangers of the era become little more than a stylish backdrop of iconic images; moreover, as if to reinforce the sense of illusion that permeates the film, these iconic scenes frequently appear to have been drawn less from real life than from earlier films. The shadow of *To Be or Not to Be* is felt in a sequence in which a brave Deneuve, who has gone to German headquarters, rejects the advances of a Nazi officer; *Casablanca* comes to mind in a nightclub scene in which a Parisian *chanteuse* entertains German soldiers. Underscoring the insistent reminders of old Hollywood films that reverberate throughout *Le dernier métro*, Richard Grenier, one of the very few critics hostile to the film, pointed to still other cinematic echoes. "I suspect," he wrote, "that the notion of the hidden Jew in the cellar was suggested by *The Diary of Anne Frank* (the film, not the book); the idea of a stage director secretly guiding the performances in a stage production by a comparable device in the Fred Astaire–Ginger Rogers musical *The Barclays of Broadway*; and the florid declaration of a minor actress's naked ambition by the character of Anne Baxter in *All about Eve*."[39]

Le dernier métro differs, of course, from old Hollywood movies in one critical respect: it alludes to the dark zones of the French past—the presence of collaboration, of anti-Semitic legislation—that had been exposed to the light in the early 1970s. But, seen against the background of earlier screen memories, these zones become part of an improbable world of illusion and make-believe. Absorbed into the fabric of melodrama, the dangers faced by Jews, for example, are surmounted with astonishing ease: the Jewish director of the troupe manages to direct the play from his hiding place; the Jewish costume designer is able to violate the curfew by draping a scarf over the yellow star she is forced to wear. As for the collaborator, a theater critic based on Alain Laubreaux, an influential drama critic for a weekly Vichy paper, *Le cri du peuple*: he is turned into a stock character of melodrama. Even Truffaut's usual care for *vraisemblance*, which lends a special charm to his films, is lacking. As Yann Lardeau points out, the Nazis do not recognize the leading man although they have seen him previously with a captured Resistance fighter; when the police arrive to search the theater, they wait for Deneuve to guide them backstage herself so that her husband has time to hide.[40] In short, never had the difficulties of the Occupation appeared more negligible—the villain of the piece is, significantly, a hostile theater critic—or, in the end, more unreal.

Le dernier métro is not, however, merely an improbable fiction, a testament to Truffaut's love of stage and screen. It is also, and most important in this context, a historical melodrama imbued with the familiar contours of the resistancialist version of the past that was challenged so dramatically by *Le chagrin et la pitié*. Truffaut's film takes us back, once again, to a reassuring world where ideological divisions scarcely existed, and where French men and women were joined in opposition to the invader. In this respect, it is telling that *Le dernier métro* virtually ignores the more troubling zones of the past. One would never know, from this film, that Parisian theater flourished during the Occupation in large part because the Germans wanted to encourage the distractions of entertainment.[41] Or that, as Colin Nettelbeck observes, France was subject at this time to a critical "divide" between Pétain and de Gaulle: a divide marked, of course, by the "fratricidal struggles" of the Occupation.[42] Only the figure of the collaborationist theater critic serves as a reminder that the "enemy" could be a Frenchman as well as a German. But the critic constitutes a striking exception in a political landscape marked, above all, by French solidarity and patriotism.

The tone of national unity and resistance that pervades *Le dernier métro* is set, in fact, early in the film in two rapid, but revealing, scenes. In one, when a German soldier brushes a boy's head in a rough caress, his mother immediately washes his hair to remove the contamination of the Nazi touch; in the other, the stage manager teaches a youngster all the deprecatory names used by the French to denote the Nazis. As the film progresses, it becomes clear that everyone in the world of theater—a world that was

hardly noted for the strength of its political courage and convictions—
shares this aversion to the Germans. So, too, and this may be even more
telling, is everyone sympathetic toward Jews. Members of the troupe do
not hesitate to rally round the Jewish costume designer and her daughter;
Jew and Gentile happily work together backstage. Despite the fact that
Jews were banned from the world of theater as early as 1942, and the film
is set in 1944, the leading man is surprised and outraged when he learns
that the theater might refuse to hire Jewish actors. Indeed, the only anti-
Semite in the film is the fascist critic who, not surprisingly, has a bizarre,
perhaps pathological, edge to him. Once more, the message is unmistakable: only twisted, disturbed beings were anti-Semitic; the vast majority of
the French did everything possible to aid the Jews.

Judging by the reception of *Le dernier métro*, this message was clearly a
welcome one. Truffaut's most successful film, *Le dernier métro* won critical
acclaim—and garnered ten *Césars*—in addition to being a giant box-office
hit. (Leading all other French films of 1980, it managed to top even *The
Empire Strikes Back*). This is not to deny that the film's success owed a great
deal to its inherent charm and artistic merit. But it is difficult not to feel
that, at least in part, it struck such a welcome chord precisely because it
resurrected comforting images of the past. One critic, in fact, made it very
clear that he was drawn to the film precisely for this reason. "Of all the
films situated in the Paris of *les années noires*," he wrote, "*Le dernier métro*
is the only one, I say the only one, that I was able to see with detachment,
amusement, emotion . . . without feeling a sense of rejection (nausea,
shame, anger) in all my being."[43] Explicitly linking the popularity of *Le
dernier métro* to its rose-tinted portrait of *les années noires*, François Garçon,
critic for the left-wing review *Les temps modernes*, sadly concluded that
(along with Fassbinder's *Lili Marleen*) Truffaut's film signaled an end to
the era of national introspection launched by *Le chagrin et la pitié*. "In
France," he wrote, "*Le dernier métro*, because of its unbelievable success,
can be considered, we believe, as the negative image of the film of Marcel
Ophuls."[44]

In one respect, Garçon was absolutely correct. As I have argued in the
preceding pages, *Le dernier métro is* permeated by the comforting view of
the past that *Le chagrin et la pitié* was so obviously determined to demolish.
But in another way, he has been proven wrong. It has become clear that,
instead of indicating the end of an era of self-examination, *Le dernier métro*
signaled a particular moment in the ongoing battle for Vichy memory. The
pendulum was to swing again. In fact, the currents of denial implicit in *Le
dernier métro* may have contributed to its next swing insofar as they played
a part in what Rousso calls the "reawakening" of Jewish memory. Central
to this "reawakening" was the sense that Jewish memory of the Occupa-

tion—a period that saw one-fifth of French Jews disappear into the "night and fog" of the camps—was, indeed, very different from French memory as a whole.

Jewish Memory

Just as a variety of factors contributed to the "explosion" of Vichy memory in the wake of '68, so, too, was the "reawakening" of Jewish memories the result of a complex blend of psychological, historical, and even demographic shifts. First of all, it should be noted that if Jewish memory had to be "reawakened" in the 1970s and 1980s, it was because it, too, had shared in the general amnesia regarding the Occupation years. "There was a deep repression of two kinds," writes sociologist Pierre Birnbaum, "that which bore on the guilt of much of France, and that of Jews who had suffered an inexplicable fate."[45] To a certain degree, the repression of Jewish memories reflects the historical situation of French Jews, a situation long marked by habits of silence. In France, Jews had always considered themselves an integral part of the larger community; they were among the most assimilated, if not *the* most assimilated, Jews in Europe. Their assimilation—the sense that they were first and foremost French and only secondarily Jewish—went back to the time of the Revolution when they were granted the rights enjoyed by other citizens of the Republic. Thus when Vichy began to pass anti-Semitic legislation, many simply could not believe that the French state would strip them of their rights, much less send them to their deaths. They had been faced, of course, with violent outbursts of anti-Semitism before Vichy; but Vichy was different in that the measures passed literally turned them into "foreigners." For this reason, as Birnbaum writes, Vichy signaled "not only the end of the process of Jewish emancipation begun by the Revolution [but] also the brutal destruction of Franco-Judaism."[46]

Despite, or perhaps because of, the trauma suffered by Jews under Vichy, it was not French Jews who first began to study the "brutal destruction of Franco-Judaism." That task fell, instead, to foreign scholars who—probing the nature and extent of French complicity in the anti-Semitic legislation and, especially, in the deportations—began to demonstrate the betrayal of French Jews at the hands of the Vichy government.[47] But the situation began to change toward the end of the 1960s as, increasingly, French Jews became willing to assume, and to proclaim, their identity as a group. In part, this new sense of group identity was prompted by renewed evidence of anti-Semitism. In 1967, for example, Israel's lighting victory in the Six-Day War sparked anti-Zionist feelings that often seemed to have an anti-Semitic edge. In fact, de Gaulle himself made a controversial speech in which he not only condemned the Israeli offensive but described Jews in terms that raised hackles in the Jewish community as well as among many non-Jews who had supported Israel. Referring to Jews as an "elite" and "domineering" people, the president's words seemed to cruelly mock both those who had vanished in the Holocaust and North African Jews who had been forced from their homes in the wake of the Algerian War.[48]

The converging overtones of anti-Zionist and anti-Semitic sentiments heard in de Gaulle's remarks also reverberated, in the militant climate of the late 1960s and early 1970s, throughout the rhetoric of many on the Left and, especially, the far Left. This was particularly true after May '68: impelled by Third World sympathies to view Arabs as victims of Israeli aggression, leftists sometimes referred to the Jewish state in terms that hinted at deeply rooted, if unconscious, anti-Semitic sentiments.[49] On the other side of the political spectrum, the far Right, which had begun its ascent in the late 1970s, did not hesitate to resurrect racist rhetoric and ideology associated with the 1940s. The tensions stemming from this highly charged political climate were heightened still further when, in 1980, a bomb exploded in front of a major Parisian synagogue on the Rue Copernic.[50] And to all these factors must be added the dismay felt by many Jews in the face of the media attention accorded Holocaust denier Robert Faurisson. Remarking that Faurisson's revisionist theses were publicized at a time when many aging survivors felt they had to speak out about the past before it was too late, Rousso observes that "just as victims of the genocide were beginning to reemerge from the recesses of collective memory, here they were threatened once more with extermination, just when it seemed that repression might finally be laid to rest."[51]

The continuing evidence of anti-Semitism surfaced, moreover, at a time when the Jewish community itself was experiencing a renewed sense of collective identity and solidarity, a sense that was largely prompted by two important factors. One, certainly, was the huge influx, and the increasingly influential presence, of Sephardic Jews from North Africa. Repatriated in France in the wake of the Algerian War, such Jews were frequently more observant than their long-assimilated Ashkenazi counterparts and, also, more keenly aware of their identity as a community. And the second factor bore on the fact that the 1970s witnessed the collapse of revolutionary utopianism. The demise of Marxist hopes spurred many Jews, who had formerly placed their hopes in secular messianic goals and ideals, to return to Jewish traditions, to their "roots."[52]

All these factors—that is, a new sense of Jewish self-awareness, indications of continuing anti-Semitism, mounting evidence of the atrocities suffered by Jews during the war—combined to prompt a "reawkening" of Jewish memory concerning the fate suffered by French Jews during the Occupation. Against this complex background, cinematic representations of the treatment accorded French Jews during the Vichy era clearly assume a particular relevance. In this context, two films of the late 1980s—Claude Chabrol's *Histoire des femmes* and, especially, Louis Malle's *Au revoir les enfants*—are, I think, of special interest. Neither work, and it is important that this be very clear, gives any hint of the anti-Semitic currents that had (re)surfaced at this time. On the contrary: both feature bonds of friendship between Jews and Christians even as they portray a world that is virtually free of anti-Semitic sentiments. But this very portrayal is, I think, permeated by revealing currents of denial: it goes counter to, erases, the deeply rooted feelings of French anti-Semitism that, at least to some degree, contributed to the measures taken against Jews by the Vichy government.[53]

Needless to say—and this, too, must be very clear—this is not to imply that all the French shared such feelings. Many, certainly, felt no ill will toward their Jewish neighbors; some were sympathetic toward them and their plight; others even felt moved enough to provide hiding places for Jews or means of escape. Still, it is difficult to imagine, as these films seem to suggest, that few people knew anything about Jews or the measures that had been taken against them. In a sense, this singular lack of knowledge or awareness had already made itself felt in *Lacombe Lucien*. But in later films this unawareness becomes at once more insistent and more revealing. Coming at a moment when far more was known, and acknowledged, about French complicity in the genocide, this ignorance seemed impelled by the desire, which may well have been unconscious, to hold at bay what was perhaps the most troubled zone in modern French history. The deep repression that, at first, had surrounded the camps themselves—"the return of victims from the Nazi concentration camps," writes Rousso, "was the event most quickly effaced from memory"[54]—was later transferred, it would seem, to French attitudes and behavior toward Jews.

In *Histoire des femmes*, these attitudes are treated rapidly—yet revealingly. Based on a true incident, Chabrol's film tells the story of a young French housewife and mother, Marie (Isabelle Hupert), who becomes an abortionist during the Occupation. At first, she turns to this dubious *métier* in order to support herself and her children. But soon sheer greed gets the upper hand: thus even after her husband returns from Germany, Marie continues to perform abortions. Worse still, under her husband's eyes, she takes a collaborationist as a lover. Jealous and enraged, her husband finally denounces her to the authorities. Judged by a Vichy tribunal, she is condemned to death to set an example of French "morality."

As portrayed by Chabrol, Marie is hardly a sympathetic character. Her plight may arouse our compassion; still, she herself is a mixture of shrewdness and cunning, of sensuality and greed. Given these traits, it is all the more telling that in one striking respect—that is, in regard to Jews—she is totally unworldly and innocent. Despite the fact that her best friend is named Rachel, and they live in a small town where everyone seems to know everyone else, she is unaware that her friend is Jewish. Indeed, she learns this critical detail only when Rachel is deported. And this is followed by something even more improbable. When Marie hears of Rachel's fate, *for the first and only time in the film*, this callous housewife—who despises her husband, neglects her children, and flaunts her infidelity—begins to cry.

While Marie's friendship with Rachel constitutes a subplot in *Histoire des femmes*, a similar friendship—that is, one between Christian and Jew—is at the very core of *Au revoir les enfants*. Made thirteen years after *Lacombe Lucien*, Malle's second film about the Occupation generated none of the controversy that had greeted his earlier work. In large part, certainly, this reflected a change in attitudes toward the past: by 1987, audiences had absorbed revelations about the Vichy past that might well have shocked them a decade earlier. But it is also true that *Au revoir les enfants* contains few of the moral ambiguities of Malle's earlier film. Skirting and softening the most troubling issues of the past, *Au revoir les enfants* offered what was for Malle, often considered a "cold" director, an uncharacteristically benign view of human nature. As in the case of *Le dernier métro*, it was a view that appealed both to the public and to critics. Ranked eleventh at the box office, *Au revoir les enfants* won *Césars* for best film, best director, and best script.

Set in 1944, *Au revoir les enfants* takes us back, once again, to the darkest hours of the Occupation—this time, to a *lycée* run by priests whose faith and courage prompt them to harbor Jewish refugees among their more affluent charges. The film traces the growing friendship between one such refugee, who has assumed a false name, and a Christian boy (apparently based on Malle himself). But neither innocence nor friendship can protect these friends from the ugly realities of the Occupation. When a servant is dismissed from his job at the *lycée* for black-market dealings with the schoolboys, he becomes disgruntled and resentful. Impelled by a desire for revenge, as well as a need for money, he informs the authorities about the presence of Jewish children. It is not long before members of the Gestapo march into a classroom and demand to know which schoolboys are Jewish. The Christian lad, who is aware of his friend's true identity, cannot prevent himself from glancing at the young refugee. His fearful glance is not lost on the Germans. The Jewish boy is seized; soon afterward, a voice-off tells us that he died in a German camp.

Malle has suggested that the guilt which assails the Christian boy after his incriminating glance points to the diffuse and general guilt that he, like many of his compatriots, experienced in regard to the fate of Jews. I would not question this. But such an interpretation makes it all the more telling that the film itself underscores the fact that neither the boy nor virtually anyone else is, in fact, guilty. Indeed, in sharp contrast with *Lacombe Lucien*, it is not guilt that prevails in this film but innocence. Set in a schoolboy realm of youthful innocence, *Au revoir les enfants* consistently avoids the murky moral zones of Malle's earlier film. Whereas, for example, the drama of collaboration was at the core of *Lacombe Lucien*, in *Au revoir les enfants* it constitutes a distinctly secondary theme. And while the servant who informs on the Jewish boys resembles Lucien in certain respects—he, too, is clearly a victim of class injustice and oppression—he is given even more mitigating reasons for his decision to collaborate. Born with a handicap, he has also been made the scapegoat for a crime that he committed together with the bourgeois schoolboys.

If the servant collaborator is a more sympathetic figure than Lucien, so, too, is the Jewish boy far more attractive than, say, the character of France in *Lacombe Lucien*. As if to erase the ambiguities that clung to the Jewish family in his earlier film, in *Au revoir les enfants* Malle draws the portrait of a young Jew who is endowed with every virtue. Talented at math and music, he is sensitive as well as intelligent. But he is so lovingly drawn that—and this was certainly unconscious on Malle's part—in some sense he, too, is rendered "other." Although Pauline Kael did not question why he should be so idealized, her review of the film, which was generally enthusiastic, made it clear that he was perceived as "foreign" metaphorically as well as literally. Throughout the film, she wrote, the Jewish boy is "used as an aesthetic object—spiritual, sensitive, foreign. . . . He's photographed as if he were a piece of religious art: Christ in his early adolescence. There's something unseemly about the movie's obsession with his exotic beauty— as if the French-German Jews had come from the far side of the moon. And does he have to be so brilliant, and a gifted pianist, and courageous?"[55]

It is not only the flattering portrait of the young Jew or, for that matter, the friendship between Christian and Jew, that bespeaks a determination on Malle's part to avoid the sinister moral zones explored in *Lacombe Lucien*. Marked by friendship and innocence, the schoolboy realm depicted in this film is one that seems to have been hermetically sealed against the bitter struggles and intense propaganda of the Occupation years. No one in this film seems to have heard of Jews, to say nothing of being anti-Semitic. Even the intelligent Christian boy—who comes, after all, from a bourgeois, sophisticated family—remarks that he knows nothing about Jews except that they do not eat pork and "are smarter than we are." Deeming this ignorance "singular," in a review of the film Stanley Hoffmann, who spent the war years in a *lycée* in France, observed that it ran counter to his own experience. Noting that in his own *lycée* "even ten-year-olds often lined up aggressively on one or the other side of the barricades," he went on to say that the Occupation was a time when "ideology pushed people into collaboration, or pro-Vichy organizations, or the variety of Resistance movements. . . . Especially by 1944 many of the French who worked with or for the Nazis did so out of belief more than out of social resentment— or at least they had rationalized and translated their class anger into ideological belief."[56] While granting that "sheltered schoolboys" could conceivably have been as innocent as those in *Au revoir les enfants*, Hoffmann asserted that they "would hardly have been typical of young Frenchmen at that time."

It is not only the absence of ideology that struck Hoffmann as improbable. He also expressed doubts about an important sequence in which the mother of the Christian boy invites her son, together with his Jewish friend, to dinner in an expensive restaurant. The scene is revealing because, like several tableaux in *Le dernier métro*, it harks back to the myth of French unity informing the resistancialist version of the past. The scene begins when a group of *miliciens* enter the restaurant where the protagonists are dining and start to harass an elderly Jewish man who is seated by himself at a neighboring table. Instead of looking away in embarrassed silence, the upper-class clients of the restaurant begin to protest this harassment with murmured cries of "collabo." Questioning the credibility of this exchange, Hoffmann observed that although most of the French "did hope for their liberation" by 1944, such courage seemed improbable. "Wouldn't," he asked, "the heavy, guilty silence of fear have prevailed . . . especially in an expensive establishment, where German officers were also dining?"[57]

Just as *Au revoir les enfants* gives no sign of the ideological battles that raged in 1944, so, too, does it refrain from depicting the "guilty silence of fear" that often determined French attitudes toward Jews. Indeed, far more than in most of Malle's films, the world seen in *Au revoir les enfants* is one of youthful innocence and adult courage. When evil finally shatters this sheltered realm, it is hardly surprising that it is not associated with the murky moral zones and bitter struggles of the Occupation. It is not a French *milicien* like Lucien who sends the Jewish boys to their death but, rather, anonymous German soldiers.

Au revoir les enfants was not the only film of 1987 haunted by the specter of deported Jewish children. That same year the issue was raised in a long documentary by Marcel Ophuls, *Hotel Terminus*. Ophuls's second documentary about the Occupation, *Hotel Terminus* was prompted by the trial of the so-called butcher of Lyons, Klaus Barbie, for crimes against humanity. (Gestapo chief of Lyons during the Occupation, after the war Barbie escaped to South America with the help of American officials; he was finally brought back to France, tried before a French court in 1987, and sentenced to life in prison.) Composed of segments devoted to the various phases of Barbie's life, *Hotel Terminus* concludes with a moving sequence that bears on a very grim episode of the Occupation: the deportation of forty-four Jewish children from a hiding place in Izieu, a small town near Lyons.

The contrast between the concluding sequence of *Hotel Terminus* and *Au revoir les enfants* is, I think, telling. For in probing the still-mysterious circumstances behind the deportation of the children from Izieu, *Hotel Terminus* raised the unsettling moral issue that, of course, is absent in *Au revoir les enfants*: that of French complicity and guilt. By making it clear that the children's hiding place had been revealed to the Germans by a *French* informer, *Hotel Terminus* left no doubt that Barbie and the Nazis were not the only ones responsible for their deaths. And, just as important, the film also exposed what appeared to be a continuing reluctance on the part of French officials to acknowledge the extent of French responsibility for these acts. This reluctance emerges in the course of an extensive interview with a laborer who, despite the fact that he knew both the children and the French informer, was never called to testify in the course of Barbie's trial. When the state prosecutor is questioned about this surprising omission, he is unable—unwilling?—to explain precisely why the laborer was never called to the stand. We are left to assume that the state did not want his disquieting version of events to be made public.

By the late 1980s, *Hotel Terminus* was but one, albeit the most notable, of a steady stream of documentaries, which were often the work of Jewish directors, devoted to the Occupation years. Some, deeply felt, were inspired by personal experiences. In *Weapons of the Spirit* (1989) Pierre Sauvage returned to the French town where his family had been among the many Jews sheltered by Protestants of the region; *Boulevard des Hirondelles* (Josée Yanne, 1992) is based on an autobiographical novel by Resistance fighter Lucie Aubrac; *Les enfants du Vel d'Hiv* (1992) consists of interviews with some of the very few survivors of the massive deportations of July 1942. Others sought to illuminate a specific aspect, or moment, of *les années noires*. Made somewhat earlier, *Chantons sous l'Occupation* (1976), by André Halimi, deals with the world of entertainment under the Occupation; Claude Chabrol's *L'oeil de Vichy* (1993) examines the extent and nature of Vichy propaganda. But whatever their subject, virtually all these films, in sharp contrast with their fictional counterparts, were clearly determined to confront the most difficult truths, the darkest aspects, of the past. It would be difficult to imagine a more striking contrast than that between *Le dernier métro* and *Chantons sous l'Occupation*. Both deal, of course, with theatrical life under the Occupation. But whereas Truffaut depicted a world of dedicated artists, Halimi focused on acts of collaboration, or near collaboration, on the part of performers. (Indeed, the film implicitly argues that the very act of entertaining an occupying army constitutes a form of collaboration). And while Chabrol's *Histoire des femmes* paints a far more somber picture of the period than, say, *Le dernier métro*, its denunciation of Vichy pales beside that seen in the director's later documentary, *L'oeil de Vichy*.

In the case of certain documentaries, the contrast between their view of the Vichy past and that seen in the feature films explored earlier seems to illustrate the divergence between Jewish memory and French memory as a whole. But, as suggested earlier, this contrast also mirrors a division that runs throughout much of film history: that separating documentaries from works of fiction. For unlike the vast majority of fictional films, documentaries—and this is certainly true of those dealing with the Vichy past—are frequently animated by the desire to testify, to take sides, to keep memory alive. In so doing, of course, as works such as *Le chagrin et la pitié* and *Hotel Terminus* made very clear, they often become important documents or witnesses in their own right.

Still, if fictional films are seldom consciously aware of this need, they too testify, albeit in a very different way. Indeed, if documentaries about the Vichy era reveal a great deal about the past, it is fictional works that, as I have argued throughout this chapter, best capture the mood of the moment that saw their creation. The deep tensions that are felt in *Le dernier métro* and *Au revoir les enfants*, their tendency to soften or erase the most troubling zones of the past, are at the very core of the Vichy syndrome. And, indeed, showing how well these films seized widely shared emotions, the tensions they embody were felt in two major political controversies that erupted in 1994.[58] For in both cases, the figure at the center of the storm, as well as a portion of public opinion, clung to the protestations of innocence, and to the denials, that echo throughout the most successful *rétro* films.

The first of these controversies was triggered by the trial of Paul Touvier. Deemed the "last war criminal" at the time of his trial, Touvier was, significantly, the *first* Frenchman to be tried for "crimes against humanity." (Papon, of course, would be the second.) The crimes of which Touvier stood accused followed the assassination, at the hands of the Resistance, of Philippe Henriot, a rabid pro-Nazi French cabinet officer in charge of information and propaganda. In retaliation for Henriot's death, Touvier, then a regional chief in Lyons of the infamous *Milice*, sent seven Jews to their death. (It was because he chose his victims solely on the basis of race that his actions fell into the category of "crimes against humanity.") Although Touvier maintained that he was merely following German instructions—that, in fact, he had actually saved other Jews from death—the court found him guilty. "The Resistance," wrote a commentator for the *New York Times*, "had killed Henriot, but Touvier went after Jews, because the Resistance was armed and would strike back, while Jews were powerless and could be killed with impunity."[59]

If Touvier's crimes reflect the darkest zones of the French past, his responses before the court embody the repressions and denials that have consistently fueled the Vichy syndrome. Interrogated by the judges about the past, Touvier, who had been in hiding virtually since the end of the war, and who had been shielded from arrest by members of the Roman Catholic clergy, kept insisting that he could not remember critical events.

When asked to explain illegal acts committed by members of the *Milice*, who were known to blackmail their victims and to loot and pillage the homes of those destined to be deported, he resorted to a variety of euphemisms. Hence "holdups became 'recoveries,' thefts became 'borrowing,' money received while in hiding became 'scholarships' and extortion became 'donations out of gratitude.' "[60] Denying that he had been close to Klaus Barbie, Touvier also maintained that he knew nothing about the anti-Semitic statutes promulgated by the Vichy government, although such statutes were, in fact, often carried out by the *Milice*. "There was no television," he said. "We didn't know anything about round-ups or deportations."[61] In a similar manner, he also denied his anti-Semitism. In this case, however, his protestations of innocence were flatly contradicted by his own journals and diaries. For virtually every page, even those written as recently as the 1980s, contained anti-Semitic or pro-Nazi comments.

Barely six months after Touvier's trial, a still more important scandal broke out. It was provoked by revelations concerning no less a personage than President Mitterand himself. Putting a sad coda to one of the longest political careers in French history, revelations concerning the president's behavior both during and after the Occupation cast a disturbing light on many of the positions he had taken earlier concerning Vichy controversies: his refusal, in 1992, on the fiftieth anniversary of the deportations of the Vel d'Hiv, to apologize for the French state and acknowledge its role in the deportations; his unsettling decision, made that same year, to lay a wreath on the tomb of Vichy leader Marshal Pétain; his insistence that there was "no point" to Touvier's trial. A book by Pierre Péan, *Une jeunesse française: François Mitterand 1934–1947* (Paris: Fayard, 1994), written with Mitterand's assistance, not only confirmed long-standing rumors concerning the president's Vichyite past—Mitterand had worked as a Vichy official before joining the Resistance in 1943—but offered documents and letters proving that the future head of the French Socialists had been a "pétainiste dur," a convinced Vichyite who was, as a commentator for *Le monde* had it, "righter than Right."[62] The youthful Mitterand had written xenophobic letters in the 1930s: in one the future French president expressed fears that "outside influences" were making the Latin Quarter into a "tower of Babel"; moreover, as one photograph demonstrated incontrovertibly, he had taken part in a 1935 student demonstration against "les métèques." (A derogatory epithet for foreigners, *les métèques* was a term used by demonstrators mainly to designate Polish students of Jewish origin.)[63] By 1942, Mitterand appears to have moved even further to the Right: in an article that showed the depth of ideological divisions in France, and which was published that year in a Pétainist propaganda review, he blamed France's collapse not on the German Reich or on Nazism but on *French* Republican traditions dating to the time of the Revolution. "We are the heirs," he declared, "of one hundred and fifty years of mistakes."[64] Around this same time, he also worked for *La légion française*, an umbrella group of veterans founded in 1940 largely designed to produce propaganda (much of which was anti-Semitic) to diffuse Vichy's National Revolution. (Among the slogans espoused by this group was "Contre la lèpre juive, pour la pureté française" ["Against the Jewish plague, for French purity"].) When interviewed by Péan about these activities and, in particular, about the anti-Semitic legislation passed under Vichy—that is, before the German troops marched into the unoccupied zone in November of 1942—Mitterand remarked: "I didn't think about Vichy anti-Semitism. I know that there were unfortunately anti-Semites who had an important position under the *Maréchal*, but I did not follow the legislation at the time the measures were taken."[65]

To the ears of many, Mitterand's denials had the same hollow ring as those of Touvier. Is it possible, after all, that Mitterand, then working for the Vichy government, did not "notice" the infamous roundup of the Vel d'Hiv, as he claims? Or that, although he worked in a propaganda unit, he was unaware of anti-Semitic propaganda and legislation? Indeed, as Tony Judt points out in a discussion of Péan's book, by 1942 it was virtually impossible to be unaware of what was happening to Jews. "The harsh public treatment of Jews in 1942," writes Judt, "was a turning point in public attitudes. . . . Furthermore, the anti-Jewish legislation promulgated by Vichy itself, limiting and eventually forbidding Jews access to all official and professional occupations, required public employees to affirm their non-Jewish origin. Mitterand also made a number of visits to Paris in the later part of 1942; it is unlikely that he did not notice the yellow stars that Jews were obliged by then to wear."[66] Inevitably raising questions such as these, Mitterand's weak and unconvincing denials were, in the view of several of his Socialist colleagues, even more disturbing than his past conduct.[67] In their eyes, not only did the attitude of the Socialist leader suggest a refusal to confront the past, but, it was felt, it did much to "banalize" Vichy. And they were even more dismayed, as were many of their countrymen, by still another revelation that only confirmed Mitterand's deep complicity with, or indifference to, France's role in the Final Solution. For it turned out that the president had maintained a lifelong friendship with one of the most infamous of Vichy officials, René Bousquet. As the highest ranking police officer in France from April 1942 to December 1943, Bousquet played a major role in the deportations of Jews and, in particular, in the notorious roundup of the Vel d'Hiv when zealous French police—ignoring German requests that only adults over sixteen be deported—included children among those destined for the camps.[68] (Ultimately indicted for "crimes against humanity," Bousquet was assassinated, on June 8, 1993, before he could be brought to trial.)

Providing ample evidence that the Vichy syndrome was still alive and well, the controversies that swirled around Mitterand's past, as well as Touvier's trial, also demonstrated the depth of the national fault lines harking back to Vichy. It was clear that, as *New York Times* commentator Ted Morgan wrote at the time, France was still

> divided by a line traced during the war. Two major bodies of opinion continued to confront each other. One said that Pétain had preserved the French state, and the other that he had sold out to the Germans. One said that there were atrocities on both sides, and the other that the Final Solution was different in nature from the other crimes, and that Vichy had abetted it. One said that the *Milice* and the Resistance were equals in a cycle of crimes and reprisals, and the other that the *Milice* were traitors at the service of the Nazis, while the Resistance were patriots working with the Allies.[69]

When Touvier was declared guilty, many had expressed the hope that this verdict, with its implicit acknowledgment of French responsibility for the deaths of Jews, was an indication that France had finally come to terms with its past and could now bury the bitter divisions and repressions of the Vichy syndrome. But the disputes and recriminations prompted by Péan's revelations suggested that this hope had been voiced too soon. Once again, divisions were clear: between those who argued that France had to look forward and not back, and those who felt (as one of the prosecution lawyers had phrased it at the time of Touvier's trial) that "a page of history cannot be turned before it is written." Struck by the fact that the national debate provoked by Péan's book exploded just as Europeans were celebrating the fiftieth anniversary of the end of Nazism, *Le monde* commentator Luc Rosenzweig deemed France a "schizophrenic" country that was still "incapable of confronting the past directly."[70]

Rosenzweig made these comments in 1994. Since that time, there have been striking indications that this "schizophrenia" is well on the way to being cured. More than a half-century after the war, the Vichy syndrome finally seems to be drawing to a close. It is a close made possible, above all, by the fact that Mitterand's generation—that is, the generation of those actively involved in the bitter dramas of the Occupation—is fast disappearing. (Indeed, it has been suggested that Mitterand himself, who was ill with cancer at the time the revelations concerning his past were made public, cooperated with Péan in order to have a hand in shaping the version of his life that would go down in history.) The verdict meted out to Touvier is by no means the only sign that France has found the force to look directly into the abyss and to confront the darkest aspects of the national past. Virtually every passing month brings renewed evidence that, as an editorialist for *Le monde* wrote at the time of Touvier's trial, "French society of the 1990s dares to do what would have been unthinkable in the 1960s."[71]

An important indication of a changed attitude toward the past was visible, for example, in the painful introspection that accompanied the fiftieth anniversary of the deportations of the Vel d'Hiv: documentaries devoted to those terrible events were aired on French television (though some complained that they were shown too late at night); while Mitterand himself refused to acknowledge the responsibility of the French state for the deportations, his position did not go unchallenged. The following year, long-suppressed documents revealing the extent of French-Nazi complicity were finally released.[72] Recent years have seen the erection, too, of museums commemorating the deportations: in the town of Izieu, a museum was dedicated to the memory of the forty-four children deported from there to Auschwitz; in Lyons itself, the building that formerly housed the *Milice* has been turned into a museum devoted to "the History of the Resistance and the Deportations." Most telling, perhaps, French schoolbooks now acknowledge that the worst aspects of the Vichy past were repressed for many years. "For thirty years," reads one, "the role played by the French state in the persecution and death of French Jews and foreign Jews who had sought refuge in France was deliberately masked by those in positions of political responsibility and forgotten in history textbooks."[73]

The election of Jacques Chirac as president in 1995 clearly hastened a changed attitude toward the Vichy past. Barely two months after his election, Chirac made a dramatic speech in which he renounced the "ambiguities" toward the past that had prevailed under Mitterand. At a commemoration ceremony for the deportations of the Vel d'Hiv, in sharp contrast with the position taken earlier by Mitterand, Chirac made it a point to acknowledge the collective responsibility of the French state for this "criminal" act. "To recognize the errors of the past and the errors committed by the state," declared the French president, "and not to hide the dark hours of our history—that is plainly the way to defend a vision of man, of his freedom and dignity."[74] At the beginning of 1996, this commitment to "recognizing" the errors of the past prompted two important announcements: the news that Papon would finally be brought to trial was soon followed by that concerning the formation of a committee to identify property (including valuable Paris real estate and works of art in French museums) stolen from Jews during the Occupation.[75] The following year brought even more dramatic indications that France is now willing, indeed determined, to come to terms with its past. Representatives of the twin pillars of French society, church and state, issued formal "apologies" to Jews. On September 30, 1997, French bishops asked forgiveness of God and the Jewish people for the "silence" of the Catholic Church in the face of the anti-Semitic laws of the 1940s; a week later, the nation's largest police union asked forgiveness of the "Hebrew people" for acts committed during the Occupation. A few days later an apology came from still another quarter: French doctors acknowledged that the "basic values of [their] profession" had been violated when they acquiesced in legislation that discriminated against and excluded their Jewish colleagues.[76] Underscoring the dramatic and unprecedented nature of these apologies, Pierre Birnbaum goes so far as to suggest that they may well herald the emergence of a new France—a more adaptable nation shorn of the divisive myths that have constituted a central dimension of its identity for centuries.[77]

Given the role that cinema has played in regard to the particular myths surrounding the Occupation, it is, perhaps, fitting that the winding down of the Vichy syndrome is reflected in a 1996 film, *Un héros très discret* (*A Self-Made Hero*), directed by Jacques Audiard. Surely one of the most curious films about *les années noires* made thus far, *Un héros très discret* deals, significantly, less with the Vichy period itself than with its aftermath—the deliberate creation of the resistancialist myth. In so doing, of course, it offers an important contrast with the *rétro* films discussed earlier; its real concern is not the past per se but, rather, the way(s) that past has been manipulated and remembered.

The film, which opens during the Occupation, takes as its protagonist a young man from the provinces whose family members mirror what were then the nation's deep internal divisions. While his mother decides to collaborate, the family of his young wife choose, unbeknownst to him, to join the Resistance. Upon Liberation, the young man learns the truth about his in-laws; dismayed at the lack of trust they displayed by not telling him about their Resistance work, he leaves for Paris. Once he reaches the capital city, it is not long before the young man's easy disposition, aided by a strange chain of events, allows him to infiltrate Resistance circles. The mistaken assumption, which he does nothing to discourage, that he is a former Resistance member leads to a military commission and to a tour of duty in Germany. There, he undergoes adventures both sentimental and political. On the sentimental front, he falls in love and marries again. His experiences in the political arena are less happy: he is forced to oversee the execution of several men who, prompted by ideological conviction, had joined a special divison of the German army composed of French volunteers. Haunted by their deaths, and by his continuing imposture, he finally makes a full confession. In the last scene, he is in jail; but he is not there, we learn to our surprise, for his political imposture. To save everyone embarrassment, the authorities have hushed up his crime, and he has been sent to jail not for impersonating a Resistance fighter but, instead, for bigamy: he married his second wife without divorcing his first.

An amusing satire full of old footage from the 1940s, *Un héros très discret* hardly ranks with the compelling *rétro* works explored earlier. But it is clearly of interest in the context of the Vichy syndrome. For its matter-of-fact presentation of a likable young man who cavalierly erases and rewrites his past constitutes an acknowledgment of the myths, the omissions and repressions, that surrounded the Vichy past for almost half a century. A film less about Vichy than about the Vichy syndrome, *Un héros très discret* reveals an ease with, an acceptance of, the past not seen in earlier works. It seeks neither to indict nor to deny. In other words, it lacks those very impulses that, testifying to the strength of the Vichy syndrome, made earlier films such important players in the struggle for memory that was waged throughout the 1970s and 1980s. Now that syndrome itself, *Un héros très discret* seems to say, has taken its place in the long unfolding of French memory.

IV

Bertrand Tavernier: History in the Present Tense

IN THE WAKE of May '68, *rétro* films were not the only ones to challenge long-standing images of national history. Still other works, often inspired by the new social history as well as the militant political perspectives of the 1970s, posed that challenge in terms of the nation's more distant past. In so doing, they traced what might be seen as a "counterportrait" of French history. It was a portrait that focused on the abuses of power, rather than its glories; on the internal wars and divisions that had torn the nation apart, rather than the patriotic impulses that had served to unify it; on the lives and *mentalités* of ordinary people, rather than the deeds of the famous. Avoiding the well-trodden avenues of the French past, these films ventured, instead, into its unknown recesses and its obscure, yet revealing, byways.

Nowhere has this counterportrait received more ample resonance than in the cinema of Bertrand Tavernier. Often considered the most important director of the post-'68 generation, Tavernier has not limited himself to films about the past. In the course of a long career, he has made a wide variety of films: contemporary social dramas like *L'horloger de Saint-Paul* (*The Clockmaker*, 1973); personal documentaries and semidocumentaries such as *Autour de minuit* (*Round Midnight*, 1986); and intimate portraits of family life like *Un dimanche à la campagne* (*A Sunday in the Country*, 1984).[1] Still, his historical films—which range over the long centuries of the French past from the Middle Ages to the Algerian War—may well constitute the most important dimension of his oeuvre. And, from the first such film, *Que la fête commence* (*Let Joy Reign Supreme*, 1975), to the most recent, *Capitaine Conan* (1996), Tavernier, who is deeply left-wing, has never ceased to question the "official" versions of history handed down from one generation to the next. The great French historian Jules Michelet was correct, the director assured one interviewer, when he observed that we had to learn "disrespect" for history in order to see it anew. Speaking of his own desire to strip the past of its many layers of "varnish," in a discussion of *Que la fête commence*, he asserted that in challenging "official" versions of the past we also question the present. Noting that he and his collaborators on the script for this film approached the past "in a disrespectful, insolent, manner," Tavernier went on to say that this approach was "necessary to make people question the official version of history. That is the best way of making them doubt contemporary reality."[2]

But if Tavernier's historical films reread the past, they also mirror—as this chapter seeks to demonstrate—the changing cultural and political landscape of the present. For example, over the course of time, the militant political perspectives that informed films of the 1970s such as *Que la fête commence* and *Le juge et l'assassin* (*The Judge and the Assassin*, 1976) have given way to an issue that is currently at the forefront of French historiography: that of memory. Imbued with changing approaches to history, these films also allow us to trace, as if through a palimpsest, the evolving shape of what may be the most significant ideological drama of the postwar years, what is variously called the crisis of ideology or the collapse of Marxism. Indeed, almost as Tavernier felt impelled, consciously or unconsciously, to cloak his deepest doubts and fears in the folds of history, it is in his films about the past that one senses the most profound tremors of the present.

A "seismograph" of their era, to borrow a term from the director, Tavernier's historical films also reflect some of his most deeply felt passions. One, certainly, is his love of cinema itself. Although his films marked a distinct break from those of the preceding generation of filmmakers—that is, the New Wave—Tavernier shared the ardent *cinéphilisme* characteristic of directors such as Godard and Truffaut. He, too, was an eclectic lover of cinema and a great admirer of American cinema in particular.[3] In his case, though, this admiration bore less upon the grimy *noir* thrillers beloved by Godard and Truffaut than upon Westerns and swashbuckling tales of adventure and daring. Confessing to a very un-French love of melodramatic excess, he once remarked that he "adored historical cinema, films with capes and swords. I was classified as an apostle of B films. I was delirious about melodramas."[4] Transferring this love of costume dramas into his own historical melodramas, in these works he displays a baroque taste for sound and color, for striking landscapes—the misty hills of Brittany in *Que la fête commence*, the rugged mountains of the Ardèche region in *Le juge et l'assassin*—and for outsize or "excessive" characters. The presence of towering villains, in particular, suggests that the genre itself allowed him to give full rein to impulses held in check elsewhere in his work, to indulge what he called his *côté noir*, his "dark side" with its penchant for "madness" and "excess."

Tavernier's films recall not only American Westerns, or, for that matter, Italian costume melodramas: they also hark back to earlier French models. Frequently marked by the presence of well-known performers—the celebrated actor Philippe Noiret, for example, appears in almost all of the director's historical melodramas—and the use of polished literary scripts, his films bring to mind the "cinema of quality" that was attacked so harshly by the Young Turks of the New Wave.[5] (Indeed, for the scenario of his first film, *L'horloger de Saint-Paul*, Tavernier collaborated with two veteran scriptwriters, Jean Aurenche and Pierre Bost, closely associated the "tradition of quality.")[6] But at the same time—and this points to the political passions that course throughout his cinema as well as the eclectic nature of his *cinéphilisme*—his films also owe a debt to French populist works of the 1930s, especially those by Jean Renoir. Indeed, Tavernier pays explicit homage to Renoir in at least two films: *Un dimanche à la campagne* evokes the impressionist masterpieces of Renoir's father as well as a relatively late film by the director himself, *Le déjeuner sur l'herbe* (*Picnic on the Grass*, 1959); a tenants' union in Tavernier's contemporary social drama *Les enfants gâtés* (*Spoiled Children*, 1977), seems a latter-day incarnation of the workers' co-operative featured in Renoir's 1935 left-wing classic, *Le crime de M. Lange* (*The Crime of M. Lange*).[7]

Along with the cinematic and political impulses that animate Tavernier's films goes, of course, a fascination with history. Even as a boy, Tavernier told one interviewer, he was attracted to historical works by nineteenth-century French writers such as Balzac, Dumas, and Hugo.[8] This attraction would later lead to a "passion" for historical films. Referring to the film-related activities he engaged in before making his first feature, he remarked, "I have a passion for historical films; as a *cinéphile* and as an *attaché de presse*, I fought for the films of Freda, of Cottafavi, and for French directors like Renoir (for *La Marseillaise*), Allio (for *Les Camisards*) and for Ariane Mnouchkine."[9] And early in his career, he complained that, in his view, the "scandal" of French cinema was precisely its

> ignorance of history, the fact that we had to wait so long before someone like Allio made *Les Camisards*, the fact that there aren't any films on the Commune or the Middle Ages. The only successful film on the Middle Ages is *A Walk with Love and Death*; it's the only film on the Hundred Years War. . . . How long will it be before there is a film that says simply how many people were killed during the French Revolution. . . . I think that the lack of curiosity toward history is something terrible.[10]

Not surprisingly, Tavernier's own "curiosity toward history" has already led him to fill some of the lacunae mentioned in this passage. Like John Huston's *A Walk with Love and Death* (1969), *La passion Béatrice* (*Béatrice*, 1987) portrays a Middle Ages haunted by death and violence; although the director has yet to deal with the victims of the French Revolution, both *La vie et rien d'autre* (*Life and Nothing But*, 1989) and *Capitaine Conan* underscore the terrible butchery of World War I. In a still broader sense, moreover, all his historical films seem impelled by a desire to fill in the blanks, the untold stories, left by historians and filmmakers alike. Set in the early eighteenth century, *Que la fête commence* depicts the relatively unknown ruler, Philippe d'Orléans, who served as regent between the celebrated reigns of two far more famous monarchs, Louis XIV and Louis XVI; *Le juge et l'assassin* evokes one of the most traumatic, and represssed, moments of nineteenth-century history, the doomed popular uprising of the Commune. More recently, with *La guerre sans nom* (1991), the director has pierced the wall of silence that had smothered the memory of the Algerian War. In all these works, Tavernier has sought not only to reread the past but to cast off the aura of solemn veneration that enveloped it in earlier films so completely that, in his words, the very notion of "history" disappears.[11]

Hollow Moments: *Que la fête commence* and the 1970s

Set during the period of the Regency (1715–1723), Tavernier's second feature, *Que la fête commence*—the film that begins, in the words of one commentator, Tavernier's "long cinematic reflection on the History of the French and on their memory"[12]—immediately announced a distinctly post-'68 determination to reread the French past as well as Tavernier's predilection for what have been called "the hollow moments of history." For unlike the celebrated eras of national history known to every French schoolchild, the Regency, a period that saw the old feudal order gradually give way before the rising tide of mercantile capitalism, was a little-known era unmarked by fame or glory. It did not witness the dramatic clashes that characterized, say, the period of Joan of Arc or that of the Revolution; nor did it give any hint of French *grandeur*, of the onward sweep of national destiny, central to the era of Louis XIV or that of Napoleon. Instead, like virtually all the historical eras Tavernier would portray, the Regency was a "hollow" moment of transition, one in which, as Tavernier remarked in a slightly different context, "a social class, a race, a people disappear."[13] Frequently haunted by the sense of "coming after," like the Regency, these melancholy moments look back, or forward, to the more dramatic or convulsive—and, certainly, better-known—eras of the past. Thus the Regency looks *back* to the glories of the Sun King and *forward* to the bonfires of 1789; *Le juge et l'assassin* is haunted by the specter of the Commune; *La passion Béatrice* takes place in a declining Middle Ages, in a period marked by the "twilight of chivalry." Deliberately avoiding the conflagrations of history that attracted earlier directors, Tavernier portrays, instead, the unease that precedes them, the desolation that follows.

In respect to conventional images of French history, moreover, Tavernier's choice of the Regency was significant for still another reason.

That is, the Regency was not only a "hollow" or relatively unknown era; it was also one associated with a phenomenon that could only detract from French *gloire*. For the regent himself, Philippe d'Orléans, has gone down in history as a great libertine, one who (as the film indirectly suggests) may even have enjoyed a liaison with a much beloved daughter. (In its entry on Philippe, the authoritative French dictionary-encyclopedia, *Le petit Larousse*, refers to the collapse of the speculative investment scheme designed by financier John Law as it notes succinctly that the regent "compromised finances by the system of Law and public morality by the bad example of his depraved life.") And, as French critic Jacques Demeure points out, Tavernier's decision to make a film about a less-than-glorious era, and a regent of dubious morality, immediately indicated the "tone" of the film: one of "disrespect" toward the national past.[14] This "disrespect" was compounded, moreover, by the film's graphic portrayal of the orgies, the nightly *fêtes*, that were organized for the regent's pleasure. Defending this aspect of the film, Tavernier underscored both his quest for historical accuracy and his desire to probe the "hidden" corners of the French past. "If one studies the life of the regent," he observed, "one sees that every evening for about ten years he indulged in orgies. I can't help it if History has hidden them . . . as well as the fact that homosexuals were hanged and prostitutes were shaved."[15]

To portray people and circumstances long "hidden" by history, Tavernier drew upon eclectic sources; weaving together disparate strands of inspiration, he created a film that is at once a swashbuckling adventure tale, an *Annales*-inspired portrait of earlier *mentalités*, and a New Left or *gauchiste* meditation on the nature and reach of power. A romantic tale by Alexandre Dumas *fils*, *La fille du Régent*, evidencing the director's love for nineteenth-century historical novels, serves as a point of departure for a complicated subplot involving a band of rebellious noblemen; the memoirs of the duke of St. Simon (who was well acquainted with the regent) provide the basis for the film's quasi-documentary study, reminiscent of that seen in Roberto Rossellini's *La prise du pouvoir de Louis XIV* (*The Rise to Power of Louis XIV*, 1966), of life at court.[16] To these two sources must be added the work of *Annales* historians who furnished information concerning the material realities, the social and medical practices, that prevailed during the Regency. Referring to several well-known *Annales* scholars, Tavernier elaborated on some of the precise ways in which he attempted to seize, and reconstruct, the concrete realities of a distant era.

> I had discussions with history professors, I looked at paintings by Watteau and Hogarth. But then I tried to find my own interpretation. I considered it important to discover the daily relationship to objects. . . . For example, I wondered how a room was heated in order to see how the characters might have behaved.

Movement is conditioned by firewood. It was the same for lighting. . . . People speak differently according to the way they are lit. . . . Thanks to the work of Braudel, Duby, Le Goff, we learn to establish a relationship between characters and decor. An object becomes a dramatic factor.[17]

As the film begins, it is clearly the romantic strand of inspiration that prevails. For *Que la fête commence* opens with a scene that would not have been out of place in the kind of sword-and-dagger Hollywood adventure films beloved by the youthful Tavernier. Here, a horseman comes galloping over the misty coast of Brittany to rescue a young woman who is about to be kidnapped and seduced by a cunning stranger. With a blow, the horseman kills the intruder. Before long, we discover that the knight-errant is an impoverished Breton nobleman, the marquis de Pontcallec (Jean-Pierre Marielle). One of the principal characters of the film, the passionate and impulsive marquis is not only a rescuer of damsels in distress but a "crazy idealist," to use Tavernier's phrase, who is devoted to the cause of Breton autonomy. He is, in fact, the leader of a small band of rebellious Breton nobles who seek to enlist the aid of Spain in their struggle against the French state. From the outset, it is clear that their revolt, which lacks funds and allies, is doomed to failure. But nothing daunts the idealistic marquis who, in fact, sets off for Paris to press his demands upon the regent.

The scene now shifts to the figure at the center of Tavernier's historical fresco—to Philippe II, duc d'Orléans (Philippe Noiret). When first seen, the regent, a melancholy and introspective man, is grieving for a much beloved daughter who has just died. It is at least in part to distract himself from thoughts of death, as well as from a prevailing sense of spiritual unease, that the regent embraces a life of dissolute excess. Nightly orgies are carefully orchestrated and staged for his benefit: demonstrating Tavernier's attention to "objects" that reveal the material realities and social practices of the past, one royal *fête* features a magic lantern that casts pornographic pictures on the wall to titillate its aristocratic audience. When not engaged in what Tavernier described as a "mad search for pleasure," Philippe soberly goes about his everyday routines at court: he bickers with his courtiers; he slyly attempts to regain possession of a house bestowed upon a former mistress.

As these scenes suggest, the protocols of power so assiduously followed by the regent are little more than empty rituals. Indeed, real power is exercised not by the weary regent but, rather, by his ambitious and ruthless prime minister, the abbé Dubois (Jean Rochefort). It is, in fact, through the cynical and corrupt Dubois that the various strands of the film's complicated plot converge. For Dubois is engaged in negotiations with the British that indirectly seal the fate of the idealistic leader of the Breton conspiracy, the marquis de Pontcallec. That is, in exchange for financial favors, the

British demand the death of the Breton noblemen who are conspiring with Britain's principal enemy, Spain. Although the regent is loath to put noblemen to death, Dubois has his way: Pontcallec is captured and brought to trial. Prevented from taking the stand in his own defense, the Breton leader is rapidly condemned to death and rushed off to the gallows.

Disturbed by these events, Philippe seeks solace in still another orgiastic *fête*. But this last night of excess takes its toll. Upon awakening, the regent smells an odor of rotting flesh coming from his hand and hastily sets off for the doctor. As his carriage speeds through the countryside, it hurtles into a peasant's cart and kills a young boy. Philippe quickly offers money to the dead boy's sister, abandons his carriage, enters another, and goes on his way. But after the regent's departure, the boy's sister, enraged by her brother's death, exhorts the peasants who have witnessed the scene to torch the fateful carriage. As the flames rise up, she turns her brother's lifeless head to the bonfire. "Look," she commands him, "see how well the carriage of the powerful is burning." To the echo of a ballad associated with the martyred Pontcallec, the film comes to an end on this image of destruction and revenge. Imbued with the specter of class warfare, it is an image that looks ahead to the coming apocalypse of 1789 when the "rotting" world of the regent will be swept away as surely as his carriage is consumed by the flames of the peasants' bonfire.

The revolutionary fresco that concludes *Que la fête commence* constitutes, certainly, the most dramatic indication of the militant political perspectives that inform the film. But in a less direct manner, the entire film bears witness to the political climate, marked by changed perceptions of the past as well as the present, ushered in by the events of May '68. In fact, the important subplot involving Pontcallec and the Breton conspirators touches on an issue at the core of New Left or *gauchiste* thought: that is, the nature and reach of power. Pitting a marginalized group against the power of the state, the Breton conspiracy seemed, in fact, to foreshadow the movements for regional autonomy that would flourish in the wake of '68.[18] At the same time, from a still broader viewpoint, it embodied the kind of "local struggle" that, as Gilles Deleuze remarks, was central to *gauchiste* concerns.[19]

But it is, above all, in respect to Pontcallec himself that the issue of power comes into sharpest focus. For the fate he meets constitutes a dramatic illustration of ways in which power embeds itself in social institutions—in this case, that of justice itself. Not only is the idealistic marquis denied a just trial by those in power—he is literally gagged when he attempts to speak in his own defense—but he is executed, by a ruthless state, solely for political and economic reasons. His aborted trial thus becomes a central moment in the extended meditation on power and justice that Tavernier pursues throughout his first three films: *L'horloger de Saint-Paul*, *Que la fête commence*, and *Le juge et l'assassin*. Each film features a trial which, like that of Pontcallec, reveals how justice becomes a tool of those in power, a handmaiden of political expediency. In each film, as Michel Sineux observes, the plot "moves toward a trial that does not take place or that is trumped up. . . . Thus the Court, [as] the institutional place where theoretically the accused should account for himself . . . is conjured away three times."[20]

A ferocious indictment of the way the legal system is subverted by those in power, *Que la fête commence* testifies to the militant political climate of the 1970s in still another important respect. Focused on an era of expansionist capitalism—when France was beginning to establish its empire in the New World—the film paints a damning portrait of early-eighteenth-century French society. The world seen in *Que la fête commence* is marked by corruption and greed, by class oppression and exploitation. Rapid but telling tableaux leave no doubt about the harsh miseries faced by ordinary men and women at this time. The corpse of a hanged man bears a sign proclaiming that his crime was one of "domestic theft"; ordinary citizens are brutally conscripted into the army; to ensure French control of the New World, men and women are rounded up, forced to marry, and then sent to breed in Louisiana. The lot of the people is made worse by wild inflation and speculation, fueled both by Law's investment scheme to develop French colonies in Mississippi and by the paper money that is recklessly printed by the state. Greed is everywhere. France sides with England rather than with her more natural ally, Catholic Spain, because, as Dubois reminds the regent, "money is Protestant." Indeed, the whole of society bears the taint of prostitution—from the real prostitutes who attend the royal orgies to noblemen like Dubois who shed all their ideals for profit.[21]

If the new social order is set under the sign of prostitution, the old is characterized by a sense of decline. Even Philippe's elaborate *fêtes* speak less of pleasure than of illness and decay: during the orgies, for example, virile studs must stand by to accomplish what the corrupt and debauched nobles are too weary, too jaded, to complete.[22] As for the regent himself, Philippe corresponds to St. Simon's description of the ruler as a man "afflicted by a secret disgust with himself, by periodic fits of inertia."[23] This "inertia" prevents him from acting effectively, from wielding the power that should be his: although he understands the need for social reforms—the necessity of establishing state schools and of selling church lands—he does nothing to bring them about. The product, and the emblem, of a world in decline, he is prey to a paralysis that is not only personal but, as Tavernier observed, historical. In a revealing passage, Tavernier noted that the regent interested him precisely because he seemed unusual and dramatic and very modern. The Regent's story was one of a man who saw what he had to do very clearly, and because of the pressures on him and the nature of his character, was too weak to do it. It was a situation representative of the political conflicts in any transition period. You can find men like the Regent in pre-fascist as well as pre-revolutionary moments; you found them in the Weimar Republic and the 1905 Revolution in Russia.[24]

In the end, of course, the sense of paralysis and decline that haunts *Que la fête commence*—and that is embodied in the weak and melancholy regent—says as much about the mood of the 1970s as do the film's militant political perspectives. And while those perspectives have receded into the past, the mood of "hollowness" and uncertainty that clings to the film has become a widely acknowledged feature of the landscape of contemporary France. In retrospect, it is clear that a variety of factors came together to give this mood a pronounced cast in the 1970s. A period that saw France in the throes of what French sociologist Henri Mendras describes as a "second French Revolution," this era of transition also suffered from a "hollow" sense of "coming after."[25] If the Regency was shadowed by the glories of *le roi soleil*, 1970s France looked back not only to the exuberance of May '68 but, perhaps more important, to an era dominated by de Gaulle and by the "certain idea of France" that he incarnated and perpetuated. By the 1970s, this "idea" was clearly fading; but no new image of the nation, no new vision of the future, was on the horizon. Instead, as Michel Winock observes, the end of the "myth" of de Gaulle seemed, increasingly, to signal the "end of the national history that . . . gave France the sense of being a great nation. . . . The heroic age [was] over."[26]

But it was not only the "heroic age" of de Gaulle that was slipping into the past around the time that Tavernier made *Que la fête commence*. Even more important in terms of not only this film but also subsequent ones by Tavernier, this period witnessed the gradual collapse of the revolutionary hopes cherished by the Left for centuries. Battered by a combination of factors—the decline of the traditional working class, the antiauthoritarian spirit of May '68, the demands of the global marketplace, the revelation of horrors committed in so-called revolutionary regimes—scarcely a decade after May '68, the messianic hopes and ideals embraced by the students would seem as "hollow" and anachronistic as the chivalric values of the marquis de Pontcallec. In the words of intellectual commentator Sunil Khilnani, the "long" decade that stretched from the events of May '68 to the Socialist victory of 1981 witnessed nothing less than

> the most dramatic and decisive realignment in the political affiliations of French intellectuals that has occurred in recent times. The wave of dissent that in the late 1960s disturbed existing political routines across the globe, established Paris as the world capital of political radicalism: the idea of revolution there found new

and glittery life. But within a few years the bubble of revolutionary rhetoric had deflated helplessly, and by the end of the 1970s intellectual opinion had shifted sharply away from revolutionary politics.[27]

The dramatic changes described by Khilnani were not, of course, unique to France. The 1970s saw the collapse of revolutionary utopianism in all its forms—*gauchiste*, Communist, Marxist. Communist parties were in crisis around the world: in Western Europe, in former satellites of the Soviet Union, and, above all, in the Soviet Union itself. Still, as Khilnani suggests, 1968 *had* established "Paris as the world capital of political radicalism." And the end of the dream of revolution had a particular resonance in France: here, revolutionary goals stretched back not only to 1917 but, indeed, to 1789. A founding moment of national history, the French Revolution did much to define the very concept of the nation.[28] Even the enduring divisions and periodic conflagrations sparked by this decisive struggle—divisions between monarchists and Republicans, Dreyfusards and anti-Dreyfusards, Right and Left—had long constituted a defining element of national identity.

If, for these reasons, the end of the revolutionary dream affected long-standing images of the nation, it had even more direct and obvious consequences for left-wing intellectuals like Tavernier. After all, the French Revolution had served as a beacon for the Left for two centuries. The collapse of revolutionary hopes, understandably, left a tremendous void in the political imagination, an absence intensified by the relative weakness of liberal traditions in France.[29] Moreover, this collapse seemed to undermine the very identity, the *raison d'être*, of left-wing intellectuals. Since the time of the Dreyfus Affair, when Emile Zola rallied to the defense of the Jewish army officer accused of treason, French intellectuals had virtually defined themselves by engaging in political battles inspired by the dream of social progress born of the Enlightenment and the Revolution.[30] Composing what Stanley Hoffmann deems a kind of "secular priesthood," they had waged furious battles in support of Dreyfus and the Popular Front, had sustained a terrible defeat at the time of Vichy, and had emerged triumphant—with the Right silenced and compromised by the memory of collaboration—in the aftermath of World War II. In the postwar era, in fact, the very notion of a "committed" intellectual, exemplified by Jean-Paul Sartre, was someone on the Left.

It was, precisely, this sense of mission and "commitment" that began to falter in the late 1960s; a decade later, it had virtually vanished from the French political landscape.[31] By the time the Socialists finally came to power in 1981, what was often called the "divorce" between intellectuals and the Left seemed final. "Two centuries of near symbiosis between the militant consciences of humanity and the universal forces of revolution," observes Diana Pinto of this period, "trickled down to a Socialist political triumph without major intellectual engagement."[32] In 1983, when left-wing intellectuals found themselves attacked for their "silence" by a government spokesman, Max Gallo, they did not hesitate to express not only their disdain for the authoritarian bent of the French Socialist Party but also their disillusionment with the very notion of revolution. The time had come, declared François Châtelet, to break with an "apocalyptic vision of history"; "states born of revolutions," asserted Alain Touraine, "devour the revolutionaries and become concentration camps." Nor did they mince words when it came to what they saw as the cultural backwardness of the Socialist Party. "In the era of Freud and Kafka, of Popper, of Foucault and Bourdieu," complained Emile Malet, "here are Socialists churning out Rousseau, Jaurès . . . and the revolutionary epic of 1789." Attacking the very notion of "Progress" central both to Enlightenment philosophy and to Marxism, Jean-Edern Hallier proclaimed that not a single important intellectual could "accommodate himself to the petrified socialism coming from the humid cellars of the nineteenth century."[33]

Que la fête commence, of course, contains no hint of sentiments such as these. There is no suggestion of "petrified socialism," of the dangers of "apocalyptic" visions of history. Indeed, the film concludes with a fresco that lyrically evokes the very idea, and the model, of revolution. But even as this stirring sequence suggests the enormous resonance of the dream of revolution, it also appears to sense its coming end. As if to confirm Tavernier's belief that films act as "seismographs" of their era, this sequence is imbued with tensions that point, indirectly but unmistakably, to the crisis of ideology that would erupt before the end of the decade.

These tensions stem both from the nature of the scene itself and from the position it holds in respect to the body of the film. It is not only that the concluding segment of *Que la fête commence* is distanced, both temporally and psychologically, from all that precedes it. It is also—and, in some sense, above all—that this scene of dramatic action, in which angry peasants torch the regent's carriage, appears to contradict everything else we have seen. After all, throughout *Que la fête commence*, Tavernier underscores the difficulty or impossibility of action. If neither the regent nor the marquis can alter the course of events, still less can ordinary people—subject to misery and hardships, to the whims of those in power—determine the course their lives will take. (Indeed, in several important scenes, a beautiful young prostitute, played by Christine Pascal, expresses the humble resignation that appears to characterize the masses of ordinary men and women.) In light of the paralysis that afflicts both the people and their rulers, the moment of decisive action and stirring revolt that comes at the end seems to express a wish rather than a possibility or a reality. For this reason, Manfred Engelbert hardly seems to exaggerate when he remarks that the revolutionary fresco at the end of *Que la fête commence* virtually "falls from the sky." The film's conclusion, he writes, "remains unsupported in a film that, from the very first, does nothing but emphasize the powerlessness of a people exploited and oppressed by the church, by Pontcallec and the Breton nobles, by the agents of the regent, by the regent himself."[34]

In the end, of course, what Engelbert deems the "lack of historical continuity" between the body of *Que la fête commence* and its conclusion says as much, or more, about the "hollowness" and uncertainties of the 1970s as it does about those of the Regency. Analyzing the contemporary meaning of this "lack," Engelbert suggests that it reflected both the "unassuaged thirst for action" of a new generation emerging from a period of profound apoliticism and the "moral uncertainties of a bourgeois intelligentsia caught in a crisis of modernization that [was] badly understood and viewed as a revolution."[35] That may well have been the case. But above all, I think, it constituted an implicit, and perhaps an unconscious, acknowledgment that the dream of revolution was precisely that—a dream. And indeed, in his next film, Tavernier would acknowledge, far more concretely and explicitly than in *Que la fête commence*, that the revolutionary hopes rooted in 1789 had come to an end. Amplifying both the counterportrait of French history and the *gauchiste* meditation on power seen in *Que la fête commence*, in *Le juge et l'assassin* the director would also bid adieu to the ideal of revolution.

The Triumph of Power: *Le juge et l'assassin,*
   La passion Béatrice

In light of the growing "silence" of French intellectuals toward the end of the 1970s, the setting of *Le juge et l'assassin* assumes a particular interest. For Tavernier's second historical melodrama, which opens in 1893, takes place at the time of the Dreyfus Affair: that is, during the period when left-wing intellectuals first embraced the leading public role they would play for much of the next century. It was, in fact, Emile Zola's famous pamphlet *J'accuse* (1898)—in which the novelist argued that the authorities had conspired to frame Dreyfus for giving military secrets to the Germans—that sparked what Michel Winock deems the birth of an "intellectual Left." Noting that Zola's pamphlet moved thousands to demand a new trial for Dreyfus, Winock writes that it also prompted "the massive participation in a public affair of those who, from then on, would be called intellectuals."[36] (Found guilty at a second military tribunal in 1899, Dreyfus was finally cleared by a civil court in 1906.)

Marked by the "massive participation" of intellectuals, the Dreyfus Affair also called into play the bitter ideological divisions that would reverberate throughout much of the following century. Animated by opposing views of *la patrie*, both Dreyfusards and anti-Dreyfusards believed they were engaged in a struggle for the very soul, the identity, of the nation. On the Left, Republicans and socialists felt they were championing not only the innocence of a single individual but the legacy of the French Revolution—the cause of Justice, Truth, and Individual Rights—against the narrower interests of the state. On the Right, in monarchist, Royalist, and many Catholic milieux, the stakes were equally high. In their determination to preserve the "honor" of the army, an honor that, in their view, extended to that of the nation itself, many anti-Dreyfusards embraced a new kind of militaristic and xenophobic nationalism. In their eyes, they were defending the values of French civilization against the threat of modern "decadence" and the menace posed by "foreigners" living both within and without the nation's borders. Hence the animosity they felt toward Dreyfus, who, as a Jew, was the very symbol of the "stranger" or "other" who was gnawing away at the foundations of French society. Hence, too, the centrality of anti-Semitism both to the Dreyfus Affair and to the nationalism (often deemed one of "exclusion") it sparked. Observing that this nationalism was defined, above all, by its "phobias"—by its hatred and fear of liberal democracy, of German spies, of Jews—Michel Winock argues that it is precisely because these "phobias" have (re)surfaced throughout the twentieth century that the Dreyfus Affair constitutes such a defining moment in the history of modern France.[37] Strains of the xenophobic passions that emerged in the 1890s were heard at the time of the Popular Front, of Vichy, and of the Algerian War. Resounding to the present day, they echo throughout the racist rhetoric of Jean-Marie Le Pen. Changing the figure of the "other" from Jew to Arab, the leader of France's far-Right party, *Le front national*, does not hesitate to demand that foreigners be expelled from France even as he adamantly declares that the races are not "equal."

In re-creating the bitter climate of the 1890s in *Le juge et l'assassin*, Tavernier chose a period of history that, far more than that of the Regency, was obviously central to a counterportrait of France. Moreover, in *Le juge et l'assassin* he evokes not one but two critical historical eras. Although *Le juge et l'assassin* is set in the 1890s, it recalls events that took place a generation earlier: it harks back to the revolutionary Paris Commune of 1871. (Composed largely of working-class Parisians, the Commune, modeled on the revolutionary government established in 1792, was established, in the wake of the French defeat of 1870, in opposition to the official French government at Versailles.) Implicitly linking the repressive climate of the 1890s to the fear of anarchism engendered by the Commune, *Le juge et l'assassin* is punctuated by songs and allusions that mournfully recall the terrible hardships endured by the Communards before their movement was brutally crushed. With Paris besieged by the Germans, they lived through fearful months of bitter cold and near famine—people resorted to eating not only cats and dogs but also rats, as well as animals from the zoo— before seeing their rebellion suppressed by troops sent from Versailles. In the course of the terrible week, the so-called *Semaine sanglante*, that saw the end of the Commune, tens of thousands of Parisians were killed in street warfare as official government troops seized control of the rebellious city *quartier* by *quartier*. Toward the end, the last holdouts among the Communards were executed in front of the *Mur des fédérés* at the cemetery of *Père Lachaise* and thrown into a mass grave. In the course of the following decade, the place where they fell would gradually become a "site of memory," a gathering spot for left-wing rallies, even as the Commune itself became an iconic moment for the Left. Indeed, this doomed popular uprising, marked by barricades and by hand-to-hand combat in the streets of Paris, would figure strongly in the imagination of many young radicals of '68.

Emotionally charged and deeply polemical, both the Dreyfus Affair and the Commune were also, not unexpectedly, conspicuously absent from French cinema before the 1960s. "Only Jacques Becker," writes Marcel Oms in a discussion of filmic representations of the Commune, "in *Casque d'Or* (1952) evokes this slice of History by means of a real incident that permitted him to portray believable workers whose bodies, and memories, were imprinted with the repression of the Commune and the . . . struggles that nourished anarchism."[38] Nor, as Oms also points out, was the situation different for the Dreyfus Affair. "With the exception of the Méliès film made at the time of the affair, in 1899," writes the French critic, "our national production remained sterile on this issue. Unless, of course, silence itself is taken as a confession of cowardice."[39] This "silence," of course, is not difficult to understand. Giving the lie to the myth of French unity, both the Commune and the Dreyfus Affair testify to the deepest, and most persistent, divisions in French society. In the case of the Commune, these divisions led to scenes of class warfare and slaughter on the streets of Paris; in that of the Dreyfus Affair, to xenophobic passions that would later mark some of the most shame-filled moments of recent French history.

In choosing to portray these traumatic eras, then, Tavernier displayed, as he had in *Que la fête commence*, a determination to reread the French past, to strip history of its "varnish." Once again, it was a rereading that said a great deal about the political perspectives as well as the melancholy mood of the present. Focused on still another "hollow" moment of history, one haunted by the specter of the Commune, like *Que la fête commence*, *Le juge et l'assassin* also continues the *gauchiste* exploration of power begun by Tavernier in his first two films. Far more than either *L'horloger de Saint-Paul* or *Que la fête commence*, however, *Le juge et l'assassin* makes clear how much this exploration owed to the work of philosopher Michel Foucault. Indeed, the figure at the center of this film—a homeless, half-mad "assassin"—might have stepped out of the pages of Foucault's long investigation of the ways in which society defines, and treats, those on its margins: the mad, the ill, and the criminal.

Le juge et l'assassin bears a striking resemblance, in fact, to another film made that same year, and inspired by historical documents unearthed by Foucault and a team working under him at the Collège de France: René Allio's *Moi, Pierre Rivière, ayant tué ma mère, ma soeur, and mon frère (I, Pierre Riviere, having killed my mother, my sister, and my brother).*[40] Based upon celebrated murder cases of the last century, both films explored criminality in relationship to the complex web of issues, bearing on power and marginality, central to Foucault's work. From a stylistic viewpoint, it is true, Tavernier and Allio offer a study in contrasts. Tavernier, who has always sought to reach a wide audience, incorporates aspects of popular genres like melodramas and Westerns into his films even as he relies upon well-crafted scripts and polished performances. Allio, instead, rejected commercial film for reasons that were both aesthetic and political: like Godard and other "militant" directors of the post-'68 period, Allio was convinced that traditional realistic films, exemplified by those made in Hollywood, could only perpetuate the existing social and economic order.[41] But in light of these differences, it is all the more telling, and indicative of the strength of a particular social and political climate, that *Moi, Pierre Rivière . . .* and *Le juge et l'assassin* raised almost identical issues.

At the center of both works stands a complex and fascinating criminal. In the case of *Moi, Pierre Rivière . . .* , he is a Normandy peasant, Pierre Rivière, who, in 1835, brutally murdered three members of his family— brother, sister, and mother. His crime, however, is of less interest than what occurred in its aftermath. For after he was caught and imprisoned by the authorities, Pierre Rivière proceeded to write an astonishing memoir about his life and the events that led up to his bloody deeds. (It is this memoir that—along with a transcript of the trial, medical reports, and expert testimony—was published by Foucault.) Rivière's memoir was remarkable for several reasons. In an era of widespread illiteracy, here was a coherent, indeed poetic, text by a poor peasant. Moreover, and this was particularly striking in light of the brutal madness of Rivière's murders, it was a lucid and sane document in which the assassin argued that he had had to kill his sister and mother to stop them from tormenting his father. The cogency of his argument, in fact, seemed to belie the claim, which was crucial to his defense, that he was insane. Small wonder that the experts called in on the case were baffled and divided. Some, as Foucault observed, saw the memoir as "a proof of rationality (and hence grounds for condemning [Rivière] to death)"; others, instead, viewed it as a "sign of madness (and hence grounds for shutting him up for life)."[42]

It is not difficult to see why both Allio and Foucault found Rivière's case a compelling one. For the left-wing Allio, Rivière's text, which is heard throughout the film in voice-off and in dialogues, seemed to embody the voice of the people, *la parole populaire*; at the same time, it revealed the *mentalité* of an oppressed peasant world in which unceasing misery gave rise to disastrous urges. Referring to *Les Camisards*, his earlier film about a group of persecuted Protestants living in the rugged region of the Cévennes Mountains, Allio noted that the Rivière case allowed him "to return to the peasant world in a better way than I had done in *Les Camisards*. I reserved a place for the bodies of peasants, the sounds of their voices, their accents . . . I questioned professionalism [and] the attitude of intellectuals."[43]

If Allio was fascinated by the ways in which Rivière's crimes baffled the experts and brought "professionalism" into question, so, too, was Foucault. Moreover, the fact that Rivière committed his crimes at a time when psychiatric concepts were first being applied to criminal justice raised issues crucial to the philosopher's continuing meditation on the social construction of discourses and institutions involving both criminality and madness. In fact, the nature of Rivière's crimes, together with the unresolved question of his "madness," put the Normandy peasant at the meeting point of these two domains. In Foucault's words, Rivière's case provided material for "a thorough examination of the way in which a particular kind of knowledge (e.g., medicine, psychiatry, psychology) is formed, and functions, in relation to institutions and the roles prescribed in them (e.g., the law in respect to the expert, the accused, the criminally insane, and so on)."[44]

The philosophical and social issues that drew both Foucault and Allio to the case of Pierre Rivière are precisely those that Tavernier brings to light in *Le juge et l'assassin*. Once again, the issues are seen in relationship to a nineteenth-century criminal trial—in this case, two trials. That is, the "assassin" of this film is an amalgam of two famous criminals of the last century. One, an anarchist named Ravachol, was legendary for having sung about his crimes while accompanying himself on the accordion. The other, the more important model for the assassin of Tavernier's film, was a demented social outcast named Joseph Vacher who, in the course of the 1890s, brutally molested and killed ten adolescents as well as one older woman. Combining aspects of these two men, Tavernier created one of his most unforgettable characters: Joseph Bouvier. Masterfully played by veteran actor Michel Galabru, Bouvier is, of course, the "assassin" of *Le juge et l'assassin*. Placing the encounter between the "assassin" and the "judge" (Philippe Noiret) at the center of his film, Tavernier, like Allio, created a work that rereads the French past in the light of the shapes as-

sumed by marginality—that of poverty, of madness, and of social alienation—and power.

Le juge et l'assassin begins in 1893 (a year before Dreyfus's first trial).
Against wide sweeping shots of a rugged and mountainous landscape, the
isolated figure of a man appears: kneeling at a cross, he implores the Virgin
to watch over "Louise." The supplicant, we soon learn, is Joseph Bouvier:
an ex-soldier who has been dismissed from the army because he is subject
to alternating fits of rage and religious fervor. And "Louise" is the woman
he loves and wants desperately to marry. But when, in the next scene, he
asks her for her hand, she rejects him. Distraught, he shoots and wounds
both her and himself. When next seen, Bouvier is in a hospital: his mental
condition visibly worse—he has shot himself in the head—he rants and
raves, calling himself "the anarchist of God" even as he denounces the
clergy and the church. Transferred from one institution to the next, from
psychiatric clinic to religious hospice, he is ultimately sent out into the
world to fend for himself. Although sick and demented, he cannot live, as
he is told with great condescension, "at the expense of the state forever."
Forced into a life of solitude and vagabondage, Bouvier finally falls prey to
his inner demons. Despite himself, he is driven to savagely molest and
murder young peasants he encounters on his endless journeys across the
length and breadth of France. His rampage ends only when he is caught
in the act of molesting a young shepherdess.

Once Bouvier is brought before the authorities, he encounters the man
who will seal his fate: an ambitious provincial judge named Emile Rousseau. Quick to take this case in hopes that it will further his career, the
judge is not only Bouvier's nemesis but also his social opposite. A privileged
and affluent member of the bourgeoisie, a man given to fine food and wine,
he is the embodiment of power, the staunch representative of law and
order. A determined anti-Dreyfusard, the judge counts among his friends
a disabused, anti-Semitic Royalist (Jean-Claude Brialy) who has just returned from the colonies. But despite the social chasm that separates him
from the accused, the judge, who has long been fascinated by Bouvier's
crimes, also feels a strange bond with the half-mad assassin. Under his
veneer of respectability, the judge, too, is prey to inner turmoil: deeply
repressed and neurotically attached to a domineering mother, he takes a
morbid interest in the sexual details of every atrocity Bouvier was driven
to commit. Indeed, after one particularly intense and frightening session
with Bouvier, this staunch upholder of public morality brutally sodomizes
his working-class mistress, Rose (Isabelle Hupert).

It is, ultimately, the strange bond between the two men that proves to be
Bouvier's undoing. Flattered by the attention he receives from the judge—
"Bouvier," said Tavernier, "is fascinated by the fact that for the first time
someone intelligent speaks to him, that a being from another class is inter-

ested in him"[45]—the assassin allows himself to be deceived and tricked. He believes the judge's false assurances that if he confesses, he will not be condemned as a murderer but, rather, treated as a madman. But while Bouvier keeps his part of the bargain, giving a full confession, the judge, of course, never had any intention of keeping his word. In fact, he manipulates the press so that Bouvier is judged in the court of public opinion before he ever receives a hearing. Thus despite his evident madness, Bouvier is declared sane by the medical experts and condemned to death. It is left to Rose, the judge's mistreated and long-suffering mistress, to pass judgment on her lover's actions: dismayed by the judge's perfidy toward the assassin, she decides to leave him.

But things do not turn out quite as the judge expected. His political ambitions appear to be thwarted for, in the next scene, he and his mother are seen at a right-wing political rally that is both sparsely attended and soon disrupted by protesters. As they flee the building for the street, they see soldiers heading toward a factory where a workers' uprising is in progress. The scene shifts to the factory: singing a song about the Commune, Rose, now dressed as a worker, leads a sea of workers as she holds aloft the red flag of revolution. When the soldiers who have been sent to quell their uprising arrive, she implores them to hold their fire and to join the ranks of the oppressed. The scene ends with a freeze-frame of the face of a young worker. On this note of suspended action the film comes to a close as titles fill the screen: "Between 1893 and 1898," they tell us, "Bouvier killed twelve children. In those same years more than 2,500 children under fifteen died—assassinated—in mines and textile factories."

The closing titles, of course, merely underscore the social and political message that has pervaded the entire film. Bouvier may be an assassin, but the world he inhabits—and which condemns him—is populated by assassins who are far more deadly than he. Indeed, this point is made explictly by the judge's clear-sighted Royalist friend; citing an observation taken from Octave Mirbeau, a popular author of the period, he says, "We are all assassins, at least potentially, only we channel this criminal impulse through legal means: industry, colonial trade, war, anti-Semitism." Reiterating this message in somewhat different terms, in one interview Tavernier described the confrontation between the judge and the assassin as the clash of "two violences: a crazy, tormented, uncontrollable, and unconscious violence and a legal, repressive, and hidden one."[46]

In the clash between these two "violences," there is never any doubt that the "legal violence" of the judge will prevail. Like the marquis du Pontcallec in *Que la fête commence*, Bouvier—a far more marginal and helpless figure than the aristocratic Breton nobleman—is obviously condemned less for his very real crimes than for what he is and for what he represents. "He is poor," remarks the judge's friend; "he doesn't stand a chance." His marginality, however, extends far beyond his poverty. For he is also obviously mad. And it is here, in respect to Bouvier's madness, that *Le juge et l'assassin* bears such a telling resemblance to *Moi, Pierre Rivière*. That is, like Allio's film, *Le juge et l'assassin* also investigates the ways in which criminal insanity is defined, treated, and, to some extent, created by society. If Rivière's seeming sanity baffled the experts, they proved no more perspicacious or effective when it came to Bouvier. Transferred from one medical or psychiatric clinic to another, Bouvier was mistreated, misunderstood, by a variety of "experts." He underwent, said Tavernier, "all the official possibilities of repression of the era: the army, the church, the asylum, the prison, the psychiatric hospital as well as the regular hospital. I did not invent anything: he really went through all this."[47]

Doubtless exacerbated by repression, Bouvier's madness, like that of Pierre Rivière, raises, of course, troubling questions concerning the social roots of insanity. As portrayed in the film, Bouvier is clearly an exceptional being frustrated by social and economic barriers; despite himself, he is driven to commit horrendous crimes that appall him as much as they do his executioners. Veering between moments of mad ravings and lucid incisiveness, he is often prey to acute remorse: after one murder he desperately prays to the Virgin; to avert still another, he deliberately scares away a potential victim. In addition to these indications of a moral conscience, he displays linguistic gifts that rival those of Rivière. Throughout the film, in fact, we hear extracts from his letters, based on real letters by Vacher, that reveal a talent for telling poetic and rhetorical effects.[48]

Bouvier's talents, as well as his moral sensibility, prompt the inevitable question: to what extent did the misery and solitude of his life—the hardships of a rootless existence in which he was obliged to beg for food and shelter each night—lead to violence?[49] Citing the debt he owed Foucault in respect to his exploration of this issue, Tavernier remarked that "mental illness is due to many factors which are not only psychological but also social. Sometimes madness catalyzes, to the state of paroxysm, certain traits of a society."[50] Viewed from this perspective, Bouvier's madness can be said to "catalyze" the social madness of a country in which the poor receive less compassion than Bouvier reserves for his victims. Implicitly condemned throughout *Le juge et l'assassin*, this social madness surrounds the vagabond as he tramps throughout France. In the countryside, starving peasants live in dark and cramped hovels along with their beasts; in the cities, young women—like Rose, the judge's mistress—must choose between a slow death in the factories or the bed of a wealthy man. Emphasizing the inextricable links between social misery and crime, Bouvier himself denounces the France of his time in an elegant play on words: "It is better," he declares, "to be a slaughterer than to make slaughterers."

If the madness of Bouvier/Vacher can be said to have "catalyzed" the madness of a world characterized by injustice and misery, his case also pointed to other collective "dramas" and "passions," to use Tavernier's words, of the 1890s.[51] The most unforgettable of these dramas, of course, was that of the Dreyfus Affair. And, indeed, Tavernier never lets us forget that behind Bouvier's trial lurks that of the Jewish army officer accused of treason; behind the "legal violence" of the judge, that of a society bent on restoring and maintaining order. Rapid tableaux serve as constant reminders of the violent passions that raged during the 1890s. From their pulpits, preachers denounce the arch-Dreyfusard, Emile Zola, while army battalions burn his books; a homeless man is denied food at a church soup kitchen because he is illiterate—and thus unable to add his name to an anti-Dreyfus petition. Even Bouvier's mystical outburts, in which he identifies with the martyrdom of Joan of Arc, echo a polarizing debate that was sparked by the Dreyfus Affair. On the Dreyfusard Left, anticlerical Republicans saw the Maid of Orleans as a secular patriot whose humble origins made her a daughter of the people.[52] On the Right, where hatred of Dreyfus was often bathed in anti-Semitism, Joan of Arc was not only celebrated as a "saint" but turned into the antithesis of the Jew.[53]

A battle for the very heart and soul of the nation, the conflicts of the Dreyfus Affair are, certainly, the best-remembered "dramas" of the 1890s. But they were not the only ones. And if the trial of Bouvier/Vacher evoked that of Dreyfus, Bouvier's plight reflected other pressing issues of the era even more directly. His homelessness, for example, touched on a major problem of the 1880s and 1890s: these years saw a huge increase in vagrancy due, in large measure, to an agricultural crisis that forced thousands of farm laborers and workers from their homes. (According to one study, as late as 1904, 400,000 beggars were on the roads of France.)[54] Arousing fear rather than sympathy, the armies of homeless men who took to the roads at this time evoked the specter of rising social unrest, of a second Commune. Their rootlessness represented a threat that, as historian Matt Matsuda notes in a discussion of the real Vacher affair, "struck at the heart of French 'identity,' the constituent elements of a people, the assumptions about an orderly and stable society."[55] Perceived as violent and degenerate, vagrants were considered criminals—indeed, both begging and vagrancy were punishable offenses—and social deviants.

As a crazed and brutal assassin, as well as a homeless man, Bouvier/Vacher fit the stereotype of the degenerate vagabond only too well. And he had still another strike against him. He was not only a vagabond and a killer but also a self-proclaimed anarchist. Even more than his vagrancy, his anarchism, despite its lunatic cast, was calculated to strike fear into the hearts of the French bourgeoisie. (No less than vagrants, anarchists were also subject to the clinical discourse of medical and social pathology—a

discourse that, as Robert A. Nye dryly observes, "made the killing of political criminals a more palatable affair.")[56] By raising the dreaded specter of
anarchism, Bouvier virtually sealed his doom. He was not only poor and
mad, degenerate and homeless. He also had the misfortune, as Tavernier
remarked, to live at a time when "he was forced to expiate. There were
anarchist attempts: it was necessary [to provide] guilty people."[57]

Dominated by a brutal murderer who proves more sympathetic than his
"judges," *Le juge et l'assassin* rereads a defining moment of French history
in a decidedly somber light. Stripped of its "varnish," history reveals a nation of assassins and slaughterers, a country divided by class warfare and
religious intolerance. But even as *Le juge et l'assassin* mercilessly reread the
past, like Tavernier's previous film, it also reflected some of the deepest
tensions and uncertainties—in particular, the growing crisis of ideology—
of the present. As in the case of *Que la fête commence*, its conclusion was
especially telling. For once again, a scene meant to be a "hymn to Revolution," as one critic had it, appeared, far more explicitly than in Tavernier's
previous film, to signal its death knell. Imbued with memories of the Commune, the workers' uprising glimpsed at the end of *Le juge et l'assassin* suggests the failure of not only the revolutionary goals that had inspired the
Parisian rebels of 1871 but also those embraced by the radicals of May
1968.

Unlike the revolutionary tableau at the end of *Que la fête commence*, however, the conclusion of *Le juge et l'assassin* did give rise to debate and controversy. At least two *Annales* historians found it questionable. Emmanuel Le
Roy Ladurie likened it to socialist realist art; Philippe Joutard argued that
Tavernier undermined the credibility of his film by merging what he saw
as two different historical issues: on the one hand, the ideological battles
and the anti-Semitic sentiments that swirled around the Dreyfus Affair and,
on the other, the ferocious nature of late-nineteenth-century capitalism.
Arguing that these were by no means "parallel" phenomena, Joutard declared that it was "historically questionable to lump [them] together."[58]

Not all historians, certainly, share Joutard's conviction that fin de siècle
social and ideological currents followed such divergent paths. In contrast
to Joutard, for example, Raoul Girardet believes that "Catholic reactions"
to the "secularism and anticlericalism" displayed by pro-Dreyfusards sometimes merged with "social reactions in the face of the progress of the workers' movement."[59] And Michel Winock contends that it was, in fact, the
workers' movement that nourished the first stirrings of opposition to the
extreme nationalism sparked by the affair.[60] Still, at least one interview suggests that the director apparently felt the need to respond to criticisms
directed against this scene; for, here, he offered several explanations for
his unconventional, almost Brechtian, conclusion. One explanation clearly

bore upon ideology and the nature of popular uprisings: by ending the film with a scene peopled by anonymous men and women, observed Tavernier, he meant to suggest that "if history is to continue, it will not necessarily be with the people that you've seen." Yet another explanation concerned the role played by Rose in the film. It would have cruel, remarked the director, to have her return to the judge once she sees the extent of her lover's perfidy toward the accused. But neither did he want to show the only alternative that left her: that is, unceasing labor in a factory. Pondering these dismal choices, he suddenly "had the idea for the end that wasn't at all realistic—a bit like *Threepenny Opera*."[61]

Although Tavernier does not make the point explicitly, it is obvious that he did not want to conclude *Le juge et l'assassin* on a totally somber note, with the triumph of the judge and of the repressive forces he represents and embodies. This implicit desire, however, makes it all the more significant that this scene, which was clearly designed to be one of revolutionary ardor, is not only ambiguous but also deeply pessimistic. To begin with, as in the case of *Que la fête commence*, the conclusion of *Le juge et l'assassin* seems to belie, to contradict, all that has preceded it. After all, the film has consistently underscored the many weapons that power has at its disposal to deceive and to oppress ordinary people like Bouvier and Rose. And even more than Bouvier, who derives a kind of rebellious energy from his madness, Rose is a passive creature who has submitted to the deadly weight of power in the most intimate corners of her being. Like the young prostitute of *Que la fête commence*, Rose appears crushed by, resigned to, oppression. (As if to reinforce the analogy between these two characters, the actress who plays the young prostitute in *Que la fête commence*, Christine Pascal, is among the workers seen at the end of *Le juge et l'assassin*.) Given Rose's passivity, her long-suffering nature, the conclusion becomes even more improbable: it asks us to believe that this soft creature finds the will, the determination, to embrace the cause of class warfare and revolutionary action.

If the revolutionary role that falls to Rose is problematic, so, too—and this may be even more telling—is the nature of the uprising she leads. It is here, in fact, that one senses a distinct difference between *Que la fête commence* and *Le juge et l'assassin*, a difference that points to the rapidity with which long-held political hopes crumbled in the course of the 1970s. For if both films end on a note of revolutionary ardor, the popular uprisings they evoke differ in nature and kind. To begin with, the final tableau of *Que la fête commence* looks *forward*—to the very real revolution that ushered in the modern world. *Le juge et l'assassin*, by contrast, looks *back* to an uprising that failed—and the very failure of which helped prompt the repressive regime that condemns Bouvier to death. Rose may implore the soldiers to hold their fire; but we know that the troops from Versailles slaughtered the rebellious workers of Paris. The revolutionary song that is heard may affirm the hope that the next workers' uprising will meet with success; but, in truth, the defeat of the Commune is often interpreted as the end of a period of revolutionary activity.[62]

And to these fundamental differences must be added still another. Although less obvious, it may be even more important. For the end of *Que la fête commence* takes place on the same plane of reality as the film that precedes it: that is, the angry peasants who torch the regent's carriage inhabit the same world as do the regent and his court. The end of *Le juge et l'assassin*, instead, deliberately leads into a nonrealistic realm marked only by memory and desire. From the standpoint of reason and logic, it is not possible that Rose would be leading the factory workers, or that they would be singing a song about the Commune twenty years after that unhappy event. The very elements that render this scene so moving—the collapse of past and present, the presence of Rose amid imaginary soldiers and workers, the intense theatricality of the scene's visual composition—also render it iconic rather than real. What we see, then, is the embodiment of a mythic revolt that exists only in the world of the imaginary. Far more explicitly than in *Que la fête commence*, this sequence leaves us not with political hopes for the future but, instead, with nostalgia for a past when revolution, incarnated in the class struggle, seemed a realizable dream. Despite its revolutionary ring, this scene represents not a vision of things to come but the nostalgic echo of a time when one could still believe in the reality, the necessity, of revolution.

Tavernier's next two historical films left little doubt that the end of *Le juge et l'assassin* did, indeed, signal an adieu to revolution: a farewell to a vision of history informed by the Marxist view of class conflict and revolution. For neither *Coup de torchon* (*Clean Slate*, 1981) nor *La passion Béatrice* hints at the social impulses, the hope of solidarity and collective action, that inform the "hymn to Revolution" seen at the end of both *Que la fête commence* and *Le juge et l'assassin*. With the disappearance of that hope, moreover, has come a new note of apocalyptic violence and despair.[63] The spiritual unease that ran below the surface of earlier works has given rise, in these somber melodramas, to a Manichaean world dominated by evil. Here, corruption and sin are located less in human institutions—which, it was formerly hoped, might be changed through social action and class struggle—than in the immutable depths of human nature itself. Without the utopian belief that a "sense of history" exists, that history itself can be altered for the common good, the world has become a place of demonic power and utter despair.

This despair is seen at its most extreme in *La passion Béatrice*. Set at one of history's darkest hours, amid the desolation and the slaughter of the

Hundred Years War, *La passion Béatrice* features a medieval nobleman, François de Cortemart, who manages to combine the legal, repressive violence of the judge with the instinctive savagery of Bouvier. A powerful nobleman who is lord and master of his domain, Cortemart is doubtless the most excessive monster in Tavernier's gallery of outsize characters. He is also, significantly, the only one whose murderous instincts are totally innate: as the preface to the film tells us, Cortemart's evil deeds are driven by a "poison in the blood."

In *La passion Béatrice*, the "poison" that affects Cortemart manifests itself when he is still a child. At the age of nine, he spies his mother with a lover and coolly kills the intruder; soon afterward, when he learns of his father's death at war, he cries out, "I hate you, God!" Later, this "hatred" inspires the adult Cortemart to transgress every moral and religious code. He brutally sodomizes a feverish peasant woman who has just given birth; cruelly humiliates his son whom he views as a coward; steals and pillages from neighboring castles. The worst of his violence is directed, however, against his beautiful and pious seventeen-year-old daughter, Béatrice: not only does he rape and impregnate her, but he forces her to wed him in the most unholy of ceremonies. And, in the end, he robs his daughter of her very soul: he goads Béatrice into killing him with his own dagger.

Reflecting upon the transgressive instincts, the currents of passion and violence, that give *La passion Béatrice* the frenzied cast of an Elizabethan revenge tragedy, Tavernier remarked that he wanted the film to pose "brutal and primordial questions."[64] In posing such questions, the director ventured deeper than ever before into the shadowy recesses of the human psyche, into a primordial zone where each character becomes, in his words, "a part of the global character that is our unconscious."[65] The site of a savage war between good and evil, this primordial zone is one in which power displays its most naked, intractable face to us even as it gives the lie to all hopes for social change and progress. Here, nothing—no bonds of solidarity, no collective struggle or popular revolt—can check the dark forces that well up from the unconscious.

A chilling coda to the meditation on power Tavernier had begun fifteen years earlier, *La passion Béatrice* also adds the blackest brush strokes yet seen to the counterportrait of France traced by the director's historical works. The image of medieval France that emerges from this film could hardly be in starker contrast with the traditional portrait of *la douce France* associated with medieval romances and miniature paintings. In the savage patriarchal world of *La passion Béatrice* women are neither *belles dames sans merci* nor gracious ladies waiting to be wooed and won; instead, they are objects of desire and/or exchange to be possessed, often brutally, by husband or father. In this respect, even the noble Béatrice is as helpless as the lowliest of her servants.

But it is especially in respect to medieval faith that *La passion Béatrice* distances itself from conventional images of the national past. It gives little evidence of the radiant faith portrayed, say, in a long tradition of French films—stretching from Méliès's early silent down to Jacques Rivette's *Jeanne la Pucelle* (1993)—about Joan of Arc. In the savage landscape of *La passion Béatrice*, Christian faith goes hand in hand with a belief in superstitions and black magic. (Commenting on this aspect of the film, in an enthusiastic review of *La passion Béatrice*, medieval historian Jacques Le Goff declared that Tavernier captured the spiritual malaise of a tragic, death-haunted age.)[66] The pious Béatrice may share Joan's mystical faith; still, she not only consults a witch but constructs an effigy of her father in hopes that he will be destroyed by the forces of black magic. Above all, though, it is Cortemart, who "hates" a God in whom he cannot quite believe, who reveals the dark underside of medieval spirituality. In his twisted hatred of God, he calls to mind, perhaps, not only Sade's imaginary libertines but the historical figure of Gilles de Retz. (A marshal of France during the Hundred Years War, Retz was a real-life monster who sacrificed hundreds of children in black magic ceremonies after first sadistically molesting them.)[67]

If, like Retz, Cortemart demonstrates how faith can be transformed into blasphemy and transgression, the brutal nobleman also reveals the fragmented nature of fourteenth-century French society. In this respect, too, the contrast between earlier films about the Middle Ages, especially those dealing with Joan of Arc, and *La passion Béatrice* is particularly sharp. It is obviously not patriotic fervor that sends Cortemart off to war but, rather, a desire to prove himself and/or to defend land and wealth. Quick to pillage and destroy neighboring castles, he belongs not to a unified nation but to a splintered world of warring fiefdoms. Desolate and crumbling, his castle has little connection with the surrounding region, much less with the more abstract notion of a "country." Indeed, Joan's "France" is as alien to the vicious Cortemart as are the codes of chivalry that might protect his daughter.

War Memories: *La vie et rien d'autre, La guerre sans nom*

A somber portrait of a death-haunted era, *La passion Béatrice* seemed to signal the end of a certain cycle of Tavernier's films. This is not to say that the director has ceased to reread the national past or to add new dimensions to the counterportrait of France which he began in *Que la fête commence*. Quite the contrary. Since concluding *La passion Béaatrice*, Tavernier has made two historical melodramas—*La vie et rien d'autre* (1989) and *Capitaine Conan* (1996)—concerning the era that Tavernier, like many historians, considers the "most important epoch of our century": the First World War.[68] Reminiscent of antiwar classics such as Abel Gance's *J'accuse* (1919) and Lewis Milestone's *All Quiet on the Western Front* (1930), both films portray men who have been, in the director's words, unalterably "damaged" by the violence of war. A similar concern with the human cost of war also permeates what is probably Tavernier's most compelling film of recent years, *La guerre sans nom*, a 1991 documentary about the Algerian War.

In these films, however, the impulses that dominated earlier historical works—the insistence on past *mentalités*, the revolutionary perspectives and *gauchiste* preoccupation with power seen in *Que la fête commence* and *Le juge et l'assassin*, the melodramatic paroxysms of *Coup de torchon* and *La passion Béatrice*—have faded from view. The towering villains, the stark clashes between good and evil, have also disappeared. The protagonist of *Capitaine Conan*, a soldier who has been turned into a killing-machine by the necessities of war, is, significantly, far more morally ambiguous than the villains of earlier films.[69] In contrast with, say, *Le juge et l'assassin* and *La passion Béatrice*, *La vie et rien d'autre* does not feature a confrontation between adversaries. The protagonists of this film, instead, form a couple in love; far from engaging in a deadly duel, they help one another recover from the ravages of war in the knowledge that, in the end, there is "life and nothing but."[70]

Marked by what might be seen as a new humanism, by an increased awareness of moral complexities, these films emerge from the claustrophobic universe inhabited by monsters like Bouvier and Cortemart. At the same time, they leave behind the "strangeness" of the distant past for a closer look at defining moments of modern French history. As they do so—suggesting that the absence of ideology is finally being lived as a liberation rather than a loss—they ask new questions of history even as they explore issues that are still very much alive. Underscoring the long reach of the past, they highlight the issue currently at the forefront of contemporary French historiography: the ways in which the national past is remembered. Indeed, one of these works, *La guerre sans nom*, was widely hailed as a significant contribution to the meditation on French history and memory that is currently underway.

Even before making *La guerre sans nom*, however, Tavernier explicitly addressed the issue of memory in *La vie et rien d'autre*. For the film is not only a rereading of a critical era of the French past but an investigation of the divergent ways in which that moment has been remembered. Just as Tavernier's earlier works had implicitly challenged reigning images and myths of the national past, *La vie et rien d'autre* questions the "sites of memory" charged to transmit such images. Indeed, the film is informed by an implicit contrast between the patriotic memories of World War I that are embodied in "official" sites—in monuments and holidays, in battlefields and statues—and the way(s) in which the war was experienced, lived, by individuals.

Set, in 1920, on the blood-soaked and sodden plains of Verdun, the very landscape of the film constitutes a fundamental site of French patriotic memory. One of the worst killing fields of history, Verdun witnessed an endless series of battles in which most of the French army saw action, and nearly half of those who fought were killed or wounded as they sought to repel the invader. Ever since, it has held a special place in French memory: it is seen not merely as one battle among others but, instead, as historian Antoine Prost writes, as "*the* battle that sums up, by itself, the Great War." The memory of Verdun is so highly charged, as Prost proceeds to observe, for two critical reasons. It was not only a battle in *defense* of the country, one that allowed France to "remain herself," but also one in which the French army fought bravely under indescribable conditions. For both these reasons, observes Prost, Verdun became a "sacred place: a place of sacrifice and consecration."[71]

The patriotic resonances that inhere in the very soil of Verdun also cling to two other sites of national memory evoked in *La vie et rien d'autre*. In contrast to Verdun, both were deliberately created after the war. Through an important subplot concerning a sculptor, Tavernier alludes to the construction of the monuments, which grace every French village and town, to those fallen in World War I.[72] And the construction of the most important of such monuments, the Tomb of the Unknown Soldier in Paris, becomes the subject of ferocious satire in the film. Tavernier emphasizes the impossible nature of the task that confronted army officials who had to make sure that the anonymous corpse buried in this hallowed resting place would be that of a French soldier and not that of an Englishman, a German, or, worse still, an African.

Even as Tavernier gives a distinctly grotesque cast to the military maneuvers involved in creating this imposing monument, he also draws an insistent contrast between the "official" memories it embodies—memories that dignify war even as they exalt the values of patriotism and sacrifice—and the brutal realities of a struggle that drained France of a generation of young men. These realities are built into the gruesome task that has been assigned to the film's upright protagonist, an army officer named Colonel Dellaplane (Philippe Noiret). For Dellaplane heads a military unit that, two years after the end of the war, has been established on the plains of Verdun to search for traces of those still missing. Sometimes the men themselves, wounded in body or mind, are found in grim hospital wards. More often, though, it is only pitiful remains—an identifying medallion, a cup—that are brought forth from the blood-soaked earth. And the thousands still missing, of course, are a fraction of all those who died. The enormity of the slaughter and the hollowness of "official" sites of memory are under-scored, in fact, by a striking image that comes at the end of the film. Here, Dellaplane, who has resigned from the army in disgust at empty victory celebrations and official lies, writes a letter to Irène, a beautiful woman he met while still stationed in Verdun. After acknowledging his love for her, a love that he was unable to admit or express earlier, he concludes his letter with a scathing description of the military parade designed to honor the Unknown Soldier. If all those soldiers who were killed in the war were to march along the Champs-Elysées, he tells her, the parade would not last three and one-half hours (as it did) but, instead, *eleven days and nights*.

The specter of soldiers killed in battle also hovers over *La guerre sans nom*. And this film, too, is about memories of war. But this time the memories are those of actual veterans. For *La guerre sans nom*, which was made in collaboration with Patrick Rotman, is almost entirely composed of inter-views with soldiers who fought in the Algerian War. There is no sign, here, of the "official" war memories that evoke Dellaplane's wrath. Indeed, al-most as if even newsreels or photos would be too "official" (or too partisan) a source of memory, with the exception of some early newsreel footage of antiwar demonstrations the only images from the past seen in *La guerre sans nom* consist of photographs taken by the soldiers themselves.

In sharing their memories of Algeria with the viewer, the soldiers inter-viewed in *La guerre sans nom* resurrect a struggle whose psychic scars, like those of Vietnam in the United States, are still very far from healed. Proba-bly the most divisive war in modern French history, the Algerian conflict, which lasted from 1954 to 1962, was denied even a "name"—hence Ta-vernier's title, "the war without a name"—because de Gaulle refused to admit that France could be at war with one of its own *départements*. Shrouded first in censorship, and then in a shamed silence, the guerrilla war that effectively ended France's reign as a great colonial power is only beginning to find its place in the nation's memory. Writing in 1989, com-mentator Nicole Lapierre noted that it had become less difficult to "re-member" the divided France of the Vichy years than the country which had been torn apart by the struggle in Algeria. "The screen memories of a France that resisted are cracking," observed Lapierre, "leaving space for a history of Vichy or, rather, for a history of the memory of Vichy. [The history] of the Algerian War, on the other hand, remains buried."[73]

The year after these words were written, Tavernier began shooting the film that would dramatically create a "space" for the history of the Algerian War. Reactions to the film could hardly have been more enthusiastic. *La guerre sans nom*, Marcel Oms declared, was nothing less than "*the* film on the Algerian War and the indelible imprint it left on the lives of those who fought in it";[74] referring to the terrible trauma inflicted by Algeria, Michel

Cadé declared that "only Bertrand Tavernier knew how to find the words and images to say the unsayable."[75] Observing that *La guerre sans nom* finally pierced the "thick wall of silence" that had enveloped the memory of the Algerian War for thirty years, a reviewer for *Le monde* compared it to no less a work than *Le chagrin et la pitié*, Marcel Ophuls's 1970 groundbreaking documentary about the Occupation.[76] Echoing this sentiment, Italian critic Sergio Arecco writes that Tavernier's film "harks back to great . . . antiwar documentaries, in particular, to Marcel Ophuls's *Le chagrin et la pitie . . .* and to Claude Lanzmann's *Shoah*."[77]

It is not difficult to see why *La guerre sans nom* should have prompted comparisons such as these. Like Ophuls's film, *La guerre sans nom* is both an exploration of history and a historical document in its own right; it, too, uses the oral testimony of witnesses to uncover, to "remember," traumatic and repressed zones of the past. But there is also a telling difference between the two films—one that points to a changed political and social climate as well as to Tavernier's own evolution. Deliberately polemical, Ophuls was determined to undermine, to challenge, the "myth of the Resistance" that had held sway since the end of the war. Making use of archival material (newsreels, photos) to undercut the testimony of certain witnesses, *Le chagrin et la pitié* created, as suggested earlier, what many saw as a counterlegend of the Occupation years. In contrast with *Le chagrin et la pitié*, *La guerre sans nom* displays no polemical impulse. Indeed, contrary to what might have been expected given the highly partisan cast of Tavernier's earlier films, in *La guerre sans nom* the director never appears to take sides. Treating all interviewees with the same respect and sympathy, both those who supported the war and those who opposed it, he neither judges nor invites us to judge. (Significantly, though, the film contains no interviews with officers or generals, those who might well have rationalized or "explained" the war.) Implicitly denouncing the way the army has treated many veterans of Algeria—since the Algerian conflict was never deemed a "war," many veterans have been denied the benefits accorded soldiers who fought in "official" wars—the film recalls Jean Renoir's pacifist classic, *La grande illusion* (*Grand Illusion*, 1937) in the immense sympathy it displays for ordinary soldiers sent to slaughter and be slaughtered.

Tavernier's resolutely nonpartisan approach is all the more striking in light of the fact that the Algerian War—or, more precisely, its legacy—is a source of continuing divisiveness and conflict. The emotional charge that still clings to the war may be one of the reasons, in fact, that the director chose not to further dramatize it through a work of fiction. In any case, *La guerre sans nom* is, certainly, one of the most sober and restrained of all Tavernier's works. It gives no hint of the baroque excesses and stylistic flourishes, the sweeping pans and lyrical camera movements, that mark the director's historical melodramas. The camera barely moves from the faces of the men as they relate their experiences, their long-buried fears and terrors, to Tavernier and Patrick Rotman. Under their quiet but insistent questions, interviewees recall memories that still have the power to make them weep—memories all the more vivid, perhaps, because they have been repressed for decades.

As they respond to questions about the past, most of the soldiers appear grateful for the opportunity to finally describe what they saw and endured. This holds true even when they are asked about what are, surely, the most guilt-ridden memories of the war: those bearing witness to the army's routine use of torture to extract information from prisoners. (Implemented little over a decade after the end of World War II, such practices appeared to many as a chilling reminder of Nazi atrocities.) Here, responses vary: some men shrug off the memory of torture or search for justifications; others are disturbed and distressed. Like many who served in Vietnam, interviewees seem prone to lingering, paralyzing anguish: one cries and says that nightmares lasted for years; another has "flashes" of dead or mutilated comrades. Even the most stoic seem eager to remember, to break the uneasy silence imposed on them for most of their lives. "They felt," said Tavernier, "a terrible resentment about the way a black wall had been erected over this part of History. I believe that a grave fissure in French society can be traced back to this."[78] As he interviews the men, Tavernier encourages all to remember experiences at once intensely individual and yet shared; eschewing a single view of the past, he creates a film that is a kaleidoscope of divergent memories. Troubling the very notion of collective memory, this kaleidoscope—and this will be the focus of the next chapter—points to the impossibility of incorporating the Algerian War into a single "official" version of national history.

Like many distances, that between Tavernier's first historical films and his most recent varies according to one's perspective. From one line of sight, little has changed: all his films about the past attempt to draw lessons for the present; all indict powerful and often deadly social institutions. The director has never ceased to amplify his counterportrait of French history; to explore the margins rather than the center; to denounce abuse and injustice; to focus on "official" hypocrisy and lies. But seen from another perspective, the differences between *Que la fête commence* and *La guerre sans nom* are as significant as the resemblances. Separated by the ideological chasm occasioned by the collapse of Marxism, by what has been called the "tragedy of the French Left,"[79] these films approach history, and its representation, in very different ways. In *Que la fête commence*, faith in the future was sustained by the revolution to come; in *La guerre sans nom* this faith has given way to something far more modest and yet, perhaps, more difficult: a desire to explore memory and to come to terms with the past.

The film thus questions not only the particular shapes assumed by national memory but the very notion of a collective—rather than individual—past. Suggesting that it is no longer enough to substitute a *gauchiste* version of history for that which has gone before, it is marked by a tone not of revolutionary ardor but of sympathy for all those caught in the relentless meshes of history.

In respect to this shift in sensibility, the trajectory taken by Tavernier might be compared to that which marked the career of Jean Renoir in the 1930s. In the course of the brief but tumultuous period surrounding the victory of the Popular Front, each successive film by Renoir was more militant, more ideologically charged, than the one preceding it. Hence *Toni*, a 1934 work about the plight of immigrant workers, was followed by *Le crime de M. Lange*, a parable about the evils of capitalism. And *M. Lange* was followed by two films that were even more explicitly didactic: *La vie est à nous* (1936), a propaganda film made for the Communist Party; and *La Marseillaise* (1938), a historical epic, commissioned by the C.G.T. (Congress of Trade Unions), which infused the Revolution of 1789 with all the euphoria and exuberance surrounding the Popular Front. But when the Popular Front came to an end, so, too, did Renoir's period of ideological militancy. And it was at this time that the director made two of his greatest works: *La grande illusion* and *La règle du jeu* (*The Rules of the Game*, 1939). While class distinctions continue to play a critical role in these works insofar as they shape character and determine destiny, in contrast to an earlier film like *Le crime de M. Lange*, such distinctions are no longer seen in the context of struggle and solidarity, of revolt and revolution.

Significantly, the revolutionary *élan* that sweeps through certain of Renoir's films is nowhere to be seen in Tavernier's cinema. The melancholy that pervades even *Que la fête commence* marks Tavernier's oeuvre as one that belongs to the twilight moment following revolution and not the euphoric one preceding it. Still, just as the political curve of Renoir's films mirrored the swiftly evolving climate of the 1930s, so, too, as I have attempted to show, does the course charted by Tavernier correspond to profound changes in the political sensibility of the last quarter-century. If these changes are less dramatic and exhilarating than the ideological battles of the 1930s, they may prove even more profound. While the 1930s witnessed major battles in the long-running French war between Right and Left, recent decades have seen the demise of revolutionary hopes and ideological certainties dating back to the Revolution. We have reached the point, Tavernier's recent films appear to suggest, to go beyond such battles, to forgo revolutionary dreams in favor of the modest yet difficult task of simply telling the "truth." Paraphrasing George Orwell, in the course of an interview concerning *La guerre sans nom,* Tavernier observed that the "first revolutionary virtue" for the historian is "to say: 2 + 2 = 4. Until now, no one did the addition . . . and we didn't know what they added up to. The important thing was not to ask."[80] It is surely this "virtue"—this determination to "ask" questions of the past with dispassion and lucidity—that currently animates the director.

V

Memory and Its Losses: Troubled Dreams of Empire

Colonial Legacies

While the *rétro* years dominated historical films of the 1970s, by the end of the following decade still another traumatic and defining moment of the national past, the turbulent postwar era of decolonization, was finding a second life on-screen. Nearly fifty years after the decisive battle of Dien Bien Phu—a defeat that ended French rule in Indochina (and that set the stage for American involvement)—and more than thirty years after Algeria won its independence, films seemed intent on bringing this difficult period to life. In addition to Bertrand Tavernier's documentary, *La guerre sans nom*, the year 1992 alone saw three other major works devoted to the years of empire: Jean-Jacques Annaud's *L'amant* (*The Lover*, based on the novel by Marguerite Duras), Régis Wargnier's *Indochine*, and Pierre Schoendoerffer's *Dien Bien Phu*.

As in the case of films about the Vichy era, works such as these clearly tapped into, and fueled, widely shared impulses. A striking number reflected, although in an indirect manner, what seemed to be a deep-seated nostalgia for the days of empire or, more precisely, for what that era represented. After all, the colonial era marked a period of history in which the nation was more powerful, and far surer of itself, than it is today. Not yet humiliated by defeat and occupation, France questioned neither its civilizing mission nor the central role it played upon the world stage. Using a term that refers to mainland France (as opposed to its colonies), Jacques Julliard observes that "for a long time the French [considered] the Hexagon the epicenter of an idea destined to reach, by successive waves, the borders of the universe: this idea was France herself."[1] It is this "idea" of a powerful and civilizing France that was so painfully shattered by France's defeat at Dien Bien Phu and, especially, by the 1962 treaties according Algeria its independence. (Noting that the Algerian War was "infinitely more acutely felt" than France's withdrawal from other corners of its empire, including Indochina, Philip Dine observes that *le drame algérien* "came to symbolize the process of decolonization as a whole.")[2] And it is also this "idea," now receding into the folds of the past, that gives rise to such tremendous nostalgia for the days of empire. The more uncertain the present, the stronger the glow of an imperial past. "No matter how they do it," observed a commentator for the *New York Times* in 1992, "they [the French] obsess on their lost colonial role at a time when their place in the new Europe is being debated."[3]

But this "obsession" is not the only one that sets its mark on films about the colonial past. Many also point to the prominent role that memory has assumed in the contemporary French historical imagination. Foregrounding an issue that was only implicit in most *rétro* works, some of the most noteworthy films of the colonial "cycle" explicitly filter the past through the screen of memory. This is the case, for example, of no less than three of the four films released in 1992. As suggested in the previous chapter, in *La guerre sans nom* veterans of the Algerian War describe their memories of that unhappy struggle; in both *L'amant* and *Indochine*, an aging narrator thinks back to a life spent in the colonies—a life recalled through the flashbacks that constitute the body of each film.

There is no doubt, as I have just suggested, that the role played by memory in these works points to a shift in historical consciousness. But at the same time, it also suggests the controversial and divisive nature of the struggles in Indochina and, especially, in Algeria: in other words, the fact that these wars left, in their wake, a legacy of divergent memories. This issue—as well as the indirect but insistent nostalgia that characterizes many films about the years of empire—is brought into particularly sharp focus in the two films that I would like to explore at some length in these pages: *Le crabe-tambour* (*The Drummer Crab*, 1977), by Pierre Schoendoerffer, and *Outremer* (*Overseas*, 1990), by Brigette Roüan.

Like many films about the colonial past, *Le crabe-tambour* and *Outremer* filter the past through the memories of individual men and women. But what distinguishes these works from better-known films such as, say, *L'amant* and *Indochine*, and what draws me to them, is that here the individuals portrayed belonged to clearly defined social groups. Thus *Le crabe-tambour* views France's humiliating defeat in Indochina and, later, her loss of Algeria from the perspective of the military; *Outremer* portrays the Algerian War from the viewpoint of the community of French settlers, who would later be known as *pieds-noirs*, who made Algeria their home.[4] Not only were both groups particularly affected by the Algerian War and its consequences, but both have formed and nurtured collective memories that, it is generally acknowledged, are marked by the unchanging contours, the repetitions, that characterize "myths"—or, to borrow a term from Raoul Girardet, "legendary narratives"—about the past.

It is precisely the shapes and the implications of these myths that I would like to explore in terms of *Le crabe-tambour* and *Outremer*. In respect to these myths, it is noteworthy, I think, that in the case of both films, the director had strong ties to the group whose memories are portrayed. Brigette Roüan grew up in a *pied-noir* community;[5] Pierre Schoendoerffer shares the military background of his protagonists. (After enlisting in the army in 1952, Schoendoerffer served as a military photographer in Indochina; captured as a prisoner of war at the time of Dien Bien Phu, he remained in Indochina after his release to cover what would become known as the Vietnam War for *Life* magazine.)[6] This is not to say that Roüan and Schoendoerffer endorse every aspect of the myths or "discourses," to use another commonly applied term, that inform *Le crabe-tambour* and *Outremer*. But, in both cases, the deeply felt nature of the memories portrayed—the ways in which they obscure or soften the most troubling aspects of the colonial past by weaving themselves, as if unconsciously, into the formal strategies of the films—suggests that, at least to some extent, the directors share the perspective of their protagonists.

The presence of these discourses in both films opens onto a series of questions that bear not only on cinema but also on history and memory. Suggesting the power that cinema lends to the expression of historical and/ or political myths, both *Le crabe-tambour* and *Outremer* reveal how individual memories are shaped and transformed by a shared vision of the past that is driven by its own logic and desire. In so doing, they indicate the role that "collective subjects," to use a term proposed by critic François de la Bretèque, may play in the creation of a film. (Arguing that the relationship between a cinematic text and the reality it represents is never "direct," de la Bretèque declares that it is, instead, subject to a "whole series of ideological, discursive, and mental mediations—elaborated by collective subjects and the social groups to which the various 'authors' of a film belong.")[7] At the same time, the memories that come to life in these works testify to historical realities past and present. Revealing the powerful cluster of emotions that still surround the Algerian War, they also point to some of the troubling contemporary issues that have emerged in the shadow of the nation's colonialist past.

To fully appreciate the shape taken by the memories seen in *Le crabe-tambour* and in *Outremer*, one must keep in mind certain aspects of the Algerian War itself. As suggested earlier, the divergent memories embodied in these works serve as a potent reminder that this prolonged and deeply controversial struggle, which lasted from 1954 to 1962, was experienced, and remembered, in markedly different ways by various segments or groups of the population. Reopening fault lines that stretched back to the Dreyfus Affair, France's last colonial war left in its wake not a shared sense of the national past but, rather, a host of different, and often opposing, memories. "What do these memories have in common?" asks a leading historian of contemporary Algeria, Charles-Robert Ageron, "those of the *pieds-noirs*, those of francophile Algerians and of the *harkis* [the Algerian troops who fought for France], those of enlisted soldiers or members of the professional army? The 'Nostalgeria' of the former, the contrasting . . . recollections of the others are sometimes so different that, confronted with this kaleidoscope of splintered memories, a future historian might begin to wonder about the concrete reality of French Algeria, this engulfed Atlantis, this lost Paradise."[8]

From the very first, the war that gave rise to such "splintered memories" was both unpopular—draftees protested against being sent to the front as early as 1956—and shrouded in denial. Because de Gaulle would not admit that France was at "war" with one of its own *départements*, the war was referred to by a variety of euphemisms: it was a "peace-keeping operation," a "police action," the "Algerian drama." Although fought on soil considered an integral part of France, for the vast majority of French people it remained a distant struggle: one devoid not only of emotional resonance but, above all, of a clear and compelling message.[9] And it was this, above all, as historian Robert Frank observes, that rendered, and continues to render, commemoration so difficult. "The survivors," writes Frank, "could celebrate the fact that they did not die for nothing. But by honoring the memory of their fallen comrades, they would implicitly be asking the terrible and, by definition, the most taboo of questions: why did they die? . . . It is because this question is basically unbearable that this war is uncommemorable."[10] One of the most striking indications of the difficulty of commemorating the Algerian War is the fact that veterans groups have not been able to persuade their countrymen to agree on a date to honor those fallen in battle. In the eyes of many, accepting the date often proposed— March 19, the day the treaties were signed in 1962—would be an admission that a real war, and a real defeat, had indeed taken place.[11]

Once the humiliating struggle in Algeria came to an end, the vast majority of the French asked for nothing better than to push it into the past as quickly as possible. But, of course, matters were very different for those who, like the settlers who had lived in Algeria and the soldiers who had fought there, had been directly touched by it. Indeed, the fact that others wanted to forget made it all the more imperative, perhaps, that *they* remember. And, in truth, they had much to remember: for them, the war was a trauma that could never be forgotten. For the *pieds-noirs*, the French defeat in Algeria represented the loss of home and country, the abrupt end of a cherished way of life. After years of protracted violence and anguish, they were forced to leave everything behind and flee to a "mother country" many had never seen. For the military, Algerian independence signaled the end of the empire that they had forged and continued to cherish. In their eyes, Algerian independence represented nothing less, in the words of Benjamin Stora, than "the end of a historical experience, of a world history with France at its center."[12]

The trauma experienced by both groups, as well as the chasm separating their memories from those of the vast majority of their compatriots, had still another dimension. For both the *pieds-noirs* and the military felt that they had been "betrayed" by their country, that France did not do all that was necessary to retain Indochina and, especially, Algeria. And this sense of betrayal, of estrangement, was further exacerbated in the aftermath of the war. Far from receiving a warm welcome when they arrived in France, *pied-noir* refugees frequently found themselves blamed for an unpopular war—in truth, without the settlers there would have been no war, or, at the very least, France would have resolved the terrible conflict much sooner—and cast in the role of "other" that they themselves had formerly assigned to Arabs.[13] And returning veterans often met the same unhappy fate as did those who came back from Vietnam. They were greeted by an uneasy, embarrassed silence; as Resnais's *Muriel* and Tavernier's *La guerre sans nom* make clear in very different ways, they felt that no one wanted to hear about sufferings endured and inflicted in a war "without a name."

As time went by, moreover, the world associated with, upheld by, both the *pieds-noirs* and the military—that is, the empire itself—came to seem increasingly anachronistic. As it did so, they themselves became, as Philip Dine observes, "unfortunate reminder[s] of colonial ambitions which had been discarded in favor of a new, 'hexagonal', vision of France and its future role in the world."[14] A 1979 poll taken in France revealed how dramatically attitudes had changed in regard to the Algerian War and the very notion of empire: only 16 percent of those polled felt that the war had been justified, while 58 percent were convinced that France had been wrong to fight in Algeria.[15] These changing attitudes inevitably rendered the experiences and the memories associated with both the military and the *pieds-noirs*, memories that had always been colored by the shame of a humiliating war, more marginalized, more difficult to express, than ever before. In a postcolonial world, how could one defend imperial adventures? or express nostalgia for a colonial order now perceived as unjust and racist?

I would argue that it is precisely this critical dilemma—the difficulty of remembering and of representing a past both unforgettable and yet inadmissible—that gives the memories, the myths, seen in both *Le crabe-tambour* and *Outremer* their special cast. Neither film leaves any doubt about the traumatic nature of the past that haunts its protagonists: permeated by a deep sense of melancholy and loss, both films depict survivors for whom time has stopped, men and women who are unable to live in the present because they cannot forget the past. But at the same time the precise nature of the events that shattered their lives, together with its weight of guilt and unease, has become blurred. Although the emotional charge of remembered events could hardly be stronger, the events themselves have been absorbed into a subjective and unchanging landscape characterized not by the continuities and the causal relationships of history but, instead, by the private symbols and mysterious allusions of dreams at once collective and individual. Against this landscape, the most troubling and "guilty" aspects of French colonialism fade from view; as they do so, the past beckons less as a specific moment of French history than as a vague and ill-defined "golden age." In these works, as critic Alain-Gérard Slama has observed of several novels dealing with Algeria, nostalgia and desire impel memory not to "confront" but, rather, to "reject" history.[16]

But even as these films "reject" history, they also point, albeit indirectly, both to the weight of the past and to the shadow it casts over the present. For the troubled historical zones they seek to eclipse, zones marked not only by colonial racism and injustice but by the very notions of identity and "otherness," continue to make themselves felt in contemporary France. In this respect, it is important to remember that the fall of empire bears directly, and dramatically, upon one of today's most pressing issues: the nature of French identity. Indeed, the most obvious legacy of the French imperial past—that is, the huge influx into France of *Maghrébins*, or native inhabitants of former French colonies in North Africa—is at the core of debates about what it means to be "French" in a multicultural and multireligious society. For those who feel that a sense of national identity depends upon a homogeneous population, marked by a shared religion and culture, the presence of nearly five million Muslims is a cause for alarm. Will a huge Muslim population, it is asked, destroy the very fabric and traditions of French culture and society? Is Islam compatible with the principles of the French Republic? Can one be Muslim and French at the same time?[17]

French fears about African immigrants, and about what their presence implies for French identity, have also contributed to the disturbing rise of the largest extreme-Right party in Western Europe, *Le front national*.[18] In terms of the party itself, too, the long reach of the colonialist past is very much in evidence. Led by Jean-Marie Le Pen—a man who served in an elite paratrooper unit (not unlike the Green Berets) in Indochina and who never forgave de Gaulle for "losing" Algeria—*Le front national* has resurrected the racist mentality and rhetoric that marked French rule in Algeria.[19] Playing on the memory of France's humiliating defeat in that country, Le Pen is prone to warlike rhetoric suggesting that France is now being "invaded" by the forces of Islam.[20] Even as he urges a return to what Benjamin Stora, in an important study of the legacy of the Algerian War, calls the "mythic purity" of French identity, Le Pen embraces a brand of xenophobia in which it is no longer the "Jew," or no longer principally the Jew (Le Pen is by no means free of anti-Semitism), who threatens "eternal" France but, instead, the "Arab."[21]

If the colonialist past determines the current shape of xenophobic passions even as it fuels fears about French "identity," the "splintered memories" it left in its wake point to still another contemporary phenomenon: the shattering of national historical memory into the shards, the myths, embraced by particular social groups. This phenomenon is discussed at length in an important essay by Pierre Nora, "Entre mémoire et histoire," that I would like to explore at the conclusion of this chapter. For Nora's essay does not merely shed light on the rise of "private" memories like those seen in *Le crabe-tambour* and *Outremer*; it also shares with these films, I think, the melancholy longing for a vanished "golden age." And, far more explicitly than either *Le crabe-tambour* or *Outremer*, "Entre mémoire et histoire" makes clear the national contours—the lost tradition of memory and history that nourished "a certain idea" of France—of this longed-for past. In other words, whether consciously or unconsciously, "Entre mémoire et histoire" removes the veils that the myths permeating *Le crabe-tambour* and *Outremer* place over some of the most troubling zones of national history.

Legendary Narratives: *Le crabe-tambour*

In the "kaleidoscope" of memories concerning the struggle in Algeria, none, probably, has been more deeply felt, or more controversial and marginalized, than that associated with the military. The military discourse about Algeria has been "impossible," writes historian Claude Liazu, not only because it was "refused by other memories of French society" but also, and above all, because it contradicts "the nation's conscience and its national historical imaginary."[22] In large measure, what Liazu deems the "impossible" nature of the military discourse can be traced back to the conflict in Indochina. For it was at that time that military leaders first began to feel "betrayed" by a civilian government perceived as vacillating and weak—a government that denied them, in their eyes, the support necessary for victory. "It was in fact during the conflict in Indochina," writes historian Alain Ruscio, "that the 'army's malaise' began, an army betrayed by the civilian population, by politics, by defeatists."[23] Giving free rein to this "malaise," in a scathing 1956 memoir, General Henri Navarre, who had led the French forces in Indochina, warned that the country's loss of Indochina might presage a similar defeat in Algeria. Charging that the nation's statesmen and politicians had "never dared to show the country that there was a war in Indochina," Navarre accused them of stabbing "the army in the back" and of turning its soldiers into "sacrificial lambs."[24]

The "malaise" Navarre expresses so forcefully here become still more acute during the Algerian War: indeed, many military leaders viewed *le drame algérien* as a bitter replay of what had occurred in Indochina. The bravery and sacrifices of an entire generation of career officers, like those who figure in *Le crabe-tambour*, were rendered vain, they felt, by the nation's elected government. These profound feelings of bitterness finally erupted into dramatic confrontations between the military leaders in Algeria and the civilian government in Paris. On two occasions—the first in 1958, the second toward the end of the war in 1961—generals seized power in Algeria and threatened the elected government in Paris with a military coup d'état. Faced with the possibility of a coup in 1958, a frightened nation turned to General de Gaulle, the man who had "saved their honor" decades earlier, for leadership; three years later, in order to quell the second putsch attempt, which figures prominently in *Le crabe-tambour*, de Gaulle was compelled to issue radio appeals to enlisted men asking them to ignore the orders of rebellious officers.

Around the time of the second coup attempt, moreover, disaffected soldiers had begun to form a "secret army": the O.A.S., or *Organisation de l'armée secrète*; this group embraced violent tactics in its determination to maintain a "fraternal and French Algeria." Although perceived by others as terrorists—the O.A.S., writes Philip Cerny, was the "closest one can come in the history of twentieth-century France to identifying a genuine terrorist movement"[25]—they saw themselves as patriots not dissimilar to those who had served in the Resistance. "For us," recalls a former *pied-noir* who sympathized with the Secret Army, "the O.A.S. was the Resistance. . . . We were heroes, patriots. We were going to defend France who was in danger and who was losing her Empire. We were there to get France back on the right track."[26] To "get France back on the right track," the O.A.S. engaged in a spiral of violence that became increasingly frenzied, both in Algeria and on the mainland, as the war drew to an end. Showing the depth of the passions that prompted many to join the O.A.S., thirty years after the end of the war a former official, still unrepentant, justified its terrorist campaign thus: "We carried out some operations," he remarked. "Five thousand dead, perhaps six thousand. It is horrible but everything is horrible in a war."[27]

Passions so intense that dedicated patriots were moved to treason and terrorism are, not surprisingly, passions that have left indelible memories. And it is these memories that infuse the melancholy landscape of *Le crabe-tambour*. But at the same time, as suggested earlier, Schoendoerffer's film softens, transforms, these "impossible" memories so that the most disturbing aspects of the military discourse recede from view.[28] While the aborted coup is the emotional focus of remembered events, the events surrounding it remain indistinct and shadowy. What comes to the fore, instead, is the cluster of emotions—of solidarity and bravery, of betrayal and loss—associated with the military experience. Here, history is absorbed into an epic, timeless landscape of myth and legend even as the moment of imperial *gloire* becomes a kind of lost "golden age."

Like many of Schoendoerffer's characters, the leading protagonists of *Le crabe-tambour* are, or were, military men. As the film opens, two of them are stationed aboard a vessel of the French merchant marine that is crossing the North Atlantic. One, who narrates much of the film, is the ship's doctor; the other, a man whose mortal illness ensures that this will be his last journey, is her captain. Slowly, they become friends as they reminisce about their experiences; as they do so, flashbacks disrupt the present and transport us to the past that so clearly obsesses them. It was a time, we gradually learn, dominated by a former comrade of theirs named Wilsdorf. Presently captain of a fishing boat, Wilsdorf served with the doctor in Indochina and with the captain in Algeria.

As fragments of the past are brought to life—fragments to be pieced together with difficulty—we learn of the bleak and traumatic moment that dramatically altered both the captain's life and that of Wilsdorf. This critical moment was that of the aborted putsch of April 1961. At this time, the paths of the captain and Wilsdorf diverged radically: unlike the captain, Wilsdorf chose to join those comrades who rebelled against the Republic, an act that led to imprisonment and expulsion from the navy. While the captain refused to join the rebels' ranks, the sympathy he felt for their cause prompted him to promise Wilsdorf that, whatever the outcome of the putsch, he would leave the military. His subsequent failure to keep this promise, a failure he sees as a kind of betrayal, has troubled him ever since. On this, his last voyage, he wants nothing more than to bid his former comrade-in-arms a final adieu. In what is probably the film's climactic moment, the captain's wish is granted: for a brief instant his ship passes Wilsdorf's fishing vessel on the high seas, and the two men speak, from afar, one last time.

Even this brief summary suggests, surely, some of the deep-seated emotional currents that hint at the "impossible" discourse of the military. The protagonists, especially Wilsdorf, clearly resemble those veterans who came to be known as *les soldats perdus*: that is, the "lost soldiers" whose lives were shattered by their experiences in Indochina and, especially, Algeria. Behind their melancholy stoicism, one senses the bitterness and "malaise" of those warriors who felt abandoned, betrayed, by their country. Memories of sacrifices made in vain, of ambitions thwarted and crushed, haunt them. Reading from a cherished Bible, the captain repeats the question that must obsess them all: "Qu'as-tu fait de ton talent?" he sadly intones, "What have you done with your gifts?" Exiled from home and country, these former soldiers exist in a kind of limbo as they unceasingly journey from one end of the globe to another.

Aboard ship, the military virtues that guided them in the past—the codes of honor and stoicism, of bravery and solidarity, so obviously admired by Schoendoerffer—continue to hold sway. But, now, there is no foreign foe. There is only the sea: a long and beautiful sequence of the ship's prow breaking up ice floes embodies the harshness of their struggle against freezing temperatures, gales, and high seas. (Visually striking, *Le crabe-tambour* was shot by master cameraman Raoul Coutard.) But few of these men would exchange this struggle for the ease of civilian life. This is a sentiment the director appears to share: in sharp contrast with the harsh majesty of life at sea, the single view of Paris afforded us by *Le crabe-tambour* is imbued with the sense of a civilization in decline. Here, the narrator, who has recently returned from Indochina, wanders through a desolate *quartier* of prostitutes and seedy bars, its streets lined with peeling and ugly posters.

The decaying city seen in this sequence hints, surely, at the sense of national decline that the military associated with the end of empire. And there are still other suggestions that a certain world, a civilization, is reaching its end. It is hardly coincidental that the ship is bringing mail and medical assistance to the rocky island of St. Pierre off the Canadian coast: one of France's last colonies, this snow-clad coast is a barren reminder of an empire that once extended throughout North America.[29] Or that the broadcasts which issue forth from their radio describe the last spasms of another doomed colonial struggle—that of the war in Vietnam.

But the bleaker the present, the more the past seems to assume the glowing intensity of a lost paradise, a vanished "golden age." Significantly, perhaps, of all the films dealing with the colonial period, it is *Le crabe-tambour*—which springs from the most "impossible" memories—that does most to transform the past. In no other film is the contrast between past and present so stark, the loss of youthful hope and innocence so absolute. It is a contrast that points, of course, to the myth of the "golden age"; for, as Raoul Girardet observes in *Mythes et mythologies politiques*, this myth is always about the present as much as it is about the past. "Every evocation of a golden age," writes Girardet, "is based on a single, fundamental opposition: that of yesterday and today. . . . The present time is one of decay, disorder, corruption. . . . The 'time before' is one of greatness, of nobility, of a certain happiness."[30]

Casting its melancholy shadow over *Le crabe-tambour*, the wrenching contrast described by Girardet both governs and is underscored by the film's very structure. That is, we are made aware of the terrible chasm between "yesterday" and "today" every time a flashback takes us from the bleakness of a decaying present to the greatness of a seductive past. The cold and leaden skies of the North Atlantic are that much more icy and oppressive when compared with the dazzling sunlight and lush greens of a remembered Asia; the loneliness and isolation of the present that much more acute in contrast to the warmth and solidarity experienced in the past. The vast sweep of oceans, from the seas of the North Atlantic to those off the coast of Asia, underscores, renders concrete, the distance between two opposing worlds.

Seen in terms that are at once geographical, temporal, and existential, the contrast between past and present assumes a mythic, or absolute, cast. In this respect, it is telling that the flashbacks of memory rarely lead up to, flow into, the present. Instead, dramatic cuts—which shift from one end of the globe to another, from one life to another—emphasize the radical discontinuity of these two zones. Joined only by memory, past and present thus belong not to the world of temporality and history but to a kind of absolute realm consisting of "before" and "after." Infused with a metaphysical cast, the rupture between these disparate zones signals less a historical change, from a colonial order dominated by Europe to today's postcolonial world, than a fall from grace and innocence, an expulsion from paradise.

Even as memory turns the past into a lost paradise, it also attenuates, erases, the troubled, and troubling, realities of history. Seen through the lens of an all-powerful and transforming memory, Asia is not a killing field of mud and grenades, but a dreamlike land of soft mists and hazy rivers. "All these wars," writes director Schoendoerffer revealingly in a 1969 novel, "are sadly always the same: we slogged through the mud, we waited forever, we shot, they died. That is what war is. . . . But the wind has blown away the odor of the corpses, and all that remains in our memory is the blaze of youth."[31] Just as the brutalities of war are eclipsed by the "blaze of youth," the native inhabitants of Asia—the men and women whose presence is a reminder both of French defeat and of the historical scandal at the heart of colonialism—rarely make an appearance. And when they do, it is not as threatening, and ultimately victorious, opponents; rather, they hint, albeit indirectly, at the racial stereotypes nourished by the colonial imagination. One such scene, in particular, reflects what Martin Evans calls the myth of the colonial soldier's "superior, coherent, white masculinity."[32] In this sequence, Wilsdorf is captured by a black tribe off the coast of Africa. At first, he is their helpless prisoner, exhibited in a cage like a prized and rare specimen. But before long it is clear that he is both more intelligent and a better warrior than his captors: not only does he teach them to aim their guns (and thus kill their enemies) but he becomes their talismanic leader. While this scene evokes myths of white supremacy and native backwardness, still another sequence raises the specter of Asian cruelty and barbarism. Here, Wilsdorf visits a native village only to suddenly discover that some of the faces he sees around the fire belong to decapitated heads leering at him from spikes.

A reminder of Asian "otherness," this last scene may also be a deliberate echo of a critical episode in Joseph Conrad's *Heart of Darkness*. (Interestingly, this episode inspired certain scenes in both Malraux's 1930 novel, *La voie royale*, and in another film that does much to turn a divisive war—that of Vietnam—into myth: Francis Ford Coppola's *Apocalypse Now*.) And, indeed, throughout the film, echoes of romantic tales of adventure told by nineteenth-century novelists—by Conrad and Melville, by Jules Verne—tend to overshadow and transform remembered historical events. Wilsdorf himself embodies the fusion of legend and romance, of history and myth, that permeates the film. Historical allusions are not lacking: based on a celebrated French soldier who was imprisoned at the time of the putsch, Wilsdorf displays the heroic virtues of the French soldiers, or *centurions*, who fought bravely to extend the borders of empire. But he is also a romantic nineteenth-century adventurer, a latter-day T. E. Lawrence who has put home and country far behind him. "Vieille Europe, que le diable t'emporte" ("Old Europe, to hell with you"), he cries out as he prepares to sail a Chinese junk halfway around the world. Larger than life, from the outset he is set apart from others by dress and demeanor: strikingly handsome, when first seen he is dressed in gleaming white, a black cat in his arms, as he stands aboard a vessel that is steaming down a tropical river. (The exploits of the cat, who finds his master again after the latter is captured and then released from a prisoner-of-war camp, appear to match those of Wilsdorf himself.) As the film progresses, it becomes clear that Wilsdorf has performed deeds that are known, and admired, by seamen all over the globe. Indeed, whenever his name is mentioned, someone has still another of his exploits to recount, another tale to add to his legend. As François de la Bretèque observes, this indirect way of recounting Wilsdorf's life—that is, through flashbacks remembered by different people—reinforces the legendary aura that clings to the protagonist. "This remarkable *procédé*," writes the French critic, "confers a mythic aura upon [Wilsdorf] and transforms his search into a symbolic quest. He incarnates the past of each of the protagonists and, beyond that, of colonial France herself."[33]

In addition to the "mythic aura" surrounding the figure of Wilsdorf, still other aspects of the film reinforce what de la Bretèque sees as its "symbolic" dimension. The very fact that the same few characters repeatedly meet one another in totally different parts of the world turns the film into an epic drama that takes the entire globe for its stage. "The tragic and closed universe of *Le crabe-tambour*," to cite de la Bretèque once again, "extends to the dimensions of the planet. The frame of the action goes to the edges of the civilized world, in this North Sea which might be a metaphor for the Cold War."[34] Extending to the "edges of the civilized world," the film has the temporal and spatial sweep of an epic as it takes us from youth to old age and from one end of the globe to the other. In this mythic context, the current journey it portrays—a journey that takes the men from the Old World to the New even as it leads to the final act in the captain's life (the meeting with Wilsdorf)—assumes symbolic resonance. As compelling as the search for the great white whale in *Moby Dick* or the terrifying trek Conrad's protagonist takes into the heart of darkness, this voyage leaves the zone of history for that of myth. When the captain finally meets Wilsdorf, the legendary being who has haunted him for so many years, everything in the scene—the movement of the waves, the distance that separates the two ships—heightens the epic sense that inheres in their encounter. Even Wilsdorf's ship, which bears two painted eyes upon its prow in the Asian manner, appears a fabulous sea creature as it slowly comes into the captain's line of vision. If the final adieu of these two men inevitably recalls the political events that drove a wedge between former comrades, the ordeals endured by these *soldats perdus* become part of a larger meditation on human life. Imbued with all the melancholy of approaching separation and death, their meeting speaks, above all, of failed hopes and brave sacrifices, of exile and memory, of life and death. Here, human life, seen against the boundless and eternal landscape of the sea, is as brief as the greetings exchanged by passing ships.

Pied-noir Nightmares: *Outremer*

No less than *Le crabe-tambour*, Brigette Roüan's *Outremer* also bears witness to the power of memories both individual and collective. But whereas the heroic masculine world of *Le crabe-tambour* opens onto a landscape of epic and myth, the intensely female realm depicted in *Outremer* takes us into the dreamlike depths of the psyche. Focused on the lives of three *pied-noir* sisters living in Algeria at the time of its struggle for independence, Roüan's film consists of three successive narratives, each reflecting the viewpoint of a different sister, that return, as if driven by obsessions, to the same series of traumatic events which occurred during *les événements*.

As in a latter-day *Rashomon*, each sister's narrative casts a highly subjective and partial light on people and events: behavior that one sister views as vibrant and sensual appears, in the eyes of another, to be laced with currents of frustrated longing. This narrative strategy means that, as in the case of *Le crabe-tambour*—where the critical moment of the putsch had to be teased out of memory's folds—*Outremer* also forces us to decipher and reconstruct fragments of the past. Only gradually, with difficulty and uncertainty, do we begin to understand the complex psychological and social mechanisms that govern the sisters' inner lives and those of the colonial world in which they lived. But even as the mechanisms come into sharper and sharper focus, so, too, does it become clear that we have been presented with a certain version, a "legendary narrative," of the past. Showing how profoundly individual lives were affected by *le drame algérien*, this version points, unmistakably, to the ruling impulses of *pied-noir* memory.

The first narrative views events from the perspective of the oldest sister, Zon. On the surface, Zon leads what seems to be a highly conventional life: devoted to home and family, she is apparently deeply in love with her husband. But soon it is clear that disturbing emotional currents lie below the surface. Consumed by longing for her husband, she suffers greatly during the long periods when his duties as a naval officer take him away from home. When he is declared missing in action, Zon is unable to accept his death. Desperately unhappy, she makes a disturbing bargain with God: she will give up her children, she declares melodramatically, if only her husband will return to her. But, of course, he does not return. And, before long, Zon herself is taken ill with cancer. In a troubling deathbed scene, she is seen, dressed in her husband's uniform on the bed they have shared, writhing in spasms of agony (which have a strangely sexual cast) before she falls, lifeless, to the floor.

After Zon's death, the focus shifts to the second sister, Malène. (Malène is played by Roüan who was well known as an actress before making her directorial debut with *Outremer*.) Once again, on the surface all is well: Malène has made a "good" marriage with a wealthy man who adores her. But here, too, appearances are deceiving. Malène's husband turns out to be an ineffectual dreamer, and so, despite herself, she is forced to play the "man": that is, she must make all the decisions and do all the work on their beloved farm. It is, in fact, her attachment to this farm, which she refuses to leave despite escalating violence, that ultimately causes her death. For soon after she announces her determination to remain on the farm at all costs, she is killed in the course of an ambush—shot through the head by a bullet that was doubtless intended for her husband.

Only the third and youngest of the sisters, Gritte, refuses to follow the conventional path taken by her sisters. Spurning eligible and attractive suitors, she takes a Muslim rebel as a lover. But moral bravery does not spare her from violence and death. Quite the contrary. For she loses her lover, who is killed by French soldiers while coming to see her one night, as well as her sisters. The psychic toll of all the horror she has endured is made very clear in the final scene of the film. In a dramatic temporal ellipse, the violence-filled past finally gives way to the present: a scene of Gritte on the verge of leaving Algeria is followed by one of her standing, years later, in a Parisian church where she is about to be married. As the camera explores the vast nave, the past comes to life: the whispering voices of her dead sisters are heard even as their ghostly faces take shape, superimposed on the stone walls of the church. In this haunted atmosphere, all the death and violence Gritte has experienced seem to reach out into the present and smother it. Asked to take the marriage vows, Gritte cannot utter the necessary words; she is obviously unable to begin life anew, to put down new roots to replace those so brutally severed in the past. She remains mute, paralyzed. On this note of paralysis and suspended action, the credits appear on the screen, accompanied by the voices of little girls singing the ditties of childhood.

The conclusion of *Outremer* clearly recalls what might be seen as the formative historical moment of *pied-noir* memory: the traumatic instant when, like Gritte, thousands of men and women abandoned all they held dear to begin life anew as exiles. Describing this chaotic and desperate moment—when, in the summer of 1962, the ranks of *pied-noir* refugees arriving in France swelled to a million—Benjamin Stora writes that their departure took on the "magnitude of a human tide. Thousands of people, lost, stunned, totally destitute, awaited the boats. They had to flee as quickly as possible from this country to which they would remain attached in every fiber of their being."[35] But if this moment of exodus embodies the powerful charge of loss and exile at the heart of *pied-noir* memory, it is also a moment that, in *Outremer* as in other *pied-noir* narratives about the past, is almost always accompanied by a number of other distinct impulses or themes. Forming the "legendary narrative" of *pied-noir* memory, these impulses bear, not surprisingly, on the most troubling aspects of the colonial experience: the racist attitudes that allowed the settlers to seize the lands of native Algerians and to treat the latter as inferiors. Designed to veil or repress the most guilt-ridden facts of history, these impulses were aimed, in the words of Philip Dine, at legitimizing "European minority control of the colony."[36]

Even before the Algerian War came to an end, Pierre Nora, the future historian of national memory, probed the psychological mechanisms that, informing these themes, would later shape the contours of *pied-noir* memory. In a work published in 1961, *Les français d'Algérie*, Nora examined the conscious and unconscious system of emotions and beliefs underlying the racism displayed by *pieds-noirs* toward those whom they referred to as "Arabs." It was Nora's conviction that this racism was fueled by a complex mix of emotions—by guilt and fear, by repression and denial—that stemmed from the settlers' uneasy possession of Algerian lands. That is, in Nora's view, the *pieds-noirs* suffered, on the one hand, from the repressed knowledge that they had stolen the Arabs' land; and, on the other, from the unacknowledged fear that what had been stolen might be repossessed at any moment. Prey to this continual and often unacknowledged anxiety, the Europeans in Algeria, observed Nora, became ever more fiercely attached to their beloved farms and homesteads. But at the same time, the fear and guilt they experienced toward this stolen land also gave rise to repression and denial when it came to Arabs themselves. Thus Europeans tried to ignore the presence, the very being, of those whom they had wronged. "The French of Algeria," observed Nora, "have refused [to give] any independent reality to Arabs [and] have denied their existence."[37] This meant—and here Nora described the basic impulse not only of *pied-noir* racism but of all racism—that the *pieds-noirs* viewed Arabs as a group but never as individuals. Their racism, he declared, "is a way of not seeing an Arab except through the distorting prism of his group—of a group from which nothing in the world can pry him loose."[38]

Little more than thirty years after Nora wrote these lines, historian Anne Roche set out to discern the general shapes that *pied-noir* memory had assumed. To do so, she conducted a series of interviews with former *pieds-noirs* who had settled in France. Her interviews allowed her to observe an important phenomenon that, for Nora, was still well in the future. That is, Roche was struck by the depth and the persistence of trauma in *pieds-noirs* who had come to France more than a generation earlier.[39] But in other respects her findings appear to confirm the observations Nora had made toward the end of the war. In other words, her interviews pointed to the persistence of the complex mechanisms of repression and denial, of guilt and racism, that were probed so subtly in *Les français d'Algérie*.

For example, when Roche questioned her subjects about their former lives in Algeria, it was clear that repression was still very much at work: they felt impelled to deny the enormous social gap that had separated colonizer from colonized in Algeria. Hence they remembered Algeria as a "paradise without colonial sin," as a land where everyone, Arabs and Europeans alike, lived in harmony and plenty. When confronted with the obvious discrepancy between these happy memories of an "idyllic world" and the brutal facts of rebellion and war—between what Nora calls "the kind Algeria" of everyday life and the "cruel Algeria of History"—they attempted to reconcile the two by establishing a dichotomy distinguishing a few individual "good" Arabs (who proved that French rule was a beneficient one) from the vast majority of Arabs who belonged to what they saw as "a mass [that was] undifferentiated, confusing, and probably manipulated."[40] (In Nora's view, the perceived need for "good" Arabs whose presence might justify the colonial system was so keenly felt that Europeans would have "invented" such beings had none existed.)[41] Not unexpectedly, when it came to the Arabs' struggle for independence, the weight of denial and repression was most in evidence. Although, for example, Roche's subjects could recall the details of daily life in Algeria with "myopic concentration," their recollections of historical and political events were hazy and confused. Prone to ignore the precise outlines of the convulsions that had overtaken Algeria, they lacked, writes Roche, a sense of the "different phases of the war [and] a synthesizing view of the forces at work."[42]

The complicated mechanisms of repression and denial explored by Roche and Nora—especially in those critical areas that bear upon *pied-noir* attitudes toward Algerians and the historical nature of their struggle for independence—are, I think, central to *Outremer*. This is not to say that the film embraces every aspect of *pied-noir* memory. On the contrary: in certain respects, *Outremer* criticizes *pied-noir* attitudes or, at the very least, takes an ironic stance toward them. This is the case, for example, when it comes to the sisters' desire to see themselves as "French." (What Philip Dine describes as "a preoccupation with being French and loving France" was, in fact, widespread in the *pied-noir* community. As he observes, the "Frenchness" of the *pieds-noirs* provided a source of communal identity even as it legitimized France's control of Algeria.)[43] Although the sisters consider themselves French, they regard a visitor from France as an "outsider" who cannot really understand their problems or share their perspective. They may speak of France in tones of awe and longing, and emulate French fashion, but the viewer is well aware that it is Algeria which is their real home, their true country. It is Algerian soil to which, as in the case of the second sister, the *pieds-noirs* are so passionately attached. Their modes of behavior and thought, their deepest concerns, are those of a separate community, of a people distinct from their compatriots on the mainland. Recurrent shots of the ocean that separates them from the mainland, and which renders them a colony that is "overseas" or "outremer," serve to underscore their distance, at once emotional and geographical, from France.

But the critical distance that the film maintains in regard to the "Frenchness" of the sisters vanishes, I think, when it comes to other, more emotionally charged, zones of the past. It is here than the uneasy mixture of emotions discerned by Nora and Roche comes into play. For behind the obvious ambivalences voiced by the characters in respect to France, or the conflicting feelings of superiority and inferiority they experience as "colonial" subjects, lie still other ambivalances. Frequently embedded deep within the formal strategies deployed by the film, these ambivalences— which are unacknowledged, perhaps unconscious—lead into the most guilt-ridden zones of the colonial past: that is, they bear upon the all-important relationship between the Europeans who settled in Algeria and the native inhabitants of that land. And it is when *Outremer* touches on these vital zones that, significantly, the objective or critical distance which allowed us to judge the characters' attitudes toward lesser matters (such as, say, their presumed "Frenchness") seems to disappear. Here, instead, we are led into some of the darkest layers of memory even as the director's vision merges, almost imperceptibly, with that of her characters. Drawn into the intensely subjective and private universe of the sisters, we are made to see the world through their eyes—eyes that softened, transformed, the most brutal realities of the historical past.

To a large degree, the very form of the film is designed to promote ambivalences, to erode a sense of critical or objective distance. For virtually every aspect of *Outremer* works to draw us away from the shared realm of history, characterized by temporal markers and a conscious chronology, into the subjective world of memory and dream. In this respect, the differences between *Outremer* and, say, a film such as *L'amant*—which also views the past through an intensely female perspective—are telling. Unlike *Outremer*, *L'amant* frames the past with sequences set in the present: in this manner, it creates an objective distance or space from which long-vanished events and feelings can be evaluated. For example, as the elderly narrator in *L'amant* thinks back to a passionate affair she had with a Chinese man when she was barely an adolescent, she creates a distance between the woman she has become and the young girl she once was. She remembers not only the intensity of their affair but also the racial caste system that infiltrated and undermined passion itself.

Outremer, in contrast, offers no similar objective space from which the past can be confronted. Instead, the obsessive repetitions inherent in the tripartite narrative structure, as well as the elliptical and mysterious nature of each narrative, give rise to an atemporal world of primal moments infused with love and passion, with longing and desire. Shifting perspectives and temporal gaps, mysteries that are not always elucidated by a subsequent narrative, all work to disorient the viewer and to deny him or her the sense of a clearly defined context, an ordered chronology, necessary to a historical overview. True, certain critical dates—1947, 1949, 1957—are mentioned; extracts are heard from a famous speech de Gaulle made to the *pied-noir* community in which he gave them ambiguous reassurances that were later taken as a sign of his "betrayal." But these fleeting historical allusions mean little to the viewer who is not already conversant with the Algerian past. While the film portrays a climate of escalating violence, the complex nature of this violence—the precise sequence of events, the clash of opposing forces, the ideological conflicts—is never brought into focus.

All this means that the vision of the past emerging from *Outremer* is one marked not by the precise contours of history but, instead, by the displacements and ellipses, the repetitions and fragmented images, of dreams. The oneiric cast of Roüan's film is dramatically announced in its mysterious opening sequence; repeated at critical junctures throughout the film, this dreamlike sequence becomes a kind of haunting leitmotif. A shot of barbed wire glimpsed through the credits is followed by one of three young women in a small boat waving to someone. Abruptly, this gives way to a close-up of a man in a white military uniform. For a moment, it seems as if the young women were waving to this man; but the next shot, in which the same man is seen in a black uniform on the deck of a ship, makes it clear that this was not the case. Instead of establishing us in space and time, this opening has given rise to a series of perplexing questions: Who and where are these women? to whom are they waving and why? Long before these questions are answered, the cluster of emotions conveyed by the images—a sense of limbo (a directionless boat on the open sea); of claustrophobia (the barbed wire); of lost innocence (the three young girls in the boat); of exile and separation (the sea)—will have imprinted themselves on the viewer.

Marked, as this sequence suggests, by the logic of dreams, *Outremer* also bears upon intimate memories whose very nature leads away from the outer world and into the hidden corners of the psyche, to the disturbing impulses that lie below the surface of everyday life. It is almost as if the convulsions of history have been repressed on a conscious level only to turn inward and to invade the sisters' very bodies. Hence the women seem prey to uneasy sexuality, to violent urges that well up from the depths of the unconscious. Obscure sexual currents give rise to disturbing, little-understood, behavior: despite her seemingly intense attachment to her husband, the oldest sister encourages the attentions of another man (and then chastises herself for being "abnormal"); prompted by frustration and anger, the middle sister sets fire to the farm she loves; the youngest sister refuses to sleep with her fiancé and then gives herself to a rebel she hardly knows. Focused intently on the innermost lives of the sisters, *Outremer* takes us away from the public realm and into hidden crevices of fear and desire where feelings condition perception itself. Even time is subject to the play of emotions, the pull of fear or desire. "Sometimes," writes critic Jacques Siclier, "time is suspended in illusions, sometimes it stretches out as a result of specific dangers and changes in the Franco-Arab relationship."[44]

As Siclier suggests, *Outremer* is obviously at its most subjective, its most ambiguous and elliptical, when it comes to the most guilty, and most repressed, zones of memory: those scenes that portray the relationship between *pieds-noirs* and native Algerians. And it is here, significantly, that the power of cinema to express political myths which resist clear articulation comes into sharpest focus: largely through formal strategies, the film itself reveals, embodies, the fundamental pattern of repression and denial that *pieds-noirs* displayed when confronted with the reality of Muslims and their struggle. On the surface, of course, *Outremer* appears to criticize these attitudes, to condemn racism. Thus not only does it appear to mock the sisters' racist remarks, but it depicts a love affair, between a European woman and an Algerian native, that breaks one of the most fundamental taboos of the colonial system. Still, when it comes to what we *see* rather than what we hear or are told, disturbing ambiguities and omissions begin to make themselves felt. Racist remarks may often appear ludicrous; still, when Algerians themselves are seen, they invariably correspond to *pied-noir* stereotypes: shadowy and menacing, they suddenly materialize from nowhere and mutter among themselves in a conspiratorial fashion. It might be argued, of course, that we are seeing them from a *pied-noir* perspective: that is, they *appear* menacing to the sisters and other Europeans. But there are no indications that we are seeing Algerians through their eyes, through their fears. Without such indications, we have no reason to question the reality of what is seen. This means that for us, too, native Algerians lose all individuality and become faceless members of a conspiratorial and frightening group or, as Roche has it, an "undifferentiated mass."

The suspicion that this portrayal of Algerians reflects the director's own ambivalence(s), whether conscious or unconscious, is confirmed, moreover, by several critical scenes. At one point, for example, the laborers on the middle sister's farm begin to express discontent, to mutiny, when they receive their meager wages from her. Confronted with their anger, the sister expresses great surprise and protests that she cannot help them; it is her husband, she says, who determines their wages. Although our initial reaction is one of sympathy—she is, after all, a woman in danger—upon reflection disturbing questions come to mind. For the film has clearly established that she, and not her husband, runs the farm. Why, then, does she immediately blame him? Since she appears genuinely shocked and distressed, it is difficult to take her response as a calculated and self-protective lie. But that leaves only one conclusion: she *believes* in her professed innocence precisely because she desperately wants to ignore, to repress, the terrible truths of social injustice. Like those interviewed by Roche, she too wants to believe that everyone in Algeria, including the laborers on her farm, lived in harmony and plenty. And doesn't the profoundly ambiguous nature of this scene, which invites us both to believe her and to sympathize with her plight, suggest that the director herself shares this thirst for innocence?

In this respect, it is telling that the scenes depicting the forbidden love affair between the youngest sister, Gritte, and the Muslim rebel are the most ambiguous and elliptical of the entire film. It is true, of course, that the affair might well be seen as a star-crossed, tragic love which sets into stark relief the absurdity and brutality of the war. But even if it is interpreted in this fashion, it nonetheless hints at one of the most disturbing myths of the colonial imagination: that which bears upon Arab sexuality. "There is a knife," declares philosopher Cornélius Castoriadis, "between the Algerians and the French. . . . And this knife is the French *imaginaire* about *Maghrébins* and, in particular, about Algerians in connection with murder and sexuality."[45] To a limited extent, this "knife" was undoubtedly sharpened by historical circumstances: that is, the rebels did use rape and multilation as terrorist tactics. But fears of Arab sexuality began long before the outbreak of war and bore almost exclusively on scenarios that were

imaginary rather than real. As historian John Talbott points out, contacts
between European women and Arab men—contacts at the very heart of
such fears—were virtually nonexistent. Noting that marriages between Europeans and Arabs were "rare" and that "illicit relationships were unheard
of," Talbott writes that "sexual encounters between Europeans and Algerians were limited to the furtive meetings of homosexuals and the commercial transactions of prostitutes."[46]

In portraying an "unheard-of" relationship between a European woman
and a native Algerian man, *Outremer* might seem to be denouncing European fears and myths about Arab sexuality. But closer observation reveals
that the image of the *Maghrébin* as powerful sexual "other" does indeed
hover, indistinctly but unmistakably, over Gritte's passionate affair. Significantly, the Arab rebel is portrayed differently from the other men in
the film. For unlike the others, Gritte's Muslim rebel lacks a clearly marked
identity, a psychological profile that would define him as more than an
"Arab," more than a "lover." Mute and spectral, he is but an icon of passion,
a symbol of the double threat—of sexuality and of violence—that clung to
Algerians in the European imagination. Silent, rough, and grimy, in what
appears to be the couple's second encounter (although even this is not
made clear), he suddenly appears on the road next to Gritte and wordlessly
pulls her toward him as if he meant her bodily harm. After this episode,
they are seen together for the briefest of sequences. Since Gritte's sisters
have been depicted with their husbands in intimate moments, this omission
is telling and disquieting. Does it mean that even the director cannot imagine how an Algerian and a Frenchwoman would behave together? Or what
they would talk about? Or does the silence of the film reflect the taboos
clinging to the affair? Furthermore, it is odd that in a film which dissects
the slightest tremor of the psyche, the motives for this crucial affair remain
opaque: is her passion for him mixed with rebellion? guilt? And his love
for her is even more mysterious. Is it motivated by revenge? the color of
her skin? These questions remain unanswered for at least two important
and telling reasons: first, because we never see them interact as a couple;
and second, because the man is deprived of those traits that would bring
him to life not only as a lover but, indeed, as a human being.[47]

The mysteries and ambiguities surrounding Gritte's love for an Arab rebel
reveal, I think, how profoundly *pied-noir* memory infuses *Outremer*. Bearing
witness to the pattern of denial and repression observed by historians such
as Nora and Roche, this aspect of the film suggests that, perhaps despite
herself, the director cannot, or will not, confront the darkest zones of the
past, the most inadmissable of historical truths. In this sense, the silence
that shrouds Gritte's doomed and passionate affair corresponds to the absence of the putsch in *Le crabe-tambour*. In both instances, erasures and

silences, which blur and repress the most troubling zones of the past, point to the divide between the brutal events of history and the transformations wrought by memory. At the heart of the divergent memories seen in *Le crabe-tambour* and *Outremer*, these transformations become increasingly fixed or "ritualized," as Benjamin Stora has it, with each new retelling. In this sense, these memories, which always feature the repetition of certain moments and events that take their assigned place in a "legendary organization of the past," resist evolving meanings and changing interpretations. Bearing on history and memory, they involve nothing less—as Stora remarks of several autobiographical books dealing with Algeria—than a "sterilization of historiography" and "the decline of real memory."[48]

Golden Ages: "Between Memory and History"

To a great degree, the shape assumed by memory in *Le crabe-tambour* and *Outremer*—its distance from history, its ritualized and private cast, the melancholy nostalgia it exudes—is analyzed at length, albeit in a very different context, by Pierre Nora in his introductory essay to *Les lieux de mémoire*: "Entre mémoire et histoire." But this is not the only reason that I would like to turn to this very influential essay at this point. For "Entre mémoire et histoire" does more than explore the nature and function of ritualized memories like those seen in *Le crabe-tambour* and *Outremer*; as suggested earlier, it also displays some of the defining impulses of both films. Permeated by the mood of inexorable decline that haunts these works, "Entre mémoire et histoire" is filled with melancholy longing for a lost "golden age." And, far more explicitly than either film, Nora's essay makes it clear that this vanished moment is one that corresponds to a certain era of the national past.

In fact, despite its title, "Entre mémoire et histoire" is less an analysis of the relationship between "memory" and "history" than an elegiac meditation, in which both terms assume a variety of guises, on the loss of a tradition of national historical memory and on the disappearance of a "certain idea of a France." "Everything is good when it emerges from the hand of the Creator," declares Rousseau in the well-known opening paragraphs of his treatise on education, *Emile*; "everything degenerates in the hands of man." Echoing both these Rousseauistic cadences, as well as the philosopher's evocation of a lost "golden age," Nora begins "Entre mémoire et histoire" with a ringing declaration of loss. But here, what has been lost is not Rousseau's natural paradise but a tradition of memory. "We speak so much about memory," Nora declares, "only because it is no longer there."[49]

To examine why memory "is no longer there," Nora, like Rousseau, casts his gaze backward in time as he surveys the stages of loss. He begins by

describing what might be seen as an Edenic moment of memory, one
marked by the "true" memories of "primitive" or "archaic" peoples. "True"
in that such memories fulfilled what Nora sees as the archetypal function
of memory: that is, they transmitted values from one generation to another.
In so doing, they connected people not only to their immediate ancestors
but, beyond them, to "the undifferentiated time of heroes, origins, and
myths."[50] With the collapse of traditional rural societies, and the "acceleration" of history, however, "true" memory received mortal blows. Expelled
from the original paradise of "true memory," man was forced to enter the
world of history: a world devoid of memory's "lived link with an eternal
present." Describing this original fall from grace, in an eloquent passage,
Nora draws the following contrast between "memory" and "history."
"Memory," he declares,

> is life, embodied in living societies. . . . History, on the other hand, is the recon-
> struction, which is always incomplete and problematic, of what no longer exists.
> Memory is always a phenomenon of the present . . . history a representation of
> the past. . . . History, because it is an intellectual and secular phenomenon, calls
> for analysis and critical discourse. Memory installs recollections in a sacred con-
> text. . . . Memory is rooted in the concrete: in spaces, gestures, images, and ob-
> jects. History is bound to temporal continuities, to evolutions, and to relations
> of things. Memory is absolute while history is . . . relative.[51]

This passage leaves little doubt that Nora considers history but a poor
cousin, a lifeless relation, to memory. Memory is alive, concrete, sacred;
history, instead, is an intellectual exercise, a mere reconstruction of the
past. But despite this fundamental divide, there was a period, continues
Nora, when history managed to draw close to memory. Describing this
period, Nora takes us from the universal past of "archaic" peoples to the
stage of French history. In doing so, he gradually allows us to see that his
real concern is not memory per se but, instead, the transformations which
have changed the shape of *French* memory and history in the course of the
last century. As he examines these transformations, it becomes clear that
the "golden age" which shines so brightly in this essay is less the mythical
moment of "true" memory than it is the shape and role assumed by memory—or what Nora calls "*histoire-mémoire*"—in nineteenth-century France.

The very term *histoire-mémoire*, or history-memory, is telling: indeed, it
suggests why Nora looks back with such nostalgia to the last century. For
Nora believes that, at that time, the nation's history provided the sense
of unity and continuity, the dimension of "sacredness," that had formerly
accrued to "true" memory. This was especially true, he believes, during the
era of the Third Republic, when the trauma of defeat and virtual civil war
prompted a period of intense national soul-searching and a meditation on
the very meaning of *la patrie*. "By means of history and in terms of the

Nation," writes Nora, "a tradition of memory seemed to crystallize in the . . . Third Republic."[52] Providing the sense of deep continuity once furnished by the memories of "archaic" peoples, national historical memory or *histoire-mémoire* saw the history of France as a continuum stretching from the Greek and Roman "cradle" of the nation's birth to its most glorious years of empire. During this period, every aspect of the nation, "the political, the military, the biographical, and the diplomatic," became a "pillar" of continuity. The sense of "sacredness" that clung to the nation extended to its history—"Histoire sainte parce que nation sainte"—even as the historian, as the guardian of this sacred tradition, was both "priest" and "soldier."[53]

But, like all "golden ages," the happy moment of *histoire-mémoire* that marked the Third Republic was not destined to endure. The fall from grace was gradual but inexorable. As the idea of the Nation as a sacred entity, based on shared traditions and values, gave way to that of a diverse and secular "Society"—or to what Americans might call a multiethnic and multicultural society—France's historical memory lost both its national role and its sacred dimension. It was, Nora implies, during the intense ideological conflicts of the 1930s, under the "pressure of a new secularizing force," that "history was transformed, spectacularly in France, from the tradition of memory that it had become into the self-knowledge of society."[54] In losing its "national identity," history also lost, as a consequence, its pedagogical vocation and its sacredness. Unable to transmit values, it no longer served as a vital bridge, a link, interconnecting past, present, and future. No longer imbued with the "conscience of the collectivity," or enrolled in the service of the nation, "history became a social science; memory a purely private phenomenon."[55]

The void left by the disappearance of national historical memory has been filled, continues Nora as he nears the present day, by the rise of "private" memories, or what he calls "les mémoires particulières." Such memories differ from the *histoire-mémoire* of the last century in that they reflect the experience, and ensure the continuity, not of the nation but of different social groups. ("The end of history-memory," writes Nora, "has multiplied individual memories that demand their own history.")[56] Bound together by virtue of a shared historical experience (like that which unites the *pieds-noirs*), or by religious or ethnic affinities, such groups depend upon "les mémoires particulières" for a vital sense of communal identity and cohesion.[57] But while acknowledging the critical role such memories play in this respect, Nora leaves no doubt that they represent a loss, a decline, when compared to the tradition of *histoire-mémoire* that characterized France in the last century. Not only are these shards of "private" memories more limited in scope than national historical memory, but, says Nora, they are also different in kind. For in losing its national character and mission, memory also underwent, he asserts, a fundamental metamorphosis. Tracing the beginnings of this transformation back to the era of Proust and Bergson, Nora declares that when memory left the realm of the nation, it underwent a shift from the "historical to the psychological, from the social to the individual. . . . The total psychologization of contemporary memory has led to a conspicuously new economy in the identity of the self, in the mechanisms of memory, and the relationship to the past."[58]

As this last remark suggests, what Nora views as the "new economy" of memory manifests itself in three distinctive ways. The first of these bears upon what he calls the "identity of the self." He maintains that whereas collective memory offered a spontaneous link with the past, people experience *la mémoire particulière* as a "devoir" or a "duty" precisely because they depend upon private memories for a sense of identity.[59] And this "duty" to remember leads, in turn, to what Nora considers the second defining characteristic of contemporary memory. That is, impelled by the "internal coercion" to remember, people create "archives" or "sites of memory" in which to preserve every shred or fragment of the past. But the very creation of such sites—which range from monuments and museums to symbolic commemorations and celebrations—is imbued with a terrible paradox: the conscious and deliberate attempt to preserve the past means that we are irretrievably distanced from it.

It is precisely this sense of "distance" that constitutes the last—and, in some sense, the most important—defining characteristic of contemporary memory. For the "distance" from the past that prompts the dutiful creation of mnemonic "sites" also suggests the futility of our attempts to truly remember, to seize and capture the past. Characterized by their "distance" from the past, contemporary "sites of memory" offer neither the spontaneous link with the past that distinguished the "archaic" memories of traditional societies nor the sense of sacredness that historical memory drew from the Nation. Instead, they bear witness to the absolute discontinuity that separates us from what has gone before. "We no longer study the nation," declares Nora; "we study its celebrations."[60] As hollow as they are monumental, the "places of memory" are but reminders, vestiges, of what has vanished. They are, declares the historian in a revealing passage,

> the testimonial markers of another age, illusions of eternity. That is what makes these pious undertakings seem like exercises in nostalgia, sad and lifeless. They are the rituals of a society without ritual. . . . Sites of memory are born and nourished by the sense that there is no spontaneous memory, that archives must be created. . . . that without commemorative vigilance, they would be quickly swept away by history.[61]

Hence not only is modern memory lived as a "duty" and embodied in "sites" and "archives," but, despite everything, it is marked by a "distance" from the very past it strains to embrace. Underscoring this sense of distance, an eloquent Nora declares that modern memory views the past as "radically other; it is the world from which we are forever cut off. And the essence of memory lies in showing the extent of this separation."[62]

In describing the "essence" of contemporary memory, Nora might well be discussing the ghost-haunted memories of *Le crabe-tambour* and *Outremer*. For there is no doubt that both films illustrate what Nora views as the "new economy," the "total psychologization," of contemporary memory. Marked by constant blurrings of the historical context, by an insistence on primal moments, by private and subjective images, the memories seen in these films turn away from the shared stage of national history. Embodying the "mémoires particulières," the "legendary narratives," vital to specific social groups, these memories emphasize not the continuity between past and present—the sense that the past can offer guidelines and inspiration for the present and, indeed, the future—but the absolute rupture between these two zones. In both works, past and present are separated by a radical discontinuity: a traumatic moment divides the world of "before" from that of "after."

But if *Le crabe-tambour* and *Outremer* testify to a sense of absolute rupture, of discontinuity, so, too, I think, does "Entre mémoire et histoire." That is, as suggested earlier, I believe that Nora's view of the French past and of the changing forms assumed by national memory and history is itself imbued with what he sees as the defining features, so vividly illustrated in *Le crabe-tambour* and *Outremer*, of *la mémoire particulière*. No less than either film, "Entre mémoire et histoire" is punctuated by a sense of rupture, of "distance," from a cherished past. Moreover, far more than either film, Nora's essay brings into relatively sharp focus the disquieting political issues that surround the nostalgia for a vanished world permeating both films. In so doing, it brings us back to an issue that, as suggested earlier, is deeply rooted in France's colonial past: that of French identity.

Of these various currents, the sense of radical discontinuity between past and present that marks Nora's essay is, perhaps, the most obvious. For there is absolutely no doubt in Nora's mind that an unbreachable chasm separates French "historical memory" of the last century from the multiplicity of today's social memories. Nor does he harbor any doubt that this represents an irreversible degradation of memory and history. In this sense, like both films, "Entre mémoire et histoire" also bears witness to what Raoul Girardet describes as the fundamental "theme" of the myth of the "golden age": the "apprehension of human history as a process of irremediable decadence."[63] The contrast between the "sacred" tradition of *histoire-mémoire* that flowered in nineteenth-century France and the profane and hollow shards of contemporary French memory is as absolute, as wrenching, as that which separates the survivors of both films from their former lives. Nora's very vocabulary is calculated to underscore the absolute nature of this divide. The "rituals of a society without rituals," contemporary *lieux de mémoire* are, he insists, the "vestiges" and "traces" of a past that is "definitively dead" and "radically other."

In "Entre mémoire et histoire," of course, the melancholy contrast between the plenitude of the past and the emptiness of the present—a contrast that indicates, and embodies, the "irremediable decadence" of history—is discussed in terms of memory. But it is clear that the downward path traveled by French memory points to a much broader social and political phenomenon: the decline of the nation itself or, at least, the decline of a "certain idea of France." In other words, "Entre mémoire et histoire" is imbued with the deep sense of national decline that permeates not only *Le crabe-tambour* and *Outremer* but other films of the colonial cycle. The "historical memory" Nora describes in such glowing terms was rooted in, belonged to, a "sacred nation" with a "sacred history." In contrast with contemporary France, marked by a proliferation of heterogeneous social groups and varying private memories, the nineteenth-century nation described in "Entre mémoire et histoire" was one in which children were taught to venerate *la patrie* even as historians, charged with transmitting the nation's *histoire-mémoire*, became its soldiers and its priests.

Transformed into a kind of "golden age" of French memory and history, in "Entre mémoire et histoire" the Third Republic begins to assume a mythic hue. Just as *Le crabe-tambour* and *Outremer* softened the brutal realities of recent French history, Nora's essay similarly draws a veil over the difficulties and struggles that marked the late nineteenth century. Indeed, his essay seems to confirm Girardet's observation that in France the myth of the "golden age" often goes hand in hand with still another fundamental French myth: that of "unity," or what Girardet describes as "the dream of a fraternal community, liberated from internal divisions."[64] For Nora's portrait of the Third Republic, this "golden age" of memory and history, never refers to the deep national fault lines that erupted at this time. From "Entre mémoire et histoire" one would never know that the Third Republic was born in the ashes of the Commune, or that it set the stage for the bitter battles of the Dreyfus Affair.

Even as the mythic portrait of the Third Republic that emerges from "Entre mémoire et histoire" ignores the fault lines of the past, it also points to some of the most hotly debated questions of the present. It is here, in fact, that Nora's essay brings into focus some of the disquieting political and social issues that only hover around the edges of *Le crabe-tambour* and *Outremer*. For unlike those films, in which the period of "before" is bathed in a haze of longing and desire, Nora locates it in a specific era of the French past; at the same time, he endows it with definite political and social contours. As described in "Entre mémoire et histoire," the "golden age" of French history and memory is essentially defined by cultural and religious homogeneity. And the nostalgia that Nora so obviously feels for this period of homogeneity—when "symbiotic" links connected the "nation" to its "memory" and its "history"—raises the very issues that are at the heart of contemporary debates bearing upon cultural diversity and French identity.

To begin with, Nora appears to ignore the price paid for that homogeneity. In other words, confident that the *histoire-mémoire* of the nation is superior to the "private" memories of different social groups, he makes no mention of the divergent and/or marginal social groups that have lost their memories, and their identities, with the advance of French civilization. For historians who set less value on the homogeneity of national memory, that loss is a significant one. For example, casting a jaundiced eye on the kind of all-encompassing national memory extolled by Nora, Marc Ferro points out that "national consciousness was born from the annihilation of the specific past of different communities. Like the economic and social revolution of the nineteenth century, schools, railroads, and centralization have ruined the social memory of entire communities . . . they have seen their language devalued, their identity dissolved."[65]

Looking at this same issue from a somewhat more theoretical viewpoint, American historian Robert Gildea calls into question the very notion of a single tradition of French national memory or *histoire-mémoire*. In contrast with Nora, Gildea argues that there have always been "competing" memories in France—the very kind of "private" memories that, in Nora's view, have arisen only in recent decades. Moreover, Gildea insists on the political imperatives behind all memories. Toward the beginning of a study of French history and memory, *The Past in French History*, Gildea tells us that his work is based on the following two premises: "First, that there is no single French collective memory but parallel and competing collective memories elaborated by communities which have experienced and handled the past in different ways. And second, that the past is constructed not objectively but as myth, in the sense not of fiction, but of a past constructed collectively by a community in such a way as to serve the political claims of that community."[66]

It seems to me that Nora's vision of the French past is, in the end, firmly rooted in what Gildea would call the realm of "political claims." On the one hand, his glorified portrait of nineteenth-century France, of a country dominated by a single tradition of memory and history, draws perilously close to what Stora, in a remark cited earlier, called the "purity of mythic identity." On the other, the dismay seemingly inspired in him by the sight of the proliferating memories of diverse social and cultural groups raises disquieting social and political questions. One wonders, for example, how *Maghrébins* living in France today would respond to Nora's implicit lament for a traditional society of homogeneous people and values. Or how they would feel about his suggestion that *les mémoires particulières* of different groups are inferior to the "true" collective memory of the nation-state. The specter of right-wing thought that infuses Nora's paean to *histoire-mémoire* is reinforced, moreover, by a passage in which he appears to blame the loss of a tradition of national memory (what he calls the "demise of national history") not on the decline of French prestige since the 1940s but, instead, on the "ideological battles of the 1930s." In other words, it would seem that it is not the humiliation of defeat and Occupation, or the loss of empire, that has provoked the discontinuities of contemporary memory but the socialist and Republican ideals of the Popular Front.[67]

Far more explicitly than in the case of either *Le crabe-tambour* or *Outremer*, then, Nora's essay reveals some of the disquieting political implications behind today's longing for a "golden age" of the national past. But even as "Entre mémoire et histoire" opens onto the political landscape of contemporary France, it also illustrates, perhaps, an observation Nora himself made years earlier. "Historical memory," he declared in 1974, "filters, accumulates, amasses, and transmits; collective memory momentarily preserves the remembrance of an experience that cannot be transmitted, erasing and recomposing it at will and in accord with the demands of the moment, the laws of the imaginary, and the return of the repressed."[68] It is, I think, this "recomposition" that is effected not only in *Outremer* and *Le crabe-tambour* but in "Entre mémoire et histoire" itself. In all these works, memory—as if reacting to contemporary anxieties and to an overwhelming sense of decline—creates the vision of a lost and mythic world more real, perhaps, than the present. In so doing, it leaves no doubt that memory is about not only the past but also, and perhaps above all, the present.

VI

A la recherche du temps perdu: The Specter of Populism

The "Cinéma du Look"

The melancholy contrast between past and present that permeates the works discussed in the preceding chapter also characterizes the films that I would like to turn to at this point: notably *Diva* (1981) and *La lune dans le caniveau* (*The Moon in the Gutter*, 1983), both by Jean-Jacques Beineix, *Les amants du Pont-Neuf* (1991) by Leos Carax, and *Delicatessen* (1991) by Jean-Pierre Jeunet and Marc Caro. But here the past that gives rise to such intense nostalgia has become even more remote and spectral. For unlike virtually all the films discussed thus far, those explored in the following pages are concerned not with the "real" past but, rather, with that of cinema itself. Filled with allusions to beloved classics of the 1930s—to films by René Clair and Jean Vigo, and by Jean Renoir and Marcel Carné—they hark back, in fact, to what is often seen as the "golden age" of French cinema. But in evoking this "golden age" of cinema, they also recall the social fabric in which it was embedded. In so doing, they call to mind an earlier France even as they demonstrate how surely that country has vanished. Compelling us to think in terms of "now" and "then," they suggest how powerfully cinema itself functions as a "site of memory."

The cinematic echoes that punctuate works such as *Diva* and *Les amants du Pont-Neuf* are at the core of what might be seen as a shared and defining aesthetic. Designed, above all, to create a stylized "look," this aesthetic—which is marked by a taste for striking visual effects, for glossy sets and hyperreal studio shots—creates a world that is at once intensely theatrical and deliberately "false." These qualities have earned for these films various sobriquets. For example, borrowing a term from art history, Raphaël Bassan qualifies Beineix and Carax—along with Luc Besson (director of the very successful 1987 film *La femme Nikita* and, most recently, *The Fifth Element* [1997])—as "neo-baroque" directors.[1] (Although some French critics consider Carax, who is the least well known in the United States, more "serious" than Beineix and Besson, the three are often referred to as a kind of trio: thus René Prédal speaks of "the Beineix-Besson-Carax syndrome.")[2] For others, the glossy and seductive surfaces of these films owe more of a debt to the world of advertising than to that of baroque art.[3] In fact, the evident affinities between these films and the arresting images of sophisticated commercials have given rise to labels such as "cinéma pub" (for "publicité," or "advertising"), "cinéma média," and, most commonly, "cinéma du look." Emphasizing the way in which advertising techniques permeate the glossy and unreal universe of these films, a critic for *Les cahiers du cinéma* defines "look"—a word that has passed, significantly, into French—as the "belief in the image as a pure seduction of the surface, the triumph of appearances."[4]

In the eyes of a more philosophically minded commentator like Alain Bergala, the "triumph of appearances" embodied in the "cinéma du look" has a still deeper significance. In his view, this "triumph" constitutes nothing less than one of the principal traits separating cinematic modernism from what Anglo-American critics tend to call postmodernism. The French critic argues that what is now viewed as the period of "historical modernity" or of high cinematic modernism, a period exemplified in France by the New Wave of the 1960s, was characterized, above all, by a search for "truth," by a passionate investigation of the relationship between cinema and "life." It was, observes Bergala, this "fetishistic" quest for the "true inscription of reality" that prompted Godard to explore what lay "behind" the image, what "really" took place in life. To this end, Godard used techniques associated with documentary (location shooting, improvised or seemingly improvised sequences, synchronous sound, the use of "real" people) and allowed his camera to linger on faces and objects as if to make them reveal their ontological reality, their innermost being.[5] And, continues Bergala, it is precisely this search for "truth," this desire to breach the wall between the "image" and the "real," that is missing in the work of directors such as Beineix or Besson. Whereas New Wave directors were disturbed by the "falseness" of the image—one remembers the bitter edge in Godard's observation that an "image is just an image"—directors like Beineix revel in proclaiming the "untruth" of cinema, in creating films based on the "pure and simple forgetfulness of the principle of reality."[6] Such directors begin, observes Bergala, "with the same logic: if the image is ontologically false, there is no point in resisting this falseness. You may as well make the most of it, and get the best out of it—that is, its theatricality."[7]

One of the most important ways in which these films proclaim their "theatricality" and their "falseness" is, of course—and this bears upon the issue of principal concern here—through their insistence on cinematic allusions and echoes. For such allusions serve as constant reminders that we have entered a world of "pure appearances." Not surprisingly, like the very "falseness" of these films, their use of borrowed images has generated a great deal of critical comment. While the self-conscious *cinéphilisme* of directors like Beineix and Carax has prompted some critics to view them as the "new wave" of the 1980s, others take a harsher view of their incessant borrowings from, and allusions to, earlier works. English critic Susan Hayward, for example, speaks of "necrophiliac trends in French cinema";[8] a number of French commentators interpret this "falseness" as the sign not only of a crisis in cinema but of a deep-seated social malaise. French director Olivier Assayas refers to an "art of crisis—that of the recycling of appearances";[9] Alain Bergala argues that the indiscriminate borrowing from the past seen in these films constitutes a "degraded" or "obtuse" form of mannerism symptomatic of a "hollow" moment in film history: a moment when the enthusiasms and innovations of the New Wave have given way to exhaustion. Experimentation has been replaced by stylization, spontaneity by affectation and excess. The "absence" of real subjects, declares Bergala, impels directors like Beineix and Besson to look to the past for "old, worn out, motifs . . . that are given a new appearance by a mannerist treatment."[10]

It is difficult, I think, to quarrel with Bergala's observations. These films do seem to lack "real" subjects even as they give off a "hollow" ring. But it seems to me that their use of "old motifs" signals more than a "crisis" in cinema. I would argue that the nature of their cinematic allusions—especially the fact that so many are drawn from classic French films of the 1930s—points to deep-seated currents of nostalgia and longing. I realize, of course, that it is sometimes difficult to extract "meanings" from films that constantly proclaim their own "falseness," or to interpret allusions and echoes that, at times, seem randomly drawn from a vast memory bank of remembered images. I do not question that, in this respect, the filmic allusions informing the "cinéma du look" are very different from those that gave a special cast to films by New Wave directors such as Godard and Truffaut. In films like Godard's *A bout de souffle* (*Breathless*, 1959) or Truffaut's *Tirez sur le pianiste* (*Shoot the Piano Player*, 1960) cinematic echoes from the past clearly invited a meditation not only on different filmic traditions, especially those of France and the United States, but also on psychological and philosophical issues. To take a well-known example: the many references to American *film noir* in Godard's first feature, *A bout de souffle*— especially the way in which the protagonist admires, and imitates, Humphrey Bogart—have a resonance at once cinematic, cultural, and psychological. An obvious homage to Hollywood action films in general, and to those of Bogart in particular, they express nostalgia for a classical cinema that, as the very presence of *Breathless* demonstrates, no longer exists. Belmondo's gestures point not only to the difference between the self-conscious and world-weary protagonist of this film and the American tough guy he so admires, but also to the contrast between action American-style and French existentialist *ennui*. To use a term Truffaut applied to the unconventional mix of genres in *Tirez sur le pianiste*, one might say that Godard's borrowings do nothing less than "explode" the detective genre within the context of a complex reflection on film.

It is precisely this complex web of self-conscious meanings that the cinematic borrowings in the "cinéma du look" appear determined to subvert, to mock. Here, cinematic allusions and echoes seem to embody what Fredric Jameson defines as the exhaustion of pastiche rather than the satirical edge of parody. "Pastiche," writes Jameson in a well-known essay, "is, like parody, the imitation of a peculiar mask, speech in a dead language: but it is a neutral practice of such mimicry, without any of parody's ulterior motives, amputated of the satirical impulse."[11] The lack of what Jameson deems "ulterior motives" is made very clear, for example, in the last scene of Luc Besson's second and highly successful film, *Subway* (1985). Set, as the title suggests, in the Parisian *métro*, Besson's film refers both to *Breathless* and, as in a palimpsest, to Godard's American models. Mimicking the end of *Breathless*, *Subway* concludes as its protagonist is gunned down by a policeman or private eye while his girlfriend runs to his side. But the resemblances end there. For the conclusion of *Breathless* is still very much in the disabused, yet neoromantic, tradition of *film noir*: "What a bitch," the dying protagonist manages to murmur, referring to the faithless woman whom he has loved and who has betrayed him. In contrast, the last words of the hero in *Subway* highlight the air of punk insouciance and total unreality that pervades the entire film. Echoing the last of three curious citations used as epigraphs to the film—"To be is to do" (Socrates). "To do is to be" (Sartre). "Do be do be do" (Sinatra)—the dying hero turns his face to the audience, winks, and repeats, "Do be do be do." Reminding us that nothing we have seen is real, this scene undercuts emotion even as it subverts meaning and resists interpretation. Is it an homage to Godard? A tongue-in-cheek parody of a parody? A way of evoking and yet avoiding the tragic cast of Godard's film? A reference to Orpheus, whose descent to the Underworld is perhaps mirrored by the musician protagonists of this film, dwelling in the sunken labyrinth of the Paris *métro*? Or simply a way, as Susan Hayward suggests, for *Subway* to establish itself as "a film of the *Nouvelle Vague* generation?"[12] Teasing and opaque, mysterious and overdetermined, the reference may mean any of these things . . . or none.

As this scene suggests, the borrowed and avowedly "false" images of the "cinéma du look" seemed designed to defy, to subvert, the search for layers of meaning deliberately called into play by New Wave films. But if, from this perspective, they lack the "ulterior motives" that inhered in the cinematic allusions in a film like *Breathless*, viewed from still another perspective, they *are* revealing. That is, while individual scenes (like that which concludes *Subway*) may resist interpretation, the combined weight of certain allusions—together with the mood that clings to them—point to deep-seated patterns of thought and feeling. And, as suggested earlier, I would argue that the clearest indication of these patterns comes from the fact that the most striking and insistent cinematic echoes in these films are drawn from French classics of the 1930s. The prominent role played by these echoes is such that they cannot be reduced to a "neutral practice of mimicry" or taken as the sign of cinematic "exhaustion." Quite the contrary: it is a role imbued, I think, with currents of deep longing and nostalgia not only for a particular moment of French film but also for an earlier version of France itself.

Not surprisingly, cinematic allusions to remembered classics take many shapes and forms: such echoes may be totally overt and conscious or so disguised and hidden that they seem to have crept in without the director's knowledge. Sometimes, as in Beineix's *Diva* and Besson's *La femme Nikita*, the characters seem to have stepped out of a film by Jean Renoir or René Clair. At others, as in the case of Carax's *Les amants du Pont-Neuf*, famous scenes from films of the 1930s are deliberately imitated and inevitably transformed. In at least two cases, an earlier classic has apparently inspired an entire film: *Delicatessen* recalls *Le million* (1931) by René Clair just as surely as *La lune dans le caniveau*, Beineix's third film, harks back to Marcel Carné's expressionist classic, *Le quai des brumes* (*Port of Shadows*, 1938). But whatever shape they take, whether the tone is one of parody or melancholy, these allusions are as revealing as the homage paid by Godard and Truffaut to their Hollywood models. If the New Wave obsession with things American reflected a France ambivalent about a rapidly changing future, one that had already taken shape in America, the nostalgia for films of the 1930s seen in the "cinéma du look" suggests, instead, a preoccupation with, and a longing for, a "golden age" that could hardly be more French.

The Golden Age of French Cinema

To appreciate the force of this nostalgia—to understand the cluster of emotions that surround the borrowed images of the "cinéma du look"—one must keep in mind the very special place that films of the 1930s hold in French memory. Frequently growing more luminous with the passage of time, their images "float," note the authors of a study entitled *Générique des années 30*, even in the "phantasms of those who have not seen [the] films."[13] From the balletic comedies of René Clair, to the social dramas of Jean Vigo and Jean Renoir, to the symbol-laden tragedies of Marcel Carné, faces and images from these films linger in French memory just as, say, certain sequences from *Gone with the Wind* and *The Wizard of Oz* or, in a different vein, *Casablanca*, haunt the American psyche. The striking traits of Michèle Morgan in *Quai des brumes* remain as etched in memory's eye as the world-weary femininity exuded by Arletty in Carné's *Hôtel du Nord* (1938). Indicating the intensity of this memory, recent decades have seen characters and places from these films become the object of national tributes. The *cinémathèque* of the Pompidou Center in Paris is named after a famous character, the beautiful Garance, played by Arletty in Carné and Prévert's wartime classic, *Les enfants du paradis* (*Children of Paradise*, 1945); a small Parisian hotel on the banks of the Canal St. Martin has been declared part of the national *patrimoine* solely because it was featured in *Hôtel du Nord*. Not surprisingly, when Carné himself died, on October 31, 1996, despite the fact that he had been well out of the public eye for nearly forty years, his death was the lead feature on the major French television news broadcast that night.

The reverent treatment accorded artists like Carné and Arletty stems, I think, not only from their own undeniable accomplishments; it also reflects the fact that they were part of what is often deemed the "golden age" of French cinema. "In 1936," writes Dudley Andrew, "critics start to render a harmonious image of a national cinema on the verge of breaking forth in glory."[14] Marked by "glory" at home, these films were also successful abroad: as film historian Jack Ellis points out, in the 1930s French films "became the substantial body of foreign-language pictures to interest American audiences."[15] Even more important, however, at least in terms of the "phantasms" such films have left in their wake, these works were also intensely "French." That is, they seemed to capture the essence of French life, to portray ordinary men and women who might have been one's neighbors, friends, relatives. Discussing this quality of "Frenchness" in terms of actor Jean Gabin—who was, in many ways, the very icon of this cinema— Ginette Vincendeau observes that Gabin's "francicité," or "Frenchness," stemmed from the fact that he was the star of a realist French cinema that involved the "detailed representation of places and people anchored in a 'reality' contemporaneous with its geographical, historical, and cultural territory."[16] Acknowledging that this portrait of contemporary "reality" did make use of certain well-established visual conventions, Vincendeau proceeds to argue that even such conventions—which bore upon decor, clothes, language, and situations—were deeply connected to existing realities that were "immediately apparent."[17]

Reflecting "existing realities," these films also perpetuated, created, treasured images of France: images of people, landscapes, cities. For example, despite the fact that virtually all the films of René Clair were shot in a studio, they etched the portrait of a quintessential Paris that, in some sense, still remains our image of the city. Marked by narrow streets and steep rooftops, the Paris created by Clair and his set designer, Lazare Meerson, was a city of friendly *quartiers* populated by bustling merchants and petty thieves, by apartment dwellers who joined in with the chorus of a street singer's refrain or sang and danced together to celebrate the good fortune of a neighbor who had won the lottery. And while Jean Vigo made only one film with episodes set in the French countryside, *L'Atalante* (1934), the lyrical nature of those episodes is such that art historian Françoise Cachin includes Vigo among the ranks of artists whose works shaped what might be described as a kind of archetypal French landscape—one complete with the spire of the local village church and softly rolling hills. "In evoking the French countryside," writes Cachin, we think of "images nourished by the paintings of Sisley, Cézanne, Pisarro, Corot, Courbet, Monet, by the films of Jean Vigo or by memories of vacations."[18]

If quintessential French places emerge from the work of Clair and Vigo, it was left, as suggested earlier, to actor Jean Gabin to crystallize a sense of French identity. Gabin was known for roles, it is true, in which he played doomed heroes confronting a destiny as implacable and tragic as that faced by any Greek hero.[19] But these doomed heroes were nonetheless unmistakably French. However exotic the locale, in the most famous of his roles—as an exiled criminal far from his beloved Paris in Julien Duvivier's *Pépé le Moko* (1937), an army deserter on the run in *Le quai des brumes*, a trainman subject to murderous rages in Jean Renoir's *La bête humaine* (1938), a vulnerable factory worker in Carné's *Le jour se lève* (*Daybreak*, 1939)—Gabin remained a typical Parisian, an average working man. As Ginette Vincendeau observes, everything about him spoke of widely shared working-class origins and habits: his accent and clothes (especially his workman's cap or *casquette*), his heavy and stolid body, the bistros he frequented, and the foods he ate. His filmic image, writes Vincendeau, "was that of a human and social type: a man whose gestures, language, occupation, and/or milieu, as well as the genre of the films in which he appeared, indicated he was from 'the people.' "[20]

A man of the "people," a French working-class version of the average American portrayed by Jimmy Stewart or Gary Cooper in films by Frank Capra, Gabin was also, as commentators repeatedly suggest, someone with whom everyone seemed able to identify. "What is remarkable about Gabin's working-class hero," writes Robin Buss, "is that he is credible both as an individual and as a representative of the 'ordinary man.' "[21] In the eyes of Vincendeau, Gabin was nothing less than "a focal point for the national identity for the spectators of his country"; for Dudley Andrew, too, Gabin was "arguably the focus of identification for an entire nation."[22] More than a half-century after Gabin appeared in his most famous roles, the French public was reminded of the "mythic" national status the actor had enjoyed. What was doubtless the most important commemorative event of recent decades—the spectacular parade that took place along the Champs-Elysées in 1989 to celebrate the bicentennial anniversary of the French Revolution—contained a striking float consisting of a locomotive built to resemble one driven by railwayman Gabin in *La bête humaine*. In the driver's seat of this mock locomotive was a figure dressed, in fact, to resemble the actor as he had appeared in one of his most famous roles.

A celebration both of Gabin and of the proletarian heroes he played, this extravagant homage points, of course, not only to a defining feature of Gabin's persona but to a vital aspect of the "Frenchness" embodied in films of the 1930s: that is, their populist cast. As Robin Buss observes, one of the most striking characteristics of these films was the fact that they treated workers "as real people, 'heroes,' capable of emotions and aspirations with which the audience is expected to identify."[23] In this respect, it is telling that directors as different from one another as Clair and Renoir, or as Vigo and Carné, all made films featuring working-class milieux and proletarian heroes. Their films included men who labored on factory assembly lines (*A nous la liberté*, Clair, 1931), in stone quarries (*Toni*, Renoir, 1934), and in print shops (*Le crime de M. Lange*, Renoir, 1935); still others featured protagonists who were mechanics (*La grande illusion*, Renoir, 1937), railwaymen (*La bête humaine*), and welders (*Le jour se lève*).

It is true, of course, that so-called populist films, exemplified by those in which Gabin played a working-class hero, constituted but a fraction of the cinema of the era. And it is also true that the populist currents seen in these works were not new. From Emile Zola in the nineteenth century down to Pierre MacOrlan and Jules Romains in the 1920s and 1930s, French novelists had portrayed working-class characters and milieux. (Indeed, *La bête humaine*, the film that inspired the extravagant float seen in the bicentennial parade, is based on a novel by Zola.) Moreover, similar characters and milieux had appeared in French cinema well before the 1930s. As Italian scholars Robert Escobar and Vittorio Giacci point out, films of the 1920s such as Abel Gance's *La roue* (1924) and Renoir's *La petite marchande d'allumettes* (*The Little Matchgirl*, 1928) displayed the presence of populist motifs and iconography—"the workers' movement, the detailed description of everyday life, the *banlieue* and the bistro"[24]—that would later be featured in classics of the following decade.

Still, if populist films represented a small fraction of French cinema of the 1930s, it is clearly this fraction that has come to be associated with the entire era. "Populist films," writes Vincendeau, "dominate our idea of the French cinema of the period in defiance of statistics."[25] And if populist themes and motifs did not originate in films of the 1930s, they did enjoy unprecedented appeal and resonance in classics such as *Le crime de M. Lange*, *La bête humaine*, and *Le jour se lève*. Most important, in films such as these, populist motifs drew strength from, and reflected, a very particular political and social climate, one marked by the difficulties of the Depression, the increasing ideological gap between Left and Right, and the spirit of the Popular Front itself. As early as 1933, future director Marcel Carné alluded to many of these motifs even as he offered what would become a well-known definition of populism. "Populism," he declared, "And so what? Neither the word nor the thing frightens us. Describing the simple life of humble people, creating the atmosphere of their life of toil, isn't that better than re-creating the murky and overheated ambience of dance-halls and the unreal nobility of nightclubs that cinema has used so profitably up till now."[26]

An important indication of the strong links that bound French populist cinema to the realities of its day was the fact that it seemed to keep pace with a rapidly evolving social and political climate. In this respect, it is interesting to compare the portrait of the typical Parisian apartment house, with its many different dwellers, seen in René Clair's *Le million* with that traced by Jean Renoir four years later in *Le crime de M. Lange*. In both films, the apartment complex, marked by an animated courtyard in which private and public space merge, serves as what Robin Buss defines as a "microcosm of society." ("The courtyard in *Le crime de Monsieur Lange*," writes Buss, "the stairway in *Le jour se lève*, the two together in *La belle équipe*, natural theaters in which a small community can react to a win on the lottery and a blind man stumble across a corpse, provided writers and directors with the opportunity for marvellous inventions.")[27] But in Renoir's film this social "microcosm" assumes a political dimension that is lacking in *Le million*. While the "small community" of *Le million* is composed of neighbors who join together to celebrate a winning lottery ticket, in *Le crime de M. Lange*, made four years later, the community portrayed includes workers in a print shop who form a successful and thriving cooperative once they are freed from the tyranny of their evil capitalist boss. The difference between the two films—that is, the heightened political dimension of *Le crime de M. Lange*—was obviously due to the left-wing sympathies of Renoir and of the film's scriptwriter, Jacques Prévert. But it is generally agreed that it also reflected the climate of exuberant hope that surrounded the Popular Front (a coalition of the Left including Communists, Socialists, and Radicals) just before it swept to power in May of 1936.

Just as *Le crime de M. Lange* captured the short-lived euphoria awakened by the Popular Front, so, too, did the increasingly dark mood of the late 1930s find an echo in cinema. The ominous shadows and symbols, the brooding claustrophobia, of "poetic realist" classics such as *Le quai des brumes* and *Le jour se lève* mirrored, in the eyes of many, the pessimism of a nation beset by the loss of political hope and the increasing fear of war. Working-class protagonists continued to dominate these films; but they were now lonely outsiders—divorced from the friendly communities seen in *Le million* and *Le crime de M. Lange*. For them, home was no more than a dingy hotel room; the workplace, like the stifling and poisonous factory in *Le jour se lève*, a source of alienation and danger. Reflecting the mood of

the time, in these films Gabin himself was no longer, to borrow a phrase
from Vincendau, the "emblem of the Popular Front." Instead, he had become, as Italian critic Goffredo Fofi observes of the character he plays in
Le quai des brumes, a man who "represents the agony and end of the Front,
and the approach of war."[28]

Borrowed Images

From the "emblem" of the Popular Front to a symbol of its "end," Gabin
is the very icon of a cinema rooted in the social and political context of its
time. Throughout the turbulent decade of the 1930s—from the battles that
accompanied the rise of the Popular Front to the gloom that surrounded
its end—French cinema participated in the major dramas of the nation. As
one commentator after another has remarked, this participation may well
constitute the most striking feature of films of the 1930s. For example, in
an essay written in 1951, André Bazin attributes the "mythic" status of
films such as *Le quai des brumes* and *Le jour se lève* to what he deems a
"particular conjunction between their themes and style and the sensibility
of the period."[29] Echoing this notion of a "particular conjunction," in a
1994 study of the links between culture and politics during the era of the
Popular Front, historian Pascal Ory writes that French populist films of
the 1930s bore witness to a unique "cultural phenomenon":< "the emergence of an aesthetic influenced by a political consciousness."[30] Looking at
this "phenomenon" from a slightly different perspective, historian Christian Amalvi observes that one of the defining traits of the Popular Front
was, precisely, its concern with culture. It was characterized, he writes, "by
extraordinary artistic activity and by original efforts to create an authentic
popular culture."[31]

To jump from past to present: it is, I would argue, precisely this "particular conjuction," this "cultural phenomenon," that is evoked whenever images from the 1930s appear in contemporary films. And it is in this sense,
above all, that the borrowed images of the "cinéma du look" are such powerful bearers of memory and history. Such images bring back not only the
greatness of a certain cinema—the shape of an actor's face, the intensity of
a given scene—but also the contours of a particular era, of a very definite
social and political world. It may well be, as Ginette Vincendeau argues,
that the populist world depicted in a film such as *Le crime de M. Lange* was
already an object of nostalgia even in the 1930s. (Referring to two films
imbued with the spirit of the Popular Front, Vincendeau contends that
the "communities" portrayed in Duvivier's *La belle équipe* and Renoir's *La
Marseillaise* reflect not the "real" France of 1936 but rather "an older,
mostly obsolete idea of a community, though one which is all the more
keenly desired—in fact a *nostalgic* society.")[32] But even if this is the case,

there is no doubt that remembered images from films such as *La belle équipe* and *Le crime de M. Lange* are indelibly associated with the populist world of the 1930s. And it is this world that is evoked, however subliminally or unconsciously, when a figure from the populist past wanders into the postmodern landscape of *Diva* or *La femme Nikita*, or when remembered scenes from *L'Atalante* suddenly surface in *Les amants du Pont-Neuf*, or when the directors of *Delicatessen* and *La lune dans le caniveau* reread masterpieces by Clair and Carné. Even as the actual historical events surrounding such images recede from consciousness—it is telling, for example, that the fiftieth anniversary of the Popular Front went virtually unnoticed[33]—such images underscore the gap between past and present. Moreover, as suggested by the films to be explored here (although perhaps they are too few in number to permit such sweeping generalizations), it is a gap that widened starkly in the decade that stretched from *Diva*, whose unexpected success virtually launched the "cinéma du look,"[34] to *Delicatessen*.

Made in 1981, *Diva*, which was Jean-Jacques Beineix's first film, takes as its principal protagonist a young French postman named Jules. As the film opens, Jules, dressed in his postman's uniform, is seen entering the venerable Palais Garnier opera house in Paris to attend a performance by a black American opera singer. A great fan of the exotic and beautiful diva, Jules secretly makes an illegal tape of her performance—a tape that is particularly valuable because the singer has consistently refused to have her voice recorded. Rushing backstage after the performance, Jules manages to meet his idol; to his amazement (and ours), the young postman soon becomes the diva's friend.

But even as the wildest dreams of an opera fan are fulfilled, Jules finds himself at the epicenter of two frenetic chases and two converging narratives. Owing to a mix-up of two tapes, he is pursued both by Japanese businessmen, who are after the valuable recording of the diva's performance, and by a corrupt Paris police chief and his evil henchmen, who are desperately seeking a tape that implicates the police chief in a prostitution ring. Hardly a match for the brutal police chief, Jules is rescued by Godorish, a strange man whom he met through a chance encounter with a young Asian woman. Probably the most original character in the film, Godorish lives in a huge theatrical loft whose sparse furnishings include a bizarre machine for making waves. Strange and mysterious, the iconoclastic Godorish is also highly resourceful and intelligent: thus he is able to retrieve the tapes and to outwit, and kill, the evil police chief. Saved by Godorish, at the end of the film a repentent Jules returns the illegal tape he made to the diva. As she takes it from him on the stage of the empty opera house, we are given the impression that she has relented, that she will finally allow her voice to be recorded.

No less than the diva herself, who practices an art from the past and yet is reluctantly drawn into the modern realm of reproduction and consumerism, Beineix's film also seems poised between past and present. While the past is glimpsed primarily through allusions to earlier films, the present, instead, emerges from the film's fascination with certain aspects of modern life—the media, stardom, and high technology—that could hardly be more contemporary. This double pull, as it were, is, in fact, the subject of an essay by Fredric Jameson, "*Diva* and French Socialism." As this intriguing title suggests, Jameson analyzes the pull between past and present that informs *Diva* almost exclusively in political and ideological terms. While this focus seems a bit narrow to me, his essay provides an undeniably interesting point of departure for a discussion of Beineix's film. For in addition to its telling political observations, it touches on the issue at the core of this chapter: the emotional charge of remembered images.

In Jameson's view, the tug-of-war between past and present that permeates Beineix's film is mirrored, above all, in the characters of Jules and Godorish. A psychological study in contrasts, Jules and Godorish, asserts Jameson, clearly belong to different historical worlds. While Godorish represents the high-tech Paris of today, Jules is a creature from the city's populist past. The little postman is nothing other, says Jameson, than a "historicist allusion, the reinvention of a very traditional figure in French populist art: the *naïf*, the innocent (not going back as far as Voltaire's *Candide* or as Parzifal, but certainly back to the Popular Front, to Raymond Queneau and to Renoir's 'Monsieur Lange')."[35] While the "little postman" evokes the Paris of the 1930s, Godorish, says Jameson, belongs to the gleaming metropolis of the present day. He is totally at home in the ultramodern city seen in *Diva*, a Paris crisscrossed by expressways and dotted with former warehouses that have been converted into glossy and theatrical lofts. Polished and seductive, this modern Paris is not without its dangers: marked by international intrigue and high finance, this city is home to Japanese businessmen who vie for illegal tapes and to corrupt policemen who kill with impunity. But these dangers do not daunt the mysterious and powerful Godorish. A wizard of high technology, he is endowed with what Jameson calls a "mastery of postmodern urban space." His strange name heightens his mysterious aura—is it a play on Godot? on Godard?—even as it defies attempts to place him in any particular country. Cosmopolitan and sophisticated, he enjoys an international anonymity in sharp contrast with the obvious "Frenchness" of Jules.

The friendship or alliance between the innocent Jules and the sophisticated Godorish is, clearly, an unexpected or improbable one. In Jameson's view, it is also one imbued with ideological implications that reflect a particular historical *conjuncture*: that is, the fact that *Diva* appeared in the same year (1981) in which the Socialists came to power for the first time since the heady years of the Popular Front. At the crux of Jameson's argument is his conviction that *Diva* mirrors the crucial problem confronting the Socialists after their victory. Once in power, they were forced to make a wrenching decision: although the party remained attached to traditional populist goals nourished during decades of opposition, it had to acknowledge the necessity of sacrificing these very goals if France were to compete in a demanding environment marked by high technology and ferocious global competition.

Jameson argues that the sad conclusion reached by the party—that traditional Socialist goals had to give way in favor of a "process of modernization" which had been initiated by Gaullism[36]—is reflected in *Diva* in at least two important ways. To begin with, the diva herself, who eventually allows her voice to be reproduced and sold, is forced to acknowledge the demands, and the power, of a world ruled by technology and the marketplace. Even more important, it is made clear that Jules, this "little postman" from the French populist past, cannot deal with the difficulties and dangers of the modern world on his own. In order to do so, he needs the help of the cosmopolitan Godorish who, as an international sophisticate, understands the intricacies of technology. The essential role played by Godorish—the fact that the provincial Jules is helpless without him—turns the film, says Jameson, into a brief for the kind of modernization associated with pragmatists on the political Right. *Diva* becomes, in his words, a "political allegory, the expression of a collective or political unconscious whose terms are very consonant with those proposed by the Right."[37] Within this "political allegory" the improbable friendship between Jules and Godorish offers nothing less than the "imaginary resolution of [a] real contradiction." In other words, this friendship suggests that it is possible to embrace the pragmatism and the "process of modernization" associated with the Right without abandoning the beloved Socialist goals of the past. Hence the unlikely, but infinitely comforting, notion that Jules, the archetypal French *naif*, can form a friendship or alliance with the eminently modern Godorish.

In certain respects, I think, Jameson is absolutely correct: there is no doubt that *Diva* reflects the insistent tug of the past as well as the seductive lure of the future. Nor is there any doubt that this past is evoked through the use of filmic allusions. But it seems to me that the contours of the *conjuncture* posited by Jameson, as well as those governing the contrast between past and present, are not as precise or schematic as his essay implies. In terms of politics, for example, the difficult choices awaiting the Socialists—choices that Jameson places at the core of Beineix's 1981 film—were by no means immediately apparent when they first assumed power. Indeed, it was only later, when they tried to implement long-cherished goals, that it became clear that this course of action might harm the country's economic health and competitiveness. As Stanley Hoffmann observes, it was in 1983, not 1981, that Mitterand "had the French government shift from the old Socialist doctrine of state-controlled economic and social change to a new policy emphasizing financial 'rigor' and industrial competitiveness."[38]

But even if *Diva* did have a premonition of this profound political shift, I wonder whether the lure of the past that is felt in this film can be seen solely in ideological terms. In fact, I would argue that the nostalgia for the populist past that runs throughout *Diva* bears not only upon politics and ideology but upon the loss of an entire social, cultural, and even physical world. In this respect, I think it is telling that the figure of Jules owes less of a debt to an explicitly political film such as *Le crime de M. Lange*—which is, in fact, the only film mentioned by Jameson—than to the bittersweet comedies made by René Clair in the course of the 1930s. Both the post-man's *métier* and his childlike innocence recall not the relatively sophisti-cated M. Lange but, rather, the gentle love-struck creatures, the street-singer of *Sous les toits de Paris* or the dreamy worker of *A nous la liberté*, who populate Clair's universe. Like these innocent creatures, Jules displays a chaste reverence for the woman he adores: as if the touch of the diva's dress, or the sound of her voice, were contentment enough, the young postman gives no hint of physical passion. And the echoes of Clair embod-ied in Jules are amplified by Beineix's choice of sets and costumes. For example, the Palais Garnier opera house where a rapt Jules hears the diva's performance played a central role in what may be René Clair's masterpiece, *Le million*. In that film, the imposing nineteenth-century building was the site of converging chases that, incidentally, were not unlike those in *Diva*. Similarly, the postman's uniform that Jules wears throughout the film, even when he attends the opera, brings to mind the characteristic work clothes worn by Clair's "butchers" and "bakers." Like them, the "little postman" of *Diva*, who is referred to by one and all as *le petit postier*, is defined by the uniform he wears and the *métier* he plies.

An implicit homage to René Clair, the echoes of *Le million* that run throughout *Diva* also indicate that the boundaries of loss are wider, the contrast between past and present more complex, than "*Diva* and French Socialism" might suggest. These echoes serve as insistent reminders not only of lost political goals—like those informing *Le crime de M. Lange*—but of the disappearance of a world marked, above all, by a sense of commu-nity and warmth. Evoking the picturesque Paris of *Le million*—a city of welcoming *quartiers* where tradesmen gaily joined together in song and dance, and lovers sang to one another from different sides of the street—*Diva* also lets us see just how much that Paris has changed. For in sharp contrast with the remembered Paris of *Le million*, the modern city seen here is a place of hidden dangers and cold, alienating surfaces. The cheerful attics that sheltered Clair's writers and artists have been transformed into gentrified lofts that dwarf their inhabitants; the popular *quartiers* of bustling merchants and friendly neighbors have been razed to make way for expressways and gleaming new buildings. Even when a building appears from out of the past, it, too, seems to have been transformed, emptied, by the landscape of the present. The most striking example of this is the Palais Garnier opera house. Even in the balletic and unreal universe of *Le million*, this imposing structure seemed solid and weighty; in *Diva*, by contrast, it has become a theatrical facade, an emptied icon of its former self. Seen at night with all its gleaming lights, it resembles nothing so much as a postcard image of a once famous monument.

But it is not only the city, or even the divide between Godorish and Jules, that insistently reminds us of the contrast between past and present. In some ways, this contrast is woven into the character of Jules himself. The innocent and provincial postman may be very different, as Jameson suggests, from the sophisticated and cosmopolitan Godorish; but Jules, too, has been seduced by the lure of the present. It is not only that this quintessential French *naïf* has a distinctly contemporary side, that he lives, for example, in a striking loft decorated with postmodernist trompe l'oeil and filled with expensive recording equipment. It is also—and, in some sense, above all—that Jules is a mere shell, a reminder, of a populist character. This brings us back, of course, to the "falseness" of the film itself, to the fact that, in a world devoted to the "triumph of appearances," everything becomes a decorative motif. This is no less true of Jules than of anything else in *Diva*. The little postman may recall the working-class characters seen in films of the 1930s, but in his case the realities of work that defined the lives of such characters have vanished. Rarely seen with fellow workers, Jules is apparently not subject to the economic constraints, the social distinctions, that governed the lives of the working men and women seen in earlier films. Quite the contrary: all the attributes that characterize him— his tapes, his apartment, his passion for opera—testify to a life of financial ease and sophisticated taste. Divorced from social and economic realities, he is but the "emblem" of a populist character; his uniform, a costume like those seen on the stage of the opera house. An improbable creature of the present, he bears only the "look"—and the memory—of a vanished past.

The implicit sense of disappearance and loss that is felt in *Diva*, and that informs the character of Jules himself, is offset, in large measure, by the sprightly mood and good humor of the film. As in a romp by Clair, in *Diva* all's well that ends well. The same cannot be said for two lavish love stories of the "cinéma du look": Beineix's *La lune dans le caniveau* and Leos Carax's *Les amants du Pont-Neuf.* Made well after the *conjuncture* of 1981, these melancholy works confirm the impression that the nostalgia for the past informing *Diva* bears upon the disappearance of a lost, and longed-for, world. Once again—indeed, far more explicitly than in *Diva*—memories of this world are evoked through remembered images drawn from French cinema of the 1930s. But, significantly, this time these images come not from comedies like *Le million* but, instead, from the melancholy tales of doomed lovers brought to life by director Marcel Carné and scriptwriter Jacques Prévert in films such as *Le quai des brumes* and *Le jour se lève*. In fact, *La lune dans le caniveau* rereads one of the most successful and best-loved of Carné's films, *Le quai des brumes*; *Les amants du Pont-Neuf* evokes the equally legendary *Hôtel du Nord*.[39]

Often referred to in terms of "poetic realism," films like *Le quai des brumes* and *Hôtel du Nord* were deeply atmospheric and highly stylized tales of cruel destinies and fatal passions. Here, expressionist shadows gave rise to claustrophobia and paralysis; symbolic objects and leitmotifs insistently alerted viewers to the inexorable fate that awaited the protagonists. From the moment that the hero of *Le quai des brumes*, an army deserter played by Jean Gabin, steps out of the fog in the film's opening scene, the shadow that falls over one-half of his face lets us know that he is a doomed man. And, indeed, before long, his unhappy fate is set in motion when he falls in love with the beautiful Nelly (Michèle Morgan) whom he meets in a seedy waterfront bar in the port city of Le Havre. By the end of the film, after many twists and turns in the plot, Gabin, who is wrongly suspected of killing Nelly's former boyfriend, is about to escape from France by boarding a ship destined for South America. But destiny proves implacable yet again. When he dismbarks to see Nelly one last time, he is gunned down on the quays of Le Havre. As the film comes to its tragic close, we hear the signal that the ship which was to take him to a new life is about to depart.

Like Carné's famous tale of *amour fou*, *La lune dans le caniveau* is also a tale of doomed lovers. Set in a modern-day "port of shadows," it takes as its protagonist an impoverished dockworker (Gérard Depardieu) who falls in love with a rich and beautiful stranger (Nastassja Kinski). Their unhappy tale is a simple one: they meet, fall in love, and, for reasons that remain unclear, go their separate ways. Thematic parallels with *Le quai des brumes* are not lacking: *La lune dans le caniveau* underscores the claustrophobic nature of the dockworker's existence as well as the inexorability of his fate. But, not surprisingly, it is, above all, the mood and style of *La lune dans le caniveau* that embody the most insistent echoes of Carné's classic. For the "look" of *La lune dans le caniveau* is clearly designed to emulate the poetic and plastic effects for which *Le quai des brumes* is famous. Thus the expressionist play of light and shadow, of fog and mist, in *Le quai des brumes* finds an echo in the shimmering lights and melancholic blue tonalities seen in *La lune dans le caniveau*. (Beineix's film begins, in fact, with a shot of a dead woman lying on wet cobblestones that gleam in the moonlight.) So, too, does Beineix's film seek to re-create the insistent symbolism concerning the tragic fate that awaits the couple in *Le quai des brumes*. Perhaps the most important such symbol in *La lune dans le caniveau* consists of recurring shots of an advertising poster depicting a bottle floating in a sea of azure; a hedonistic image of the freedom the protagonist will never enjoy, its caption seems to mock his inability to change his life. "Try another world," it tells him in English.

But even as these motifs remind the viewer of *Le quai des brumes*, they also point to the enormous gap between the two films, a gap that, in turn, makes evident the contrast between France of the 1930s and that of the 1980s. As in the case of *Diva*, where populist themes were turned into decorative motifs, this gap springs from the essential "falseness" of *La lune dans le caniveau*. In respect to this "falseness," it should be said, of course, that Carné's films were themselves highly stylized. A film like *Le quai des brumes* contains few traces of the realism—the ontological weight, the psychological *vraisemblance*—that is associated, say, with the cinema of Jean Renoir. Still, however stylized, "poetic realist" films were not designed to seem "false" or "unreal." They sought, instead, to create a mood, an atmosphere, of melancholy poetry that corresponded to deeply felt emotions. Take, for example, the celebrated sets designed for Carné by the legendary designer Alexandre Trauner.[40] Although, as in the case of *Hôtel du Nord* (when Trauner had the Parisian district of La Villette, together with the canal that runs through it, reconstructed at the studios of Billancourt), Trauner frequently reconstructed real locations, his sets were designed to give an impression of reality. In fact, contemporary viewers of *Hôtel du Nord*, in particular, are sometimes astonished to learn that the film was not shot on location. And what was true of the sets was also true, in a far more general way, of "poetic realism" itself. As the well-known French critic Jean Mitry phrased it, "poetic realism" could be seen as an "attenuated Expressionism inserted within the norms and conditions of immediate reality."[41] Amplifying Mitry's definition, American critic Edward Baron Turk, author of a study of Carné's films, observes that "poetic realism" tended to "undervalue a film's direct links with the material world in order to explore the symbolic resonances which the world—when photographed—is capable of releasing." Thus, says Turk, the worlds represented in Carné's films were "at once dependent upon and disengaged from the world as it is regularly perceived."[42]

Le quai des brumes clearly illustrates the essential tension described by Turk. While the mood and atmosphere of this highly stylized work are obviously informed by "symbolic resonances," the film also portrays realities that corresponded to a particular historical and social context. If Gabin is a mythic hero in some ways, one whose tragic fate is foretold from the moment he first appears, he is also, as suggested earlier, a working-class character whose psychology and problems are very much rooted in a given time and place. Buffeted by the hardships of the Depression, disgusted with an army bent on colonial aggrandizement, he reflects the paralysis and unease that gripped France as the 1930s drew to a close.

It is, of course, precisely this grounding in a particular historical and social moment that is consistently banished from *La lune dans le caniveau*. Beineix's film deliberately dissolves the essential tension described by Turk—that between "dependency" and "disengagement" in regard to what is "perceived as reality"—even as it suppresses references to any particular time and place. Unlike the port of Le Havre in *Le quai des brumes*, Beineix's "port of shadows" is an obvious studio designed to be perceived as such. Usually seen at night, when its outlines are marked only by shimmering lights, it appears flat and two-dimensional; lacking any detail that might mark it as "real," it is the Platonic essence of a "port" rather than a real city. And, indeed, as if to underscore its artificial, almost hallucinatory, nature, toward the beginning of the film one of the characters remarks portentously, "We are nowhere." In this oneiric city that is "nowhere," physical reality itself is replaced by a play of lights; in the words of Yann Lardeau, the film presents "a world of images, a world of projections . . . [of] dreams. As if the physical and metaphysical world had completely liquefied, dissolved into images and [as if] this two-dimensional universe had conquered and subjugated the three dimensions of the human universe."[43]

In this world of images, the characters themselves assume the dreamlike quality, the flatness, of their physical surroundings. Moving through a weightless universe, they are turned into uneasy ghosts who come from nowhere to lead lives as empty as the deserted and dreamlike spaces they inhabit. In sharp contrast to the stolid workers played by Gabin, whose physical presence was strong enough to solicit the identification of an entire nation, the characters in *La lune dans le caniveau* (even when played by actors as commanding as Gérard Depardieu) appear hollow, interchangeable, anonymous. They lack the psychological depths, the social background, that would provide an identity. While the fatalism that afflicted Gabin in *Le quai des brumes* had unmistakable existential and social roots, the mysterious numbness that paralyzes the dockworker of *La lune dans le caniveau* is never explained. He remains a cipher: it is not clear why he cannot find a less oppressive job, or move to a more inviting town, or why he leaves the woman he loves. Passive and withdrawn, he resembles a strange zombie who, to cite Lardeau once more, wanders through the film "with the same gaps, the same strangeness, the same neutrality as the actors of *Tron*. . . . It may be that—his presence reduced to a mask, his body derealized into a silhouette floating in emptiness—the image has become the place of his extermination."[44]

In the end, it is the process of "derealization" and "extermination" effected in *La lune dans le caniveau*, rather than the story it tells, that accounts for much of the deep melancholy and nostalgia the film exudes. Its "hollow" images are imbued with the sense of mourning and loss that, in the eyes of Jean Baudrillard, always clings to simulation and reproduction. "Simulation," writes the French critic, "is still and always the place of a gigantic enterprise of manipulation, of control and death, just as the objective of the false object (be it primitive statuette, or image, or photo) was always an operation of black magic."[45] But if, as Baudrillard suggests, reproduction always exudes a sense of "death," it is also true that the nature of the "imitative object" changes. In the case of *La lune dans le caniveau*, of course, that object is double: that is, Beineix's film evokes not only remembered images from *Le quai des brumes* but also the world such images represented. And it is in respect to both these "objects" that the remembered images punctuating the "cinéma du look" assume their fullest resonance. Emptied of all that gives them life, they take on their deepest charge of nostalgia. The "mask" worn by Depardieu in *La lune dans le caniveau* is all the more rigid and deathlike because it recalls the expressive and deeply human countenance of Gabin in *Le quai des brumes*; the glossiness of the modern "port of shadows" all the more hollow when compared to the city portrayed in *Le quai des brumes*. Recalling a time when cinema seemed more than a game of shadows and light upon a piece of celluloid, these ghostly allusions give rise to overwhelming nostalgia even as they bear witness to a vanished world.

Both the precise nature and the force of this nostalgia are, in fact, explicitly acknowledged by Leos Carax in *Les amants du Pont-Neuf*. Densely layered with cinematic echoes, *Les amants du Pont-Neuf* pays particular homage to two of the best-loved classics of the 1930s.[46] Its dazzling set—a re-creation of a famous Parisian bridge spanning the Seine, the so-called Pont-Neuf—calls to mind the legendary set of *Hôtel du Nord*;[47] its conclusion re-creates scenes from *L'Atalante*, Jean Vigo's 1934 masterpiece about young newlyweds who live and work aboard a barge that plies its way along the Seine. But Carax does more than re-create images and scenes from these classics: his film also alludes, far more directly than either *Diva* or *La lune dans le caniveau*, to the world that surrounded them. That is, several of the filmic echoes seen in *Les amants du Pont-Neuf* clearly bear upon certain sites of national memory—in particular, the French national holiday of Bastille Day as well as the city of Paris itself—that embody the populist atmosphere and left-wing currents associated with French cinema of the 1930s. With this film, then, it is not only remembered images that are rendered hollow but also the national past itself.

Unlike the intricate web of cinematic allusions in *Les amants du Pont-Neuf*, the story it tells is relatively simple. A tale of two lovers on the edges of society, the film begins with a striking sequence in which the male protagonist (Denis Lavant), high on drugs, is struck by a speeding car whose headlights gleam in the dark and deserted streets of nighttime Paris. The scene shifts: his leg in a cast, he awakens in a terrifying clinic filled with the city's human detritus—the addicted, the mad, the homeless. He, too, it turns out, is homeless: indeed, he has been living on the Pont-Neuf bridge, which has been closed to traffic because of construction. Soon after his return to the venerable landmark he calls home, he meets, and falls in love with, a beautiful young sidewalk artist (Juliette Binoche). Like him, she exhibits the mark of physical suffering: a patch over one eye testifies to a mysterious disease from which she is slowly going blind.

Despite their physical problems and their poverty, the couple enjoys a kind of idyll together on the bridge. Under its aged parapets, they eat, sleep, and make love. But happiness is short-lived: the possibility of finding a cure for her blindness spurs the woman to leave. After a long and painful separation, both, now cured, feel impelled to revisit the place of their love. As before, they meet once again on the bridge; ecstatic at their reunion, they dance up and down on its parapets and, finally, tumble into the Seine where—in an explicit echo of a poetic scene in *L'Atalante* in which the husband sees the image of his wife floating in the river's depths—they enjoy an underwater embrace. But Carax's *hommage* to Vigo's romantic tale of young married love does not stop there. For as the lovers in *Les amants du Pont-Neuf* rise to the surface of the river, a barge, which inevitably recalls that which housed the couple of *L'Atalante*, comes by and fishes them from the Seine. Re-creating the conclusion of *L'Atalante*, *Les amants du Pont-Neuf* comes to an end as the barge, with the joyous lovers aboard, wends its way up the river.

In weaving these remembered scenes of *L'Atalante* into the conclusion of *Les amants du Pont-Neuf*, Carax clearly pays a profound tribute both to Vigo himself and to the power of filmic memories. But at the same time, as in the case of *La lune dans le caniveau* and *Le quai des brumes*, the spectral presence of these remembered images underscores the contrast between the two films. For despite its poetic and lyrical nature, *L'Atalante* is, after all, an extremely realistic work. The husband and wife are fully three-dimensional beings who come from recognizable places and engage in familiar work. In *Les amants du Pont-Neuf*, instead, everything is totally, deliberately, unreal. It is not only that the plot is wildly improbable or that the characters, to use a term proposed by René Prédal, are "opaque."[48] It is also that, like *La lune dans le caniveau*, Carax's film is one in which everything is as flat, as one-dimensional, as the sketches the female protagonist draws on the paving stones of the bridge. Marked by hard eges and bright colors, the bridge itself resembles a painting rather than a landmark worn down by the centuries; it has no more substance or weight than the oneiric "port of shadows" in *La lune dans le caniveau*. Hyperreal and obviously reconstructed—for this film, Carax had the venerable Pont-Neuf bridge rebuilt in the south of France, where bulldozers hollowed out a "false" canal made to resemble the Seine—this monument dwarfs the characters even as it serves as very emblem, the sign, of a cinema of "pure" images. Like a postmodernist landscape, the world of *Les amants du Pont-Neuf* is one in which, to borrow a phrase from Terry Eagleton, everything is "image, spectacle, simulacrum, gratuitous fiction."[49]

The "falseness" of *Les amants du Pont-Neuf* extends, moreover, beyond the "gratuitous fiction" that unfolds on-screen. As suggested earlier, it also touches upon the realm of national history and memory. To some extent, of course, the same might be said of all the films discussed in this chapter: that is, as I have argued throughout, remembered images always recall not only earlier films but also their historical and social context. But in *Les amants du Pont-Neuf*, this phenomenon comes into particularly sharp focus: for, as suggested earlier, Carax's film explicitly recalls motifs and places so deeply charged with memories of the national past that they are generally acknowledged as collective "sites of memory."

One such site is featured, in fact, in what is certainly the film's most striking sequence, one depicting the festivities that surround the annual celebration of the nation's most important holiday, Bastille Day. (First celebrated at the time of the Third Republic, Bastille Day commemorates the storming of the Bastille—and hence the outbreak of the French Revolution—on July 14, 1789.) And these festivities take place against the background of still another another powerful site of national memory: the city of Paris itself. In the context of such sites, one must bear in mind that Paris is not only the nation's political and cultural capital. It is also the very symbol of France, a place indelibly associated with French history and memory in a way that no single American city can be said to embody the history of the United States. Paris cannot be separated from "the memory of France," writes historian Maurice Agulhon, because it was here that "French history was essentially made: it is here that kings reigned most spectacularly; it is also here that they were fought most vigorously."[50] The site of revolutionary uprisings from 1789 to 1968, Paris literally incarnated, in its very geography, the nation's most fundamental political divisions: that is, at least from the Revolution of 1848 to the time of the Popular Front, its different *quartiers* reflected the incessant tug-of-war between the "two" Frances. While populist, left-wing sentiments prevailed in the city's eastern working-class neighborhoods, the conservative *beaux quartiers* in the west were usually staunch supporters of the established order.[51]

Not surprisingly, both sites of national memory featured in *Les amants du Pont-Neuf*, Bastille Day and the city of Paris, had figured powerfully in populist cinema of the 1930s. Concerned with the life of "humble" people, directors had portrayed working-class *quartiers*—La Villette in *Hôtel du Nord*, areas of Montmartre in several films by Clair—in which the very streets spoke of revolutionary traditions and long-standing national divisions. Signficantly, also, at least two important films of the 1930s portrayed this populist Paris in the midst of celebrating Bastille Day. René Clair set an entire film—entitled, in fact, *Le quatorze juillet* (*July Fourteenth*, 1933)—on the eve of July 14 in a working-class *quartier* festooned with gay decorations and marked by enchanting *bals populaires*. And, in one of the most elaborate sequences in *Hôtel du Nord*, Carné portrayed a nighttime Bastille Day celebration marked by thronging crowds and joyful dances.[52] In depicting such celebrations, these films suggested, of course, the left-wing political resonance that surrounded the national holiday until recent decades, a resonance that, not surprisingly, was very much in evidence at the time of the Popular Front. Indeed, as historian Christian Amalvi points out, the massive demonstrations that marked the Bastille Day celebrations of 1935, and that saw half a million people march from the Place de la Bastille to the Place de la Nation under the banners of a united Left, gave impetus to the victory of the Popular Front the following spring.[53]

It is precisely this tradition of memory and history—a tradition embedded in the very streets and monuments, the different *quartiers*, of Paris—that Carax evokes when he places his impoverished lovers in the heart of the nation's capital. But even as Carax evokes the weight of memories embedded in the city, he also drains them of depth and substance. For the city portrayed in *Les amants du Pont-Neuf* is not the Paris that saw the terrible battles of 1871, the massive demonstrations in support of the Popular Front in 1935, or the street barricades of May '68. Nor is it the populist Paris seen in *Le quatorze juillet* and *Hôtel de Nord*. It is true that motifs of this last Paris are present: outcast lovers, Bastille Day celebrations, barges that wend their way along the Seine. But they are just that—empty motifs. Transformed into a ghost of its former self, Paris has become an icon in the way that the "port of shadows" seen in *La lune dans le caniveau* was the icon of a remembered Le Havre. Unlike the animated, festive Paris portrayed in a film like *Le quatorze juillet*, the city that houses Carax's lovers is devoid of people, of traffic, of animation. Like the opera house in *Diva*, it is a place defined solely by gleaming lights. Although the "lovers of Pont-Neuf" live in the city's heart, they seem absolutely alone; the city surrounding them is as eerily deserted as a landscape by de Chirico or a devastated metropolis in a science-fiction film. No longer a place that embodies the nation's memory and history, it is, instead, one marked by "spectacle" and "gratuitous fiction."

The ghostly nature of Carax's Paris comes into sharpest focus, paradoxically, in the very scene that should bear witness to the weight of collective history and memory: the sequences depicting the Bastille Day celebrations. In fact, if the festive scenes that mark the national holiday in films like *Le quatorze juillet* and *Hôtel du Nord* recall the charged political climate of the Popular Front, those portrayed in *Les amants du Pont-Neuf* suggest, rather, the lack of meaning that, in the eyes of many, characterized the lavish bicentennial extravaganza of 1989. By that time, the French holiday seemed to have lost the political and ideological charge that had defined it for centuries. Stripped of that charge, the spectacle so carefully staged by the Socialists appeared, as Christian Amalvi remarks in a somewhat more general context, little more than "a routine ritual"—the stuff of "folklore" and "tourism." Surrounded by media hype, the spectacular parade along the Champs-Elysées seemed as "false," as devoid of real meaning, as the replica of Gabin's locomotive that constituted one of its most striking floats.

It seems highly probable that, consciously or unconsciously, this extravaganza influenced Carax when he conceived of the Bastille Day sequence in *Les amants du Pont-Neuf*. At any rate, he not only underscores the spectacular nature of the bicentennial celebration; he also makes explicit the hollowness—the end of a tradition of history—at its core. In sharp contrast with the holiday celebrations seen in *Le quatorze juillet*, in *Les amants du Pont-Neuf* there are no *bals populaires*, no animated crowds, no comaraderie; the only sign of the holiday consists of dazzling lights, seen in the sky and reflected in the waters, coming from fireworks. And the lovers themselves toast the holiday in a way that emphasizes their own isolation as well as the end of collective traditions. In a totally improbable sequence, they boldly water-ski down a Seine whose waters gleam with reflected lights. As the character played by Juliette Binoche swoops beneath the banks of the city, the historical resonance of the holiday vanishes even as its contemporary "touristic" quality, to borrow Amalvi's term, is reinforced by the memory of joyous vacations passed near the shore.

But even as Carax dramatically empties Paris of its tradition of history and memory, he allows us to glimpse the terrifying modern city that has replaced the animated populist world seen in a film like *Le quatorze juillet*. It is here, of course, that the contrast between "now" and "then," a contrast that haunts the remembered images evoked in *Les amants du Pont-Neuf*, is sharpest. For behind the "falseness" of the simulated Paris seen in *Les amants du Pont-Neuf*, behind the wild exuberance of the Bastille Day sequence, lurk indications of the most intractable of today's social ills. Unlike the newlyweds of *L'Atalante*, who were defined, and nurtured, by family and work, the "lovers of Pont-Neuf"—an unemployed addict, a homeless woman going blind—are marginal beings on the edges of society. They belong to the new social category of "les exclus": those "excluded" from the social whole. They are deprived of the camaraderie, the solidarity, that prevailed in traditional working-class milieux. Confronted as they are with the ills of contemporary urban life—with violence and drugs, with homelessness and alienation—it is hardly surprising that the lovers of this film do not hesitate to board the barge as it comes out of the past. In so doing, they are not merely stepping out of one film into the remembered images of still another. They are also exchanging the alienating and frightening world of the present for the reassuring warmth and love that cling to the past.

The contrast between past and present implicit in this sequence becomes, in fact, totally explicit in one of the strangest films of recent years, that is, *Delicatessen*. Made the same year as *Les amants du Pont-Neuf* (1991), *Delicatessen* offers distinct affinities with the "cinéma du look": like *La lune dans le caniveau* and *Les amants du Pont-Neuf*, it displays a taste for bizarre characters and improbable plots, for striking visual effects and extravagant mise-en-scène.[54] In *Delicatessen*, however, the dreamlike unreality favored by Beineix and Carax assumes a nightmarish tinge even as homage turns into biting parody. For this black farce is nothing other than a somber rereading, a kind of evil twin, of the comic operettas René Clair brought to life in the early 1930s.

As in the case of *La lune dans le caniveau* and *Les amants du Pont-Neuf*, the mise-en-scène of *Delicatessen* constitutes the most immediate—and, probably, the most important—clue to the lingering memory of earlier films. For *Delicatessen* is set in the kind of typical small Parisian apartment house featured in films such as *Le crime de M. Lange* and, especially, *Sous les toits de Paris* and *Le million*. But even as this set calls such films to mind, it also indicates the contrast between past and present informing the film. For the apartment house of *Delicatessen* is not part of a vibrant *quartier* alive with the bustle of merchants and housewives, of street singers and young lovers. Bleak, half-ruined, and isolated, it stands alone, the sole survivor, perhaps, of a holocaust that seems to have destroyed its neighbors as well as the city that once surrounded it. As its menacing silhouette looms out of the fog and mist in the film's opening scene, it evokes photographs and newsreels of cities destroyed by the bombs of World War II. And, indeed, this echo of World War II is soon reinforced by other aspects of the film: fashions and styles of the 1940s, as well as the presence of a thriving black market and clandestine radio messages, hark back to life during the Occupation.[55]

Along with this somber past, however, come intimations of a postapocalyptic or postnuclear future. A catastrophe seems to have prompted the inhabitants of the ruined building to regress to the behavior of primitive tribes. They group themselves, in fact, according to the food they eat: thus while beleaguered vegetarians, called Troglydytes, have taken refuge in the basement, and a strange breeder of snails lives by himself in an isolated corner of the building, the tenants of upper floors are voracious cannibals who will trade anything, including a family member in one case, for a piece of human flesh. For them, as Stephen Infantino notes in an unpublished paper, the value of human life can be measured literally by the pound. Tyrannized by a fleshy giant who, for gruesome reasons that are all too obvious, is known as the butcher—and whose garb recalls the very different "butchers" and "bakers" of Clair's comedies—they regard unsuspecting new tenants as prey to be killed and dismembered when supplies run low.

The unlikely hero of the film, a former circus clown named Louison, is, in fact, just one such new tenant. Like Jules in *Diva*, Louison displays the gentle innocence of Clair's love-struck protagonists. And, indeed, before long the gentle clown does fall in love; his inamorata is none other than the butcher's impossibly myopic, cello-playing daughter. Happily, she returns his love; thus she is quick to warn him when his life is threatened by her brutal father. With the help of the Troglydytes, the young couple manages to kill the tyrannical and murderous butcher. As the film comes to an end, the sky is seen for the first time: profiled against the horizon, Louison and his beloved are seen playing music together on the roof of the once sinister building.

Set in a future that contains more than a hint of present anxieties, *Delicatessen* is also deeply infused with images and scenes that speak of a longed-for past. It is not only the apartment house itself, or the presence of Louison *le naïf*, that recalls the bittersweet dramas of Clair's populist Paris. Louison's former profession as a circus clown is also imbued with cherished memories of a bygone era. It evokes a time when entertainment was joyous and shared—when people went to the circus together instead of sitting, as they do in *Delicatessen*, in front of flickering blue television lights in isolated apartments. And the memory of circus clowns also brings to mind the zany slapstick of early silent comedies that Clair loved, and that he later incorporated into films like *Le million*.

A taste for such slapstick—that is, for effects created by misbehaving objects, for chases and carefully timed rhythmic sequences that slowly build to a crescendo—is also very much in evidence in *Delicatessen*. But, not surprisingly, in this dark comedy, even slapstick has a somber hue. The misbehaving objects adored by Clair reveal an undertow of cynicism and violence: a "bullshit detector" explodes when it hears the words "Life is good"; the butcher's knife ricochets and kills the tyrant who threw it. And repellent carnality infuses what is certainly the film's most striking slapstick sequence. Built around audio and visual rhythms, it begins as the butcher and his girlfriend start to make love in his apartment; under their weight, the bedsprings begin to shrill in protest. Soon, heating vents broadcast the telltale noises throughout the apartment house; the escalating cacophony of sounds prompts all the tenants, who are characteristically engaged in solitary activities, to speed up whatever they are doing. Thus a grandmother knits more ferociously, a man pumps up his bicycle with renewed vigor, the butcher's daughter quickens her tempo on the cello, a painter slaps his brush with increased abandon. As the butcher and his girlfriend finally come to a climax, so, too, does everything else: the cello string breaks, the bike tire explodes, the painter's suspenders break and he falls.[56]

Recalling Clair's mastery of timing and rhythm, this inventive sequence also sums up, in a sense, the dramatic contrast between the world of *Le million* and that of *Delicatessen*. In this 1991 work, the ethereal, balletic lightness of Clair's operettas has given way to a dark and leaden realm dominated by the grossest of appetites, by a butcher who throws himself on his girlfriend with the same zeal with which he dismembers his neighbors' bodies. And whereas Clair used sounds, especially music, to create a sense of community as friends and neighbors joined together in song and dance, the sounds heard in this sequence only emphasize the isolation of each tenant. Barricaded doors and claustrophobic terror-filled apartments have replaced the shared spaces—the streets, courtyards, and bistros—that figured so prominently in *Le million*. All that remains of the once vibrant city seen in that film are the dark and confining walls of the small apartment house. Like the fragment that remains from a ruined building, these walls serve only to tell us that if "other" worlds once existed, they are no more.

Then and Now

In no other film of recent years is the contrast between past and present—a contrast embodied in the difference between the sinister apartment house of *Delicatessen* and the remembered Paris of Clair and Renoir—quite so apocalyptic. Yet *Delicatessen* only crystallizes impulses that are felt throughout the "cinéma du look." With the possible exception of *Diva*, the films discussed here display the bleak view of the present that reaches its grotesque apogee in Jeunet and Caro's sinister parable about contemporary cannibalism. Indeed, Raphaël Bassan hardly seems to exaggerate, I think, when he notes that if critics usually stop short at the glittering surface of these works, it is because of a reluctance to confront the "horribly pessimistic vision of the society of the 1980s" that lurks below.[57]

As suggested throughout this chapter, this "horribly pessimistic vision" is one that encompasses the characters as well as the world surrounding them. Prey to what Bassan calls "psychic inertia," the hapless beings who wander through the "cinéma du look" are condemned to the broken edges of modern life; cut off from the social whole, they inhabit what still another critic, Olivier Mongin, deems an "emotional twilight."[58] Although they suffer from isolation and loneliness, they are usually incapable of escaping the barriers of self and making contact with another. The "little postman" of *Diva* is curiously asexual; while the dockworker of *La lune dans le caniveau* experiences sexual desire, he is strangely unable, as Bassan observes, "to achieve a real liaison with a woman."[59] Frequently condemned to solitude, they are too numb, too paralyzed, to take charge of their own lives. For these films to end happily, a modern *deus ex machina* is needed; assistance must come from others or from destiny. Hence a cosmopolitan guardian angel, Godorish, rescues Jules in *Diva*; a remembered barge carries the lovers back to the past in *Les amants du Pont-Neuf.*

It is not surprising that this pessimistic vision of contemporary life should fuel an intense nostalgia for the past. But neither is it surprising that the remembered past which shines so brightly in these films—the world embodied in populist images from the 1930s—is also one on the verge of disappearing forever. "When the real is no longer what it used to be," writes Baudrillard, "nostalgia assumes its full meaning."[60] In this sense, it is certainly no coincidence that populist themes should be evoked so consistently, and with such evident nostalgia, at that very juncture when the traditional working class, as well as the world surrounding it, seems to have come to an end. And that world, as the authors of a work entitled *Le mouvement ouvrier* note, was not merely political and ideological. Reminding us that the workers' movement involved the "awareness of belonging to a social and cultural milieu," they proceed to observe that this movement gave rise to an "entire representation of social life in which it participated."[61]

It is, of course, this "representation of social life"—a representation at the core of populist films of the 1930s—that no longer corresponds to present realities. For those on the bottom of today's social ladder, the sense of belonging to a recognizable "social and cultural milieu" has given way to feelings of "exclusion." Traditional working-class communities— marked by shared ideological convictions and social hopes—are fast disappearing.[62] So, too, is the populist Paris they once inhabited. Beginning in the 1960s, vast projects of urban reform have destroyed the friendly *quartiers* seen in films such as *Le million* and *Le crime de M. Lange*. A Mc-Donalds now stands at the head of the romantic canal featured in *Le quai des brumes*. Towers of steel and glass have replaced once bustling streets; anonymous chains have dealt death blows to little shops and street vendors; the central market and working-class area of *les Halles* were destroyed in the creation of a vast "Forum" above a multilayered underground mall.[63] Commenting on these sweeping changes, Robin Buss observes, "Wherever you stand, in the Paris of the 1980s, in front of the Centre Beaubourg, in Belleville, in Montparnasse, on the Place de L'étoile/Géneral de Gaulle, or watching the traffic on the Quai d'Orsay, you would be struck by the discontinuities with the largely 19th-century city so often celebrated during the first six decades of French cinema."[64] Since those lines were written, still further projects—involving the construction of a new national library and a new opera house in areas of *le vieux Paris populaire*—have rendered the city more homogeneous even as they have destroyed further traces of the geographical divisions that preserved a tradition of social memory and history.

The destruction of *le vieux Paris* is, perhaps, the most visible or concrete indication of the sweeping social changes that have prompted the end of what Maurice Agulhon calls a "historical phase" of national life.[65] The magnitude of these changes is such that extinction threatens not only the populist past itself but even the sites charged with its memory. Commenting on the erosion, the disappearance, of such sites, historian Michelle Perrot observes that "in the landscape of contemporary France, the working-class world is fading without leaving many traces. . . . Dismantled factories, deserted mining towns, slag heaps transformed into landscaped parks . . . the outlines of abandoned vestiges are as difficult to grasp as those of shifting sand dunes."[66]

In enumerating the "abandoned vestiges" of working-class life, Michelle Perrot makes no mention of film. And, clearly, films *are* different from dismantled factories or deserted industrial towns. But, as I have argued throughout this chapter, French cinema has long played a critical role in regard to populist memory. While French cinema of the 1930s preserved—and, in fact, continues to preserve—memories of working-class life and culture, the "cinéma du look" reveals just how surely those memories are being erased. By incorporating remembered images into the "false" world of the present—that is, by deliberately rendering these remembered images unreal—they point to the fading of memory itself.

Unreal copies of images that once seemed real, the remembered images of the "cinéma du look" seem to exemplify the peril that Plato attributed to all simulacra. Speaking of the Greek philosopher, Gilles Deleuze observes that Plato viewed simulacra as dangerous and "degraded icons" precisely because of their power to deny "the original as well as the copy, the model as well as the reproduction."[67] Stripped of the validation inherent in the copy's resemblance to nature, such icons belonged, instead, in Plato's eyes, to a world of images where true was indistinguishable from false, and where "moral existence" was eclipsed, replaced, by one that is purely "aesthetic."

In the case of the remembered images haunting the "cinéma du look," of course, the "originals" that are evoked, and then "denied," are but images themselves. Still, in films of the 1930s, these images corresponded to, exemplified, a vital moment of French political life and culture. It might even be argued that, in their deep connection to national life, such images entered the realm of "moral existence." In contrast, in the "cinéma du look," this connection has vanished; here, remembered images lead only into an "aesthetic" realm of fading memories and overwhelming nostalgia.

In the end, though, the sense of loss clinging to the remembered images of the "cinéma du look" may well extend beyond the melancholy that penetrates the simulacrum, beyond the disappearance of a historical "phase" of national life. It is not only the populist world of Clair and Renoir that is faced with extinction but also French cinema itself. Recent independent productions hold out hope that French cinema has emerged from the doldrums of the 1980s. Still, a sense of widespread crisis is very much in the air. Directors, critics, and viewers continually lament the fact that one of the great national cinemas, which stretches back to the infancy of the seventh art and constitutes one of the glories of modern French culture, appears ill, if not moribund; trade negotiators and regulators seek to limit the influx of American films, which, they fear, will sound its final death knell.[68] Some in the industry—like Jean-Jacques Annaud, who directed films such as *In the Name of the Rose* (1986), *L'ours* (*The Bear*, 1988), and *The Lover* (1992), and who is now working in Hollywood—feel that the grim moment has already arrived. "I realized my choice was simple," remarked Annaud of his decision to work in America, "either I would stay in France making low-budget movies, or I would come here and make the kinds of movies I want."[69]

In light of the precipitous decline of French film, it is hardly surprising that memories of the "golden age" of French cinema should glow so brightly in memory's eye. In 1951, André Bazin observed that films such as *Le quai des brumes* and *Le jour se lève* "appear to us today with the ideal qualities of a cinematic paradise lost."[70] The aura surrounding this "cinematic paradise lost" is, if anything, even more intense today than when Bazin made these remarks nearly a half-century ago. The difficulties that actually confronted filmmakers of the 1930s—precarious financing, fly-by-night production companies, scandals—have been easily forgotten. What remains are images from a cinema that enjoyed widespread appeal, and that was deeply rooted in French cultural traditions and social realities: precisely the qualities that are no longer in evidence. Ominous statistics confirm fears that French cinema has turned increasingly inward and, in so doing, has lost touch with the larger public: from 1960 to 1990, film audiences in France shrank no less than 60 percent. The problem is at least twofold. On the one hand, as novelist and critic Michel Mardore remarks in an issue of *CinémAction* devoted to the crisis confronting French cinema, crowd-pleasing genre films (boulevard comedies, thrillers) have left the realm of cinema for that of television.[71] On the other, as Swiss director

Alain Tanner complains, many serious French directors appear fatally drawn to introspective musings that leave many viewers cold. "They believe only in themselves," writes Tanner of such directors, "in their little place of cinema. They never feel the need to see beyond this. Sometimes I find that disarming and desolating, as if French directors did not need anyone but themselves."[72]

To these problems must also be added changing economic and social patterns that have contributed, as in the United States, to the shrinking of the audience. Faced with the difficulties and the cost of an evening at the movies, many of the French (like their American counterparts) settle for one at home with the television and the VCR. All too often, the neighborhood cinemas that welcomed them in the past have closed because of the increased commercialization of downtown districts. The threat of urban danger poses a further deterrent. Referring to an area of Paris known for drugs, a well-known director of photography, Charlie Van Damne, remarks, "You have to be a hardened *cinéphile* to leave a cinema of *les Halles* after ten o'clock."[73]

Above and beyond these problems, moreover, stands the major hurdle referred to earlier: that is, as many argue, it has simply become impossible for French films to compete with Hollywood. How can you resist the "atomic attack of American superproductions like *Terminator*," asks Philippe Madral, "when Americans spend more to promote a film like this than we can devote to the entire production of one of our most expensive films?"[74] Once again, the statistics are all too eloquent. While French films rarely account for even 1 percent of all films shown in this country—a fact that provoked one commentator to quip that the role of French films in the United States resembles that of Albanian films in France[75]—beginning in 1986, American films drew a larger audience in France than did French ones. And even that does not tell the whole story. Among those films produced in France are many that, as critics constantly complain, are little more than international, homogenized, "products" aimed at a youthful public nourished by advertising, fast food, and MTV. More such "products" seem to be in the offing since French television companies, which are required by law to invest in French films and to broadcast a certain quota of them each year, are now pressing producers and directors to make films that will draw big prime-time television audiences.[76]

Discussing the pressures France confronts as it prepares for integration into a united Europe, Stanley Hoffmann makes the following observation. "It may be true," he writes, "that the more European and global economic integration intensify, the greater will be the temptation to defend and to mythologize all the remaining social and political components of French national identity."[77] This is, certainly, no less true of cinema than of any other important "component" of national identiy. And it suggests one last reason why French cinema, faced with the very real possibility of being absorbed and smothered by Hollywood models, should display such a marked nostalgia for images that reflect, and speak to, deep currents of national identity. "It is impossible not to feel that today's French cinema," observes critic François de la Bretèque, "sensing that the end is near, pays a frozen homage to past splendors."[78] Even as the hollow images of the "cinéma du look" embody the melancholia that inheres in this "frozen homage," the films themselves—commercial, glossy, and unreal—suggest a process that may well be irreversible. And what is at stake may be not merely an aspect of national culture but, given the role that cinema has traditionally played in France, a piece of the nation's soul.

Epilogue

TO SOME EXTENT, the insistent nostalgia characterizing so many of the films discussed in the preceding pages recalls the so-called cult of memory that flourished in the last decades of the nineteenth century. Then, as now, the preoccupation with memory and the past came at a time of great uncertainty concerning the nation's identity and destiny—a time when the national "substance" was felt to be at risk. Then, as now, those on the extreme Right urged a return to the virtues of the past to combat the perceived "decadence" of the present. Observing that the theme of "decadence" is once again "in the air," Michel Winock underscores the parallels between these two melancholy fins de siècle; parodying contemporary lamentations about the state of the nation, he writes: "France is falling apart; national identity is becoming uncertain. There are no more ideas, no more colonies, no more spelling. Corruption is spreading. Criminality is growing. Drugs and the lack of religion are corrupting youths and hastening the end of time. . . . The French have been hearing this old song since the Revolution."[1]

But if there are insistent parallels between the somber mood of late-nineteenth-century France and that which currently pervades the nation— if the "old song" about decadence is once again in the air—there are also differences. The past may continue to exert its lure, but its contours, its role, have changed. Those on the Right and, especially, the extreme Right may continue to long for a time when France was "French," but others acknowledge that a "certain idea of France" has faded, that a historical cycle has run its course. It is true, of course, that symbols from the past are still very much in evidence. The Socialists celebrated the bicentennial of the Revolution with spectacular élan; under the neo-Gaullist party of Jacques Chirac, the remains of André Malraux, a great champion of de Gaulle, were solemnly laid to rest in the Panthéon alongside those of the nation's most illustrious sons and daughters. But these very ceremonies appeared to be impelled by a desire for the perpetuation of memories that, it was frequently acknowledged, had lost much of their charge. Pierre Nora spoke for many when he observed that the endless discussions and media hype surrounding the bicentennial celebrations made it clear that "celebrating the Revolution was more important than the Revolution being commemorated."[2] Underscoring the intensely self-conscious nature of the ceremonies in honor of Malraux, philosopher Bernard-Henri Lévy implicitly made much the same point. "I think everyone," he remarked, "needs this commemoration—the Government, the media, intellectuals. . . . It is probably because the French feel their identity is threatened, that their identity is being shaken to its very foundations. So it is understandable that we hold onto our memories in times like these."[3]

The acknowledgment heard in Lévy's remarks—that it is the sense of a diminished present which prompts the French to explore and to hold fast to their past—runs throughout virtually all the films discussed in this book. In different ways, all suggest that a historical moment is coming to an end. Sometimes, the feelings of loss they emanate have specific ideological contours. On the Left, Tavernier's early historical films waxed nostalgic for an era when it was still possible to dream the Marxist dream of class struggle and revolution; on the Right, Schoendoerffer created protagonists haunted by the collapse of imperial *gloire*. At other times, however, the longing for a vanished world, a remembered past, extends well beyond the bounds of ideology. Resnais appears to long for a lost moment of plenitude in which horror and guilt had not yet created a chasm between human beings and the world. The "cinéma du look" looks back to a populist world that lingers only in remembered images.

In their insistence on images, these last works, in particular, open onto a larger landscape of absence and loss. Here, the sense of decline stemming from France's particular circumstances merges with the widespread feeling that we are at the "end" of a period of history. For many critics, this post-modernist sense of "ending," of "coming after," can be traced back to the convulsions of the 1940s: making a mockery of the Enlightenment faith in progress, the atrocities of that decade also challenged Europe's conviction that it could lead men and women everywhere into the brave new world of the future.[4] With the hollowness of its ideals, its culture, denounced by the camps, Europe became, in the words of Ferenc Fehér, a "museum," "a dead volcano." If, writes Fehér, Europe "has any conception of what lies ahead, not untypically it is the dreaded image of a universal Doomsday. It is hardly surprising in this atmosphere to find that 'European' art, if it intends to be more than a museum exhibit, cannot but flaunt its empty freedom, this Pyrrhic victory, over the bonds linking the aesthetic with other spheres, over bonds which were not all fetters but, at least in the case of some of them, genuine lifelines."[5]

As Fehér observes, the "lifelines" linking the world of culture to the broader sweep of national life seem to be disappearing throughout the developed countries of the West. Still, this disappearance, together with its accompanying sense of hollowness and loss, may have a particular resonance in France. After all, the Enlightenment ideals at the heart of European culture were born and nourished in that country. Ushering in the Revolution and the Republic, these ideals were central to what France felt to be its mission and its "exceptional destiny." If, as Michelet had it, France was to be a "Milky Way" in the eyes of the world, it was largely because it was its role and its privilege to spread, and to serve as a model for, the ideals of the Enlightenment and the Revolution. At the center of national debates ever since the Revolution, these ideals provided a vital sense of historical identity and continuity even as they gave a particular cast to what has always been considered one of the glories of French civilization: that is, its culture. "No other country," declares Pierre Nora, "has established such a close connection between the national State, its economy, its culture, its language, and its society."[6] Bereft of these ideals, it is hardly surprising if that culture, as Fehrér suggests, feels like a "museum." Nor if, like all "places of memory," this museum seeks to enshrine a past that has vanished forever.

Throughout this book, I have argued that the sense of rupture and dislocation, of absence and loss, characterizing contemporary historical memory in France has nowhere been better captured, illustrated, than in cinema. And, indeed, the sense that French culture has been transformed into a "museum," a "place of memory," finds an explicit echo in a very popular film of 1994: *Grosse fatigue*. A black farce that stars, and was directed by, the well-known performer Michel Blanc, *Grosse fatigue* revolves about an issue that marks virtually all the films explored earlier: that of identity. For in this work Michel Blanc plays both himself and a diabolical double who gradually steals his identity—indeed, his very life—from him.

The double begins by ruining the actor's reputation: claiming to be Michel Blanc, he performs in seedy nightclubs and forces himself upon women. Before long, he usurps Michel Blanc's life so totally that the real actor is shunned by all who know him. Reduced to haunting the casting studios, the despondent performer finally meets another icon of French cinema: Philippe Noiret. He, too, it turns out, has been robbed of *his* identity. As the two once-famous actors wander about the streets of Paris, they come upon a director, played by none other than Roman Polanski, who is in the process of shooting a film. When Polanski offers to cast them as extras, café waiters, they eagerly accept and don the appropriate costumes. At this point, the camera pulls back to reveal the film set where they will be working: that of a famous restaurant which has been built among streets designed to resemble—to usurp and replace?—a real Parisian *quartier*.

From museum to theme park; from an actor who loses his identity to a country that fears its national "substance" is being eroded; from the past of French cinema to that of the world which nourished and sustained it. The steps are huge—and yet perhaps not so huge. When Noiret cries out, "We'll all end up as mice in their amusement parks," he is referring, of course, to the specter of Euro-Disney, to the advancing threat of American cultural and economic hegemony. But behind those fears lurks the sense that French identity itself, based on a long tradition of memory and history, is at risk. It may be not only French cinema that, like Michel Blanc, is being robbed of its essence, but France itself.

One must hope that Noiret's cry of anguish is unwarranted. In the end, Euro-Disney has not drawn the crowds it expected; French cinema has recently seen the emergence of interesting and independent young directors. New life can be breathed into countries as well as into "museums." The present government of Lionel Jospin offers hope that it may be possible to reconcile the desire for social justice with the demands of the global marketplace. But there is no doubt that the past will be a hard act to follow.

Notes

Chapter I
Introduction

1. Pierre Nora, "Entre mémoire et histoire: La problématique des lieux," in *Les lieux de mémoire*, I, ed. Pierre Nora (Paris: Gallimard, 1984), xvii. Along with a selection of essays from *Les lieux de mémoire*, "Between Memory and History" appears, in English, in *Realms of Memory: The Construction of the French Past*, trans. Arthur Goldhammer, foreword by Lawrence D. Kritzman (New York: Columbia University Press, 1996). An earlier translation by Marc Roudebush was published in *Representations* 26 (Spring 1989).

2. Charles de Gaulle, *Mémoires de guerre: L'appel, 1940–1942* (Paris: Plon, 1954), 1.

3. Nora, "Présentation," *Les lieux de mémoire*, I, xii.

4. For statistics regarding the sale of books and journals dealing with history, see Pascal Ory, *L'entre-deux-mai* (Paris: Seuil, 1983), 144–45.

5. François Dosse, *L'histoire en miettes: Des "Annales" à la "nouvelle histoire"* (Paris: Editions la Découverte, 1987), 5. Here and hereafter, unless otherwise noted, translations are mine.

6. The first volume of *Les lieux de mémoire*, subtitled *La République*, appeared in 1984; the next three volumes, devoted to *La Nation*, were published in 1986; the last three volumes, *Les France*, appeared in 1992. All were published by Gallimard. In subsequent citations of *Les lieux de mémoire*, the Roman numerals refer to its three largest subdivisions: *La République* (I), *La Nation* (II), *Les France* (III).

7. For a discussion of the resonance enjoyed by *Les lieux de mémoire*, see Nancy Wood, "Memory's Remains," *History and Memory* 6, no. 1 (1994): 141.

8. Nora himself discusses the implications of the success of *Les lieux de mémoire* in its concluding essay. See Nora, "L'ère de la commémoration," in *Les lieux de mémoire*, III.3.

9. Henry Rousso, *The Vichy Syndrome: History and Memory in France since 1944*, trans. Arthur Goldhammer (Cambridge: Harvard University Press, 1991). Originally published as *Le syndrome de Vichy: De 1944 à nos jours* (Paris: Seuil, 1987). Benjamin Stora, *La gangrène et l'oubli: La mémoire de la Guerre d'Algérie* (Paris: Editions la Découverte, 1991).

10. James Wilkinson, "A Choice of Fictions: Historians, Memory, and Evidence," *PMLA* 3, no. 1 (January 1996): 86.

11. Pierre Guibbert, with the collaboration of François de la Bretèque and Marcel Oms, "D'Astérix à Jeanne d'Arc," in *L'histoire de France au cinéma*, ed. Pierre Guibbert, Marcel Oms, and Michel Cadé (Paris: *CinémAction*/Amis de *Notre Histoire*, 1993), 50.

12. Cited by Jean-Luc Douin in *Tavernier* (Paris: Edilig, 1988), 97.

13. Nora, "Entre mémoire et histoire," xix.

14. "A political myth," writes Girardet, "is certainly an invention, distortion, or interpretation that could be challenged by reality. But it is true that, as a legendary narrative [*récit*], it also exerts an explanatory function, furnishing a certain number of keys for the understanding of the present, [and] constituting a grid through which the disconcerting chaos of facts and events seems to assume an order." See Raoul Girardet, *Mythes et mythologies politiques* (Paris: Seuil, 1986), 13.

15. Ibid., 14.

16. Rousso, *The Vichy Syndrome*, 10.

17. Ronald Koven, "National Memory: The Duty to Remember, the Need to Forget," *France Magazine*, Fall 1994, 17.

Along similar lines, Marc Ferro argues that the only struggle which saw France united as a nation was World War I; every other conflict, he observes, involved an element of civil war: "what was clear in 1939–1945 was also [true] of the Revolution . . . of the era of Joan of Arc and the Burgundians, of Henri IV. . . . Even in [the Franco-Prussian war of] 1870, there was a party that . . . desired the defeat of those who governed the country." See Marc Ferro, *Comment on raconte l'histoire aux enfants à travers le monde entier* (Paris: Payot, 1981), 135.

18. Pierre Nora, "Nation," in *A Critical Dictionary of the French Revolution*, ed. François Furet and Mona Ozouf, trans. Arthur Goldhammer (Cambridge: Harvard University Press, 1989), 749.

19. I am thinking, in particular, of two sets of debates: the first involved the proposed Smithsonian display, in 1994, of the Enola Gay—the B-29 that dropped the bomb on Hiroshima—that was cancelled because of violent opposition from veterans' groups; the following year former Vietnam hawks and doves clashed once again in the wake of the publication of a book by Robert McNamara: one of the principal architects of the war, in this work McNamara acknowledged that U.S. policy had been "wrong."

On the suppression of the proposed Smithsonian exhibit, see Martin Harwit, *An Exhibit Denied: Lobbying the History of Enola Gay* (New York: Copernicus, 1996).

20. Wilkinson, "A Choice of Fictions," 87.

21. "In this changing and nebulous complex of the political imaginary," asserts Girardet, "there is finally no mythological constellation more constant, more intensely present, than that of the Golden Age." Girardet, *Mythes et mythologies politiques*, 98.

22. "History," observed Le Goff of Tavernier, "is the very matter that impregnates [his] films, creates his characters, and in which he channels his obsessions." See Jacques Le Goff, "Un document d'âme," *Le monde*, November 12, 1987, 11.

23. Ferro, *Comment on raconte l'histoire aux enfants à travers le monde entier*, 135.

24. Marc Ferro, *Cinema and History*, trans. Naomi Greene (Detroit: Wayne State University, 1988), 82–83.

25. Girardet, *Mythes et mythologies politiques*, 22.

26. René Allio, "Trois cinéastes en quête de l'histoire: Entretien avec René Allio, Frank Cassenti et Bertrand Tavernier," *Revue du cinéma* 352 (July–August 1980): 114.

27. Jules Michelet, *Le peuple*, introduction by Paul Viallaneix (Paris: Flammarion, 1974), 230.

28. Ibid., 238.

29. Cited by Raoul Girardet in his *Le nationalisme français* (Paris: Seuil, 1983), 66–67.

30. Michel Winock, *Nationalisme, antisémitisme et fascisme en France* (Paris: Seuil, 1990), 16.

31. "As was formerly the case for historical painting and sculptures," writes Bonnet, "for plays and etchings, but with immense means, cinema took hold of the great national *récit* that for two centuries had constituted a new civic catechism." See Jean-Claude Bonnet, "Les morts illustres," in *Les lieux de mémoire*, II.3, 237.

32. For a list of films inspired by historical figures such as these, see *L'histoire de France au cinéma*, 289–324.

33. Observing that cinema took hold of the "epic" of Joan of Arc from the beginning, historian Michel Winock writes that "the memory of Jeanne is not a neutral one [but rather] fractured, controversial, manipulated; it expresses the ideological conflicts that have divided the French since the dawn of Modern Times." See Michel Winock, "Jeanne d'Arc," in *Les lieux de mémoire* III.3, 680.

34. Noting that Napoleon is always treated respectfully in French cinema, Pierre Guibbert observes that only films made outside France portray him as a "dictator" or as a "proud and paranoid emperor who does not care about people, not even the French." See "Ces rois qui ont fait la France . . . ," in *L'histoire de France au cinéma*, 122.

35. The earlier versions—both entitled *L'assassinat du duc de Guise*—were made, respectively, by Georges Hatot (1897) and Ferdinand Zecca (1902).

36. Marcel Oms, "De la Belle Epoque à la guerre de 14–18," in *L'histoire de France au cinéma*, 178.

37. The notable exception to these generalizations concerning the representation of history in French cinema of the 1920s is found, of course, in the films of Jean Renoir. Indeed, well before Renoir gave a radical rereading of the French Revolution in *La Marseillaise* (1938), he made *Le tournoi* (1929), a historical film described by film historian Richard Abel as "one more instance of a general pattern of genre subversion in [Renoir's] work." See Richard Abel, *French Cinema: The First Wave, 1915–1929* (Princeton, N.J.: Princeton University Press, 1984), 200.

38. Abel, *French Cinema: The First Wave*, 161–62.

39. Guitry apparently remarked that "one has the right to imagine many events as long as there is no proof to the contrary." Cited by Guibbert, "Ces rois qui ont fait la France," in *L'histoire de France au cinéma*, 75.

40. Ibid.

41. The volcanic presence of the events of May–June 1968 may have been felt more immediately and more profoundly in film than in any other realm of French culture. Soon after the first barricades went up, the world of cinema reacted vigorously on two fronts: in Cannes, the annual festival was forced to a halt; in Paris, directors and other film professionals rapidly convened an assembly—named, in a dramatic echo of the Revolution of 1789, the Estates-General of Cinema—that demanded nothing less than "public ownership of the cinema" and "workers' control of production, distribution and exhibition." See "The Estates General of the French Cinema," *Screen* 13, no. 4 (Winter 1972–73): 59. For a discussion of the

militant phase of filmmaking after May '68, see Sylvia Harvey, *May '68 and Film Culture* (London: British Film Institute, 1978); Jill Forbes, *The Cinema in France after the New Wave* (Bloomington: Indiana University Press, 1992), chap. 1.

42. Arthur Hirsh, *The French New Left: An Intellectual History from Sartre to Gorz* (Boston: South End Press, 1981), 154.

Underscoring the sense of rupture created by the events of May, Keith Reader observes that "the landscape of West European politics would not be what it is today without them; the importance of sexual politics, environmental and ecological issues, workers' control and cooperative movements, and the politics of culture for the European Left became qualitatively different after May." See Keith A. Reader, *Intellectuals and the Left in France since 1968* (London: Macmillan Press, 1987), 6.

43. See Winock, *Nationalisme, antisémitisme et fascisme en France*, 432.

44. Jacques Le Goff, *Histoire et mémoire* (Paris: Gallimard, 1988), 54.

45. Michel Foucault, *Power/Knowledge: Selected Interviews and Other Writings. 1972–1977*, ed. Colin Gordon (New York: Pantheon, 1980), 116.

46. Jean-Claude Schmitt, "L'histoire des marginaux," in *La nouvelle histoire*, ed. Jacques Le Goff, Roger Chartier, and Jacques Revel (Paris: Retz, 1978), 344.

47. Jacques Le Goff, "Une science en marche, une science dans l'enfance," in *La nouvelle histoire*, 12.

48. Ibid., 13.

49. René Prédal, *Le cinéma français depuis 1945* (Paris: Nathan, 1991), 309.

50. At this time, film journals also began to explore the issue of historical representation. See, for example, *Les cahiers du cinéma* 251–52 (July–August 1974).

51. See Philippe Joutard, *Journaux camisards* (Paris: U.G.E., 1965). In addition to these diaries, *Les Camisards* also made use of Emmanuel Le Roy Ladurie's 1966 study of Languedoc peasants, *Paysans du Languedoc*.

52. "What is exciting in History," Allio remarked in the course of one interview, "is the effect of strangeness. The forms of the past are so specific, so original, so different from ours that they take us into a dream. If a time machine could transport us to . . . Versailles one morning when Louis XIV was leaving his apartment, or else to a Parisian street as it appeared to Rousseau, it would be a fantastic shock." See Allio, "Trois cinéastes en quête de l'histoire," 109.

53. For the "nostalgic radicals of May '68," notes historian Philippe Joutard, the Camisard revolt represented a "movement of popular liberation." See Philippe Joutard, "Le musée du désert," in *Les lieux de mémoire* III.1, 556.

54. Allio, "Trois cinéastes en quête de l'histoire," 108.

55. See Guibbert, "D'Astérix à Jeanne d'Arc," in *L'histoire de France au cinéma*, 35.

56. The resurgence of such genres in the 1980s may have been partially due, as Guy Austin points out, to Socialist cultural policies put in place by then minister of culture Jack Lang. See Guy Austin, *Contemporary French Cinema* (Manchester: University of Manchester Press, 1996), 144.

57. "What interested me," remarked the film's well-known scriptwriter, Jean-Claude Carrière, "was the era when the action took place, its baroque and precious dimension, everything that preceded the final blow of classicism. It was [an era] marked by an enormous ferment that began in the sixteenth century, and that came

to a brutal halt in 1650." Cited by Guibbert and Oms in *L'histoire de France au cinéma*, 85.

58. "Today," comments an editorial in the journal *Esprit*, "the past has supplanted the invocation of the future as the most important means of legitimization." See "Le poids de la mémoire," *Esprit*, no. 193 (July 1993): 5.

59. Nora, "La nation-mémoire," in *Les lieux de mémoire* II.3, 653.

60. Saul Friedlander, "The End of Innovation?" *Substance* 62–63 (1990): 33.

61. Le Goff, "L'histoire nouvelle," in *La nouvelle histoire*, 235.

62. Stanley Hoffmann, "Fragments Floating in the Here and Now," in his *The European Sisyphus: Essays on Europe, 1964–1994* (Boulder, Colo.: Westview Press, 1995), 189–90.

63. Nora, "La nation-mémoire," 653.

64. Cited by Michel Faure in "The Way We Were," *France Magazine* 35 (Summer 1995): 17.

65. Henri Mendras, *La Seconde Révolution française: 1964–1984* (Paris: Gallimard, 1988), 24.

66. Commenting on these social problems, Stanley Hoffmann writes that "with unemployment has come [a] phenomenon, familiar to Americans but new in France: *l'exclusion*—the estrangement of a wide variety of depressed and troubled people from society including the long-term unemployed, unskilled young men and women, illegal immigrants, drug addicts and criminal gangs." See Stanley Hoffmann, "France: Keeping the Demons at Bay," *New York Review of Books*, March 3, 1994, 10.

67. Michel Wieviorka, *La France raciste* (Paris: Seuil, 1992), 16.

68. Philippe Joutard, *Ces voix qui nous viennent du passé* (Paris: Hachette, 1983), 157.

69. Winock, *Nationalisme, antisémitisme et fascisme en France*, 39. Interestingly, Winock notes that his book might well have been entitled "the illnesses of the national self."

70. Nora, "La mémoire-nation," 652.

71. Adam Gopnik, "Elvis of the Elysée," *New Yorker*, June 3, 1996, 45.

72. See "France Fumes over Ban on Smoking," *New York Times*, January 11, 1997, A1,4.

73. Stanley Hoffmann, "Thoughts on the French Nation Today," *Daedalus* 122, no. 3 (Summer 1993), 77.

74. On this issue, see Diana Pinto, "The Left, the Intellectuals and Culture," in *The Mitterand Experiment: Continuity and Change in Modern France*, ed. George Ross, Stanley Hoffmann, and Sylvia Mazacher (Oxford: Polity Press, 1987), 219.

75. In fact, a decade after *les événements*, "new philosopher" Bernard-Henri Lévy traced the "death" of socialism itself to the convulsions of May. "Socialism," he quipped in in 1977, "a cultural genre born in Paris in 1848; died in Paris in 1968." Cited in *Les idées en France: 1945–1988*, ed. Anne Simonin and Hélène Clastres (Paris: Gallimard, 1989), 334.

76. For a discussion of these issues, see George Ross, "The Tragedy of the French Left," *New Left Review* 171 (September–October 1988).

77. Noting that the recession of the early 1970s pushed France to the Right, political scientist George Ross observes that "the terms of the post-war social com-

promise around consumerist economic growth, employment security, the Welfare State and Keynesian macroeconomic intervention had begun to unravel. . . . The interventionist state was targeted for 'deregulation' and 'privatization.'" See George Ross, introduction to *The Mitterand Experiment*, 4.

78. Stanley Hoffmann, "Mitterand vs. France?" *New York Review of Books*, September 27, 1984, 53.

79. Le Goff, *Histoire et mémoire*, 27.

80. Václav Havel, "The Hope for Europe," *New York Review of Books*, June 20, 1996, 38.

81. Winock, *Nationalisme, antisémitisme et fascisme en France*, 48.

Chapter II
Alain Resnais: The Ghosts of History

1. Hendrik Hertzberg, "The Nuclear Jubilee," *New Yorker*, July 31, 1995, 6.

2. Michael Roth, "*Hiroshima Mon Amour*: You Must Remember This," in *Revisioning History: Film and the Construction of a New Past*, ed. Robert A. Rosenstone (Princeton, N.J.: Princeton University Press, 1995), 92.

3. Serge Daney, *Ciné journal 1981–1985* (Paris: Cahiers du cinéma, 1986), 164.

4. Gilles Deleuze, "Optimisme, pessimisme et voyage: Lettre à Serge Daney," in Daney, *Ciné journal: 1981–1986*, 6.

For Prédal's discussion of Resnais's "lazarean" characters, see René Prédal, *Alain Resnais*, Etudes cinématographiques 64–68 (Paris: Minard, 1968), chap. 8.

5. Julia Kristeva, *Soleil noir: Dépression et mélancolie* (Paris: Gallimard/Folio, 1987), 230. For an English translation of this essay, see Julia Kristeva, "The Pain of Sorrow in the Modern World: The Works of Marguerite Duras," trans. Katharine A. Jensen, *PMLA* 102, no. 2 (March 1987): 138–51.

Kristeva proceeds to make the point that no work better illustrates this "explosion of death and madness" than *Hiroshima mon amour*. "Everything is there," she writes of this film, "suffering, death, love, and their explosive merging in the mad melancholy of a woman; but especially the combination of sociohistorical realism . . . and the X-ray of depression."

Although Kristeva views *Hiroshima* primarily as the work of Marguerite Duras, *Hiroshima* is, surely, as much the work of its director as of its scriptwriter—as central to Resnais's oeuvre as it is to that of Duras.

6. His protagonists bear a striking resemblance, in fact, to the fictional characters described by Jean Cayrol in a 1964 essay that explores the ways in which the experience of the camps has left its imprint on the postwar novel. See Jean Cayrol, "Pour un romanesque lazaréen," in his *Les corps étrangers* (Paris: 10/18, 1964).

7. Traumatized people, writes Erickson, "often scan the surrounding world anxiously for signs of danger, breaking into explosive rages and reacting with a start to ordinary sights and sounds, but at the same time, all that nervous activity takes place against a numbed gray background of depression, feelings of helplessness. . . . Above all, trauma involves a continual reliving of some wounding experience." See Kai Erikson, "Notes on Trauma and Community," in *Trauma: Explorations in Memory*, ed. Cathy Caruth (Baltimore: Johns Hopkins University Press, 1995), 183–84.

8. Peter Harcourt notes that throughout *Marienbad* "there seems a neurotic dread of actual experience, of any physical contact, of the here and now." See Peter Harcourt, "Alain Resnais: Toward the Certainty of Doubt," *Film Comment*, January 1974, 27.

9. Cited by Bernard Pingaud, *Alain Resnais*, Premier Plan 18 (Lyon: Serdoc, 1961), 88.

Observing that the "explosion of traditional psychology" and the subsequent emergence of free-floating mental states constitutes one of the most original aspects of Resnais's cinema, and the most difficult, critic Alain Ménil writes: "If the shots of *Hiroshima* still correspond to the gaze of the heroine, in *Muriel*, and even in *Marienbad*, this identity fades." See Alain Ménil, "Opus I," *Cinématographe* 88 (April 1983): 28.

10. Commenting on a central, repeated, scene of falling in *Je t'aime je t'aime*, Peter Harcourt observes: "By this short scene, many times repeated, Sternberg [the scenarist] and Resnais seem to be recreating that frightening feeling, of loss of control, that we can experience in dreams. It is a feeling of immense anxiety and personal insecurity. If it thus seems emblematic of *Je t'aime je t'aime*, I sometimes wonder if it couldn't be taken as emblematic for the whole of Resnais." See Harcourt, "Toward the Certainty of Doubt," 29.

11. Gilles Deleuze, *Cinéma II: L'image-temps* (Paris: Les éditions de minuit, 1985), 268.

12. "We read the books on Auschwitz," writes philosopher Maurice Blanchot, "the vow of everybody there, the last vow: know what has happened, do not forget, and at the same time: you will never know." Maurice Blanchot, *L'écriture du désastre* (Paris: Gallimard, 1980), 131. Cited in *Testimony: Crises of Witnessing in Literature, Psychoanalysis, and History*, ed. Shoshana Felman and Doris Laub (New York: Routledge, 1992), 117.

Addressing this same issue, Alain Finkielkraut writes, "Memory wants both to know the genocide and to recognize it as unknown; it wants it present as a guarantee against forgetting, and yet distant in order to prevent reductive explantions; it wants to make the event contemporary and yet keep it beyond our grasp; it wants to welcome it without assimilating it—and in this, no doubt, the faculty of memory might be deemed religious." Alain Finkielkraut, *L'avenir d'une négation* (Paris: Seuil, 1982), 95.

13. This quotation comes from the English translation of the script published in *Film: Book 2 (Films of Peace and War)*, ed. Robert Hughes (New York: Grove, 1962), 240.

Years later, Claude Lanzmann, director of *Shoah* (1985), a massive documentary on the Holocaust that refuses to "show" us anything, would echo these remarks, observing that he began his film "with the impossibility of telling this story." Cited by Cathy Caruth, "Recapturing the Past: Introduction," in *Trauma: Explorations in Memory*, 154.

14. Even after the events of May '68, censorship restrictions were not lifted as quickly or as completely as many would have liked. On this issue, see François Courtade, *Les malédictions du cinéma français: Une histoire du cinéma français parlant (1928–1978)*, preface by Raymond Borde (Paris: Editions Alain Moreau, 1978),

322–50. See also Jean-Pierre Jeancolas, *Le cinéma des français: La Ve République, 1958–1978* (Paris: Stock/Cinéma, 1977), chap. 2.

15. On this issue, see Anne-Monique Epstein, "La Résistance française: Evolution d'une mythologie du cinéma," in *Guerres révolutionnaires: Histoire et cinéma*, ed. Sylvie Dallet (Paris: L'Harmattan, 1984), 76.

16. A few years later, in 1966, *La guerre est finie* was withdrawn from Cannes as an "official" French selection at the request of the Spanish government.

17. Lynn A. Higgins, *New Novel, New Wave, New Politics: Fiction and the Representation of History in Postwar France* (Lincoln: University of Nebraska Press, 1996), 52.

18. Rousso, *The Vichy Syndrome*, 22.

19. Cited by Judith Miller in *One, by One, by One: Facing the Holocaust* (New York: Simon and Schuster, 1990), 140.

20. As Raoul Girardet observes, it is when historical change is particularly rapid or prone to "ruptures," or when "mechanisms" of solidarity give way, that political myths "assume clearer shapes, assert themselves with more intensity, exert more violently their power of attraction." See Raoul Girardet, *Mythes et mythologies politiques*, 178.

21. William Pfaff, "Remembering," *New Yorker*, December 7, 1987, 140–41.

22. Rousso, *The Vichy Syndrome*, 97.

23. As Peter Harcourt observes, each of Resnais's first three films "involve[s] a central character attempting to validate his own past by persuading another character to accept his account of it." See Harcourt, "Toward the Certainty of Doubt," 23.

24. Gérald Genette was one of the few to point out that such interpretations violated the spirit of the film. The events depicted in *Marienbad*, he wrote, may belong "either to a real past or a mythical past, or else to a hallucinatory or oneiric present, or even to a hypothetical future." See Gérard Genette, *Figures* (Paris: Seuil, 1966), 87.

25. Cited by Pingaud, *Alain Resnais*, 45.

Commenting on the total unreality of *Marienbad*, critic Youssef Ishaghpour calls Resnais's film the "greatest monument ever constructed to the glory of cinema as a world of images. . . . It is a veritable hymn to the camera. . . . Cinema as an imaginary world eliminates reproduction and representation: the film coincides with itself. . . . Places, characters, story, exist only on the screen, not elsewhere, not before, not afterward." See Youssef Ishaghpour, *D'une image à l'autre: La nouvelle modernité du cinéma* (Paris: Denoël/Gonthier, 1982), 194.

26. "Remembering," observes Gilles Deleuze of Resnais's cinema, "is no longer the faculty of having memories; it is the membrane that makes the levels of the past and the levels of reality communicate. . . . Both gnaw away at the present, which is merely the point where they meet." Deleuze, *Cinéma II: L'image-temps*, 269.

27. Pascal Bonitzer, *Décadrages: Peinture et cinéma* (Paris: Les cahiers du cinéma, 1987), 32.

28. Cited by Win Sharples, "Alain Resnais," *Filmmakers Newsletter*, 8, no. 2 (December 1974): 34.

29. Noting that he was a youthful fan of popular silent adventure serials such as *Judex* and *Fantomas*, Resnais once deemed himself a man of the "silent screen." See "Entretien avec Alain Resnais," *Les cahiers du cinéma* 347 (May 1983): 34.

30. Kristeva, *Soleil noir*, 231.

31. Robert Benayoun, *Alain Resnais: Arpenteur de l'imaginaire* (Paris: Stock/Ramsay, 1980), 45.

32. During the presidency of François Mitterand, a controversial decision was made to build a new national library. Thus most of the collections seen in the imposing building depicted in *Toute la mémoire du monde* are gradually being moved to gleaming new quarters.

33. Apparently, the official sponsors were not happy with the film. According to James Monaco, Resnais's film "annoyed a few people when it was released: cultural propaganda should be more didactic they thought." See James Monaco, *Alain Resnais* (New York: Oxford University Press, 1978), 24.

34. Deleuze, *Cinéma II: L'image-temps*, 159.

35. Noel Burch, "Four Recent French Documentaries," *Film Quarterly* 13, no. 1 (Fall 1959): 59.

36. Peter Harcourt, "Alain Resnais: Memory Is Kept Alive with Dreams," *Film Comment*, November–December 1973, 50.

37. Marguerite Duras, *Hiroshima mon amour*, trans. Richard Seaver (New York: Grove, 1961), 9.

38. Placing both this need and this anguish at the core of Resnais's cinema, Youssef Ishaghpour poses the issue thus: "How to forget the [past], how to live having forgotten it, and how to live while not forgetting it. This [is] Resnais's dilemma." See Ishaghpour, *D'une image à l'autre*, 186.

39. Cited by Gaston Bounoure, *Alain Resnais* (Paris: Seghers, 1962), 105.

40. Lawrence Langer, *Holocaust Testimonies: The Ruin of Memory* (New Haven: Yale University Press, 1991), 174–75. Cited by Onno van der Hart and Bessel A. van der Kolk, "The Intrusive Past," in *Trauma: Explorations in Memory*, 177.

41. Roth, "*Hiroshima Mon Amour*: You Must Remember This," 98, 100.

42. Rousso, *The Vichy Syndrome*, 20.

43. Higgins, *New Novel, New Wave, New Politics*, 49.

44. "*Muriel ou le temps d'un retour*," *Les cahiers de la cinémathèque*, nos. 18–19 (Spring 1976): 115.

45. Cited by Bounoure, *Alain Resnais*, 86.

46. Marie-Claire Ropars-Wuilleumier, *L'écran de la mémoire* (Paris: Seuil, 1970), 65.

47. Pierre Nora, "Gaullistes et communistes," in *Les lieux de mémoire* III.1, 362.

48. Despite this fundamental difference, the timing of Resnais's first features, as well as their break with cinematic conventions, often gave the impression (especially abroad) that he too was part of the so-called New Wave. As if to reinforce this impression, in 1961 Truffaut remarked to American journalists at Cannes that the New Wave was born the year that the festival included *Hiroshima mon amour*, *Les cousins*, *Black Orpheus*, and *Les Quatre Cent Coups*. See Benayoun, *Alain Resnais*, 77.

49. Eugen Weber, *The Hollow Years: France in the 1930s* (New York: Norton, 1994), 136.

50. "Between Dreyfus and Vichy, and especially at the time of the Popular Front," writes Pierre Birnbaum, "Léon Blum became the ideal scapegoat of political anti-Semitism. . . . The object of ferocious and demented hatred, his presence at the summit of political power reinforced the anti-Semitic movement." Pierre Birnbaum, "Grégoire, Dreyfus, Drancy et Copernic," in *Les lieux de mémoire* III.1, 593–94.

51. Winock, *Nationalisme, antisémitisme et fascisme en France*, 169.

52. This phenomenon is explored at some length and with great subtlety by Dudley Andrew and Steven Ungar in an article entitled "Presse/Première: *Stavisky . . . et la 'mise en page de l'histoire,'* " *Hors Cadre* 10 (1992): 102.

53. Monaco, *Alain Resnais*, 169.

54. See "Un autre point de vue sur *Stavisky*," *Positif* 161 (September 1974): 68.

55. Youssef Ishaghpour and Pierre Samson, "Resnais contre le courant," *Les temps modernes*, October 1974, 183–84.

56. Birnbaum, "Grégoire, Dreyfus, Drancy et Copernic," 566.

57. Monaco, *Alain Resnais*, 187.

58. Suggesting that Trotsky and Stavisky represent "positive" and "negative" reactions to the same problem, Ishaghpour observes that they "sought something other than the orders they helped establish and that expelled them: fascism and Stalinism." See Ishaghpour, *D'une image à l'autre*, 209.

59. Noting that the columns of many papers were indeed for sale, and that the "vast majority of the Paris press" was on the Right at the time of the Stavisky Affair, historian Eugen Weber proceeds to remark that the "Right, when not dedicated to opposing the Republic, worked to discredit republican governments in office." See Weber, *The Hollow Years*, 130.

60. Dudley Andrew and Steven Ungar point out that this sequence re-creates a series of photos that appeared in the weekly review *Marianne* in January of 1934. See Andrew and Ungar, "Press/Première," 103.

61. Resnais and his cameraman, Sacha Vierny, writes James Monaco, "spent a good deal of effort in trying to recapture a sense of the style of early thirties movies. They used only setups and shot angles that were possible in the early thirties. Resnais wanted the film to look archaic." See Monaco, *Alain Resnais*, 180.

62. Cited by Benayoun, *Alain Resnais*, 147. From an interview with Richard Seaver in *Film Comment*, July–August 1975.

63. Cited by Claude Beylie in *Alain Resnais, Le Cinématographe*, booklet published by the French Institute of Florence, to accompany a retrospective of Resnais's films, May 1986, 37.

64. Benayoun, *Alain Resnais*, 150.

65. Weber, *The Hollow Years*, 134.

For a discussion of the ramifications of the production of *Coriolanus* mounted at this time, see Andrew and Ungar, "Presse/Première," 105–6.

66. Ishaghpour, *D'une image à l'autre*, 207.

67. Monaco, *Alain Resnais*, 170.

68. Cited by Ishaghpour, *D'une image à l'autre*, 203.

69. Observing that *Providence* was a film *"about the will not to die,"* Resnais remarked that "one has the impression that if [Clive] stopped drinking or imagining, his body would dissolve in a few minutes." Cited by Benayoun, *Alain Resnais*, 232.

70. Beset by oft-repeated charges of "formalism," Resnais once observed: "I have always thought that the dichotomy between form and content displays an absurd reasoning . . . you can commmunicate only through form. If there is no form you cannot create any emotions in the viewer." Cited by Benayoun, *Alain Resnais*, 233.

71. "Entretien avec Alain Resnais," *Cinéma*, July–August 1980, 38.

Echoing this sentiment in more metaphorical terms, a few years later the director declared that "the human brain, incapable of conceiving and of apprehending the unknown, has invented dreams to reassure itself." Cited by Jean-Daniel Roob in his *Alain Resnais. Qui êtes-vous?* (Lyon: La Manufacture, 1986), 124.

72. Cited in Benayoun, *Alain Resnais*, 231.

73. Some of these ingenious interpretations are discussed by James Monaco in his *Alain Resnais*, 207–8.

74. Ishaghpour, *D'une image à l'autre*, 216.

75. Ibid.

76. Kristeva, *Soleil noir*, 264–65.

77. Ishaghpour, *D'une image à l'autre*, 216.

Chapter III
Battles for Memory: Vichy Revisited

1. Rousso, *The Vichy Syndrome*, 10.
In 1994, Rousso, in collaboration with Eric Conan, devoted still another book to the ongoing saga of Vichy memory. See *Vichy un passé qui ne passe pas* (Paris: Fayard, 1994).

2. The myth of "resistancialism" was, writes Henry Rousso, first, a "process that sought to minimize the importance of the Vichy regime and its impact on French society, *including its most negative aspects*; second, the construction of an object of memory, the 'Resistance,' whose significance transcended by far the sum of its active parts . . . ; and, third, the identification of this 'Resistance' with the nation as a whole, a characteristic feature of the Gaullist version of the myth." Rousso, *The Vichy Syndrome*, 10.

3. For an overview of this phenomenon, see Alan Morris, *Collaboration and Resistance Reviewed: Writers and the Mode Rétro in Post-Gaullist France* (New York: Berg, 1993).

4. For a list of films dealing with the Occupation years, see appendix 2 in Rousso, *The Vichy Syndrome*, 318–23. See also André Pierre Colombat, *The Holocaust in French Film* (Metuchen, N.J.: Scarecrow Press, 1993).

5. Underscoring the resemblances between the political "crises" provoked by the Stavisky scandal, by Pétain's National Revolution, and by the Algerian War, historian Michel Winock observes that "these three moments of internal French battles" were marked, above all, by ideological conflicts of "values." See Winock, *Nationalisme, antisémitisme et fascisme en France*, 168.

6. Robert Paxton, *Vichy France: Old Guard and New Order, 1940–1944* (New York: Columbia University Press, 1972), xii.

Henry Rousso points out that Paxton's book played an important role in the "explosion" of Vichy memory that was first triggered by *Le chagrin et la pitié*. "It is in no way to detract from the merits of Paxton's book," writes Rousso, "to point out that *Vichy France* profited immensely from the 'Ophuls effect' and from the new climate in France in the period 1971–1974. Although other works of similar intent were published at the time, Paxton's, perhaps more than all the rest, was deemed to lend scholarly authority to the return of what had been repressed. . . . The book was believed to provide dispassionate, objective proof of the points made with great passion in the film." See Rousso, *The Vichy Syndrome*, 255–56.

7. "The civil war," writes Rousso, "and particularly the inception, influence, and acts of the Vichy regime, played an essential if not primary role in the difficulties that the people of France have faced in reconciling themselves to their history—a greater role than the foreign occupation, the war, and the defeat, all things that, though they have not vanished from people's minds, are generally perceived through the prism of Vichy." See *The Vichy Syndrome*, 8–9.

8. Philippe Burrin, "Vichy," in *Les lieux de mémoire* III.1, 338.

9. Paxton, *Vichy France: Old Guard and New Order, 1940–1944*, xii.

10. Tony Judt, "French War Stories," *New York Times*, July 19, 1995, A15.

11. Calling de Gaulle the "last credible nationalist," Michel Winock notes that the policies he carried out while president—that is, the deliberate neutrality he maintained toward the two superpowers, his intransigence toward the United States, the alliance he sought to forge with Germany, his call for a "Québec libre," his development of a French nuclear capacity, his withdrawal from NATO—were all inspired by a desire to maintain French *grandeur* and to prevent his country from being reduced to the rank of a second-rate power. See Winock, *Nationalisme, antisémitisme et fascisme en France*, 60.

12. Jean-Pierre Jeancolas, "Fonction du témoignage," *Positif* 170 (June 1975): 58.

13. Bertrand Poirot-Delpech, "Vichy ou comment s'en débarasser," *Le monde*, special insert on Touvier, March 17, 1994, 1.

14. On this issue, see Stanley Hoffman, "Chagrin et pitié?" in his *Essais sur la France: Déclin ou renouveau?* (Paris: Seuil, 1974), 70.

15. Marcel Ophuls, *Le chagrin et la pitié* (Paris: Editions Alain Moreau, 1980), 222.

16. Jeancolas, "Fonction du témoignage," 60.

In a similar vein, film critic and historian René Prédal writes that *Le chagrin et la pitié* "took on a particular resonance in the wake of the traumatism of '68." See René Prédal, *Le cinéma français contemporain* (Paris: Cerf, 1984), 112.

17. Cited by Joutard, *Ces voix qui nous viennent du passé*, 125.

18. Cited by Rousso, *The Vichy Syndrome*, 108.

19. In the eyes of Guy Austin, the film does more than merely ignore de Gaulle; it also draws an "unmistakeable visual parallel" between de Gaulle and Pétain insofar as the first part of the film ends with an image of Pétain and the second part begins with one of de Gaulle. See Austin, *Contemporary French Cinema*, 23.

20. "With de la Mazière," writes Rousso, "a reassuring image collapses. It is simply not true that there had been only two kinds of Frenchmen, good and bad. There were those who consciously chose the camp of fascism and Nazism, and there were those who were willing to die for a certain idea of France." See Rousso, *The Vichy Syndrome*, 105.

21. Marc Ferro, "Interviews in the Works of Ophuls, Harris, and Sedouy," in *Cinema and History*, 143.

Showing how reactions differed, still other critics disagreed with Ferro's harsh appraisal of the film's portrait of two simple farmers who joined the Resistance. In the eyes of historian Anne-Monique Epstein, these brave men were the "heroes of the film . . . they are intelligent, straightforward, and upright." See Anne-Monique Epstein, "La Résistance française: Evolution d'une mythologie du cinéma," in *Guerres révolutionnaires: Histoire et cinéma*, 73.

22. Rousso, *The Vichy Syndrome*, 102.

23. Concerning the deportations of foreign Jews, historian Pierre Laborie reminds us that those "taken from the unoccupied zone and . . . sent to Auschwitz (more than ten thousand) [were] the only European Jews arrested in this manner in a nonoccupied territory." See Laborie, "La France de 1940–1942: Etait-elle anti-sémite?" *Libération*, March 13, 1993, 50.

24. Ory, *L'entre-deux-mai*, 121.

25. David Pryce-Jones, "Paris during the German Occupation," in *Collaboration in France: Politics and Culture during the Nazi Occupation, 1940–1944*, ed. Gerhard Hirschfeld and Patrick Marsh (New York: Berg, 1989), 27.

26. Jean-Louis Bory, "Servitudes et misères d'un salaud," *Le nouvel observateur*, January 28, 1974, 56–57.

27. Pauline Kael, review of *Lacombe Lucien*, *New Yorker*, September 30, 1974, 97.

28. Such insistences are found, for example, in *Malle on Malle*, ed. Philip French (London: Faber and Faber, 1993), 102–3. In these pages, Malle observes that in the region where the film was shot "people who had lived through that period knew that this film was completely true and honest about what actually happened."

In still another interview, remarking that he had done a great deal of research for *Lacombe Lucien*, the director declared, "I managed to find former *milicens*, to spend evenings with them, to try to get them to relax, to talk, in order to know why they did that." See Jean Decock, "Entretien avec Louis Malle: Un cinéma du regard," *French Review* 63, no. 4 (March 1990): 675.

29. Jean-Pierre Azéma, "Les hommes en noir de la Milice," *Le monde*, special insert on Touvier, March 17, 1994, 4.

30. Pascal Bonitzer, "Histoire de Sparadrap," in his *Le regard et la voix* (Paris: 10/18, 1976), 92. Originally in *Les cahiers du cinéma* 250 (May 1974).

31. Ibid., 91.

Phrased somewhat differently, this idea is echoed by Susan Hayward. *Lacombe Lucien* is, she notes, a film about "the *discours fascisant*. It points, in the instance, to the fact that Fascism is an 'attraction'—the first time Lucien encounters it he is positioned as an outsider looking on (as voyeur). If Fascism attracts, it is paradoxically because the image is eventually vacuous." See Susan Hayward, *French National Cinema* (London: Routledge, 1993), 251.

32. René Prédal, "François, David et les autres dans le cinéma hexagonal des années soixante-dix," *CinémAction* 37 (1986): 152. Edited by Annie Goldmann and Guy Hennebelle, this issue is entitled "Cinéma et judéité."

33. Eduardo Bruno, "L'ambiguità della favola e univocità del cinema di ritorno," *Filmcritica* 248 (October 1974): 314.

34. Ciriaco Tiso, "L'ambiguità filmica e il suo equivoco," *Filmcritica* 248 (October 1974): 330–31.

35. Malle himself notes the recurrence of this theme throughout his work from *Le souffle au coeur* and *Lacombe Lucien* to *Pretty Baby* and *Au revoir les enfants*. See Decock, "Entretien avec Louis Malle," 674.

36. Michel Foucault, "Anti-rétro: Entretien avec Michel Foucault," *Les cahiers du cinéma* 251–52 (July–August 1974): 6.

37. Michel Capdenac, "Révolte dévoyée, film fourvoyé," *Europe* 540–41 (April–May 1974): 266.

38. Christian Zimmer, "La paille dans le discours de l'ordre," *Les temps modernes* 336 (July 1974): 2496.

39. Richard Grenier, "The Aging of the New Wave," *Commentary* 71, no. 2 (February 1981): 64.

40. Yann Lardeau, "Une nuit au théâtre," *Les cahiers du cinéma* 316 (October 1980): 5.

41. On this issue, see Patrick Marsh, "The Theatre: Compromise or Collaboration?" in *Collaboration in France: Politics and Culture during the Nazi Occupation*.

42. Colin Nettelbeck, "Getting the Story Right," in *Collaboration in France: Politics and Culture during the Nazi Occupation*, 291.

43. Cited by François Garçon in "Le retour d'une inquiétante imposture: *Lili Marleen* et *Le dernier métro*," *Les temps modernes* 422 (September 1981): 544.

44. Ibid., 545.

45. Birnbaum, "Grégoire, Dreyfus, Drancy et Copernic," 602.

46. Ibid., 595.

47. Major studies devoted to this difficult and sensitive issue include: Robert Paxton, *Vichy France: Old Guard and New Order, 1940–1944*, 174–85; Michael Marrus and Robert Paxton, *Vichy France and the Jews* (New York: Schocken, 1981); Susan Zuccotti, *The Holocaust, the French, and the Jews* (New York: Basic Books, 1993); Sanford Gutman, "The Holocaust in France" in *Holocaust Literature: A Handbook of Critical, Historical, and Literary Writings*, ed. Saul S. Friedman (London: Greenwood Press, 1993).

48. "Some people," declared de Gaulle, "even feared that the Jews, hitherto dispersed, but who had remained what they had always been, an elite people, sure of itself and domineering, might, once assembled on the site of their former grandeur, transform into ardent and conquering ambition the very moving wishes that they had been formulating for nineteen centuries: 'Next year in Jerusalem.'" Cited in Rousso, *The Vichy Syndrome*, 135.

49. Such sentiments could be discerned, many believed, in several controversial editorial comments made by left-wing newspapers following the broadcast of the television series *Holocaust*: *Libération* denounced a "hierarchy of genocide" that privileged the suffering of the Jews; *L'Humanité* criticized the "exclusive focus on the Jewish problem."

The phenomenon of left-wing anti-Semitism is discussed at length, and with great subtlety, by Alain Finkelkraut in his *Le juif imaginaire* (Paris: Seuil, 1980).

50. Pierre Birnbaum notes that in the wake of this explosion Prime Minister Raymond Barre made matters worse by articulating a strange distinction between "the Jewish victims of the explosion and the 'innocent' French victims." See Birnbaum, "Grégoire, Dreyfus, Drancy et Copernic," 606.

51. Rousso, *The Vichy Syndrome*, 157.

52. Characterized by a variety of phenomena—from public rallies to a growth of Jewish schools—the rediscovery of Judaism, remarks Pierre Birnbaum, signaled a search for Jewish identity that went beyond "its religious and institutional framework." See Birnbaum, "Grégoire, Dreyfus, Drancy et Copernic," 606.

53. In a dispassionate, but ultimately condemnatory, summary of the consequences of these measures, Robert Paxton makes several important points. Observing that while the Vichy government did not foresee that French Jews would be sent to the death camps, he goes on to say that the measures taken against them— that is, the obligation to register as Jews, the loss of goods and businesses, their exclusion from liberal professions and government jobs—all "helped to render them more visible and vulnerable to the process of extermination put into place in Europe by the Nazis in the spring of 1942. If a third of the Jews in France who were murdered in the course of the genocide were of French nationality, the Vichy government was an accomplice in their fate. If a great number of Jews of French nationality escaped from this fate, it was in spite of what their government did." See Robert Paxton, "Vichy a-t-il protégé les juifs français?" *Libération*, July 13, 1993, 48.

54. Rousso, *The Vichy Syndrome*, 25.

55. Pauline Kael, review of *Au revoir les enfants*, *New Yorker*, February 22, 1988, 86.

56. Stanley Hoffmann, "Neither Hope nor Glory," *New York Review of Books*, May 12, 1988, 21.

57. Ibid.

58. That same year also witnessed a third controversy stemming from the Occupation years. It was sparked by President Mitterand's decision to invite German troops to join the traditional Bastille Day parade on July 14 as part of the newly formed Eurocorps. While Mitterand argued that one had to turn the page on the past, others—including veterans' associations, the Communist Party, the far-Right National Front, and several prominent individuals (among them minister of the interior Charles Pasqua and former president Giscard d'Estaing)—were deeply disturbed by the sight of German troops marching along the Champs-Elysées for the first time since the Occupation. Significantly, though, the polemics raised by this event were relatively mild compared to other controversies stemming from French, rather than German, behavior during the war.

59. Ted Morgan, "The Hidden Frenchman," *New York Times Magazine*, May 22, 1992, 35.

60. See Alan Riding, "At His Trial, Frenchman's Memory of Nazis Is Dim," *New York Times*, March 27, 1994, 6.

61. Alan Riding, "Frenchman Charged in Jews' Killing Says He's No Anti-Semite," *New York Times*, March 22, 1994, A6.

62. Edwy Plenel, "Les secrets de jeunesse de François Mitterand," *Le monde*, September 2, 1994, 12.

63. Writing in the protofascist review *Action française*, in 1912 Charles Maurras, a writer with strong royalist and anti-Dreyfusard sympathies, classified "les métèques"—along with Protestants, Jews, and Freemasons—as one of four categories of "internal foreigners" who posed a threat to France.

64. Cited by Claire Andieu, "Questions d'une historienne," *Le monde*, September 15, 1994, 2.

65. Ibid.

66. Tony Judt, "Truth and Consequences," *New York Review of Books*, November 3, 1994, 11.

67. For Socialist reactions to Mitterand's conduct, see "Deux heures de déchirements chez les socialistes," *Le monde*, September 9, 1994, 9.

68. The deportation of the children—more than four thousand of whom were sent to their death—was one of the major articles for which Bousquet was scheduled to be tried. Speaking of Mitterand's friendship with the man responsible for these deaths, Tony Judt observes that "there is strong suspicion that Mitterand engineered the delays that prevented Bousquet from coming to trial after his indictment in 1989 for crimes against humanity." See Judt, "Truth and Consequences," 10.

As for Mitterand, he denied knowing anything about Bousquet's role in the deportations.

69. Morgan, "The Hidden Frenchman," 78.

70. Luc Rosenzweig, "Mémoire officielle, mémoire souterraine," *Le monde*, September 15, 1994, 1.

71. "La mémoire retrouvée," *Le monde*, special insert on Touvier, March 17, 1994, 1.

72. For information on these documents, see the *New York Times*, April 7, 1993, 1, 4.

73. Jean-Michel Dumay, "La lente imprégnation des manuels scolaires," *Le monde*, special insert on Touvier, March 17, 1994, 7.

74. Cited by Marlise Simons, "Chirac Affirms France's Guilt in Fate of Jews," *New York Times*, July 17, 1995, A3. Although Jewish leaders praised this speech, they also made it clear that the families of those deported had yet to be financially compensated.

75. After a six-month trial, Papon was condemned to ten years in prison—a sentence that seemed to acknowledge that he was guilty of "crimes against humanity" but not as guilty as someone like Barbie.

76. These apologies seem to have stimulated mea culpas concerning still earlier instances of French anti-Semitism. On the occasion of the 1998 centennial commemoration of the publication of Emile Zola's famous pamphlet, *J'accuse*, President Chirac called the Dreyfus Affair a "dark spot" on French history, while the Roman Catholic daily, *La Croix*, acknowledged that its anti-Semitic editorials denouncing Dreyfus were a betrayal of its "Christian beliefs."

77. See Roger Cohen, "France Confronts Its Jews, and Itself," *New York Times*, October 19, 1997, sec. 4, 4.

Chapter IV
Bertrand Tavernier: History in the Present Tense

1. For further information concerning the whole of Tavernier's oeuvre, see Danièle Bion, *Bertrand Tavernier: Cinéaste de l'émotion* (Paris: Hatier, 1984); Jean-Luc Douin, *Tavernier* (Paris: Edilig, 1988); Sergio Arecco, *Bertrand Tavernier* (Rome: Il Castoro, 1993).

2. "Entretien," *Cinéma* 198 (May 1975): 76.

3. Tavernier has spoken of his love of American cinema in numerous interviews and articles. Many of these have been reprinted in a volume written in collaboration with Jean-Pierre Coursodon, *Trente ans de cinéma américain* (Paris: C.I.B., 1970). See also Tavernier's contributions to *Le Western* (Paris: 10/18, 1966) and to *Humphrey Bogart* (Paris: Terrain Vague, 1967).

He has also expressed his personal attraction to left-wing American directors such as Herbert Biberman, Abraham Polonski, and Dalton Trumbo. See Douin, *Tavernier*, 83.

4. Cited by Douin, *Tavernier*, 81.

5. His films seem to embody, in fact, what Ginette Vincendeau has called the "negative esthetic" of the New Wave. See Ginette Vincendeau, "France 1945–65 and Hollywood: The *policier* as Inter-national text," *Screen* 33, no. 1 (Spring 1992): 57.

6. When questioned about this collaboration, which seemed very surprising at the time, Tavernier remarked that he was drawn to Bost and Aurenche for reasons that were both political and aesthetic. Observing that they really knew how to develop or "nourish" a script in the manner of classical American or prewar French films, he went on to say that they "did not have to wait for May 1968 to discover that it was necessary to put political elements into film." See "Entretien avec Bertrand Tavernier: A propos de *L'Horloger de Saint-Paul*," *Positif* 156 (February 1974): 46.

Bost died soon after the completion of *L'horloger de Saint-Paul*; Tavernier continued to work with Aurenche—notably on *Que la fête commence*, *Le juge et l'assassin*, and *Coup de Torchon*.

7. In addition to these allusions to Renoir himself, Tavernier's first film, *L'horloger de Saint-Paul*, is dedicated to poet and scriptwriter Jacques Prévert, who wrote the scenario for *Le crime de M. Lange*.

8. See Douin, *Tavernier*, 76.

9. "Entretien," *Cinéma* 198, 75.

10. Ibid., 76–77.

11. In the course of one interview, Tavernier remarked that he wanted his viewers "to forget that they are seeing historical films a bit as they do when they go to plays by Brecht. *The Caucasian Chalk Circle* begins as a historical play, but after a time its feelings, passions, and social relationships become so clear that the notion of 'history' completely disappears." See "Trois cinéastes en quête de l'histoire: Entretien avec René Allio, Frank Cassenti et Bertrand Tavernier," 110.

12. Manfred Engelbert, "Le discours historique de Bertrand Tavernier dans *Que la fête commence*," *Les cahiers de la cinémathèque* (Perpignan) 51–52 (Summer 1989): 109.

13. These remarks were made in connection with the cinema of American director John Ford. See Bertrand Tavernier, "La chevauchée de Sganarelle," *Présence du cinéma* 21 (March 1965): 5.

14. Jacques Demeure, "Avant l'heure des brasiers," *Positif* 168 (April 1975): 2.

15. Cited by Douin, *Tavernier*, 89.

16. Underscoring the resemblances between *Que la fête commence* and *La prise du pouvoir de Louis XIV,* Italian critic Sergio Arecco writes that both films depict what he calls the "dailiness" of History. *Que la fête commence* emphasizes, he writes, "the regent's getting up, his conversations, his maneuverings with priests, courtiers, and statesmen, and even his libertinism." Arecco, *Bertrand Tavernier*, 30.

17. Cited by Douin, *Tavernier*, 88.

18. The implicit analogies *Que la fête commence* drew between past and present in this respect were so striking that Tavernier felt compelled to point out that he had not taken liberties with history. "It was a question," he said, "of Breton autonomy, of colonization, of independence, of conflicts between Catholics and Protestants, of sexual liberty, of the way homosexuals were treated. All that was there: I did not have to change or interpret anything." See "Trois cinéastes en quête de l'histoire," 114.

19. Drawing an implicit contrast between, on the one hand, "local struggles" and, on the other, the monolithic nature of the class struggle envisioned by traditional Marxist thought, Deleuze observed that "what has characterized the *gauchiste* mentality has been the renewed questioning of the problem of power. The questioning of Marxist as well as bourgeois ideas. In practice, that [has involved] certain forms of local, specific, struggles whose [inter]relationship and necessary unity no longer come from a process of totalization or centralization but . . . from a transversality." See Gilles Deleuze, *Foucault* (Paris: Minuit, 1986), 32.

20. Michel Sineux, "Temps des cerises, temps sans pitié," *Positif* 180 (April 1976): 63.

21. Along with theft, write William and Joan Magretta, prostitution is "one definitive model for relationships in [the] new economic order" portrayed in *Que la fête commence*. See William R. Magretta and Joan Magretta, "Bertrand Tavernier: The Constraints of Convention," *Film Quarterly* 31, no. 4 (Summer 1978): 29.

22. "In this mad search for pleasure," Tavernier observed of his obsessive libertines, "there was something suicidal. I tried to show that it was sinister, and totally ridiculous." See "Entretien," *Cinéma* 198, 75.

23. Cited by Tavernier in "Entretien avec Bertrand Tavernier," *Ecran* 36 (May 1975): 62.

24. Cited by Leonard Quart and Lenny Rubenstein, "Blending the Personal with the Political: An Interview with Bertrand Tavernier," *Cineaste* 8, no. 4 (1976–77): 27.

25. In fact, French critic Guy Braucourt draws an explicit parallel between the corrupt and cynical world of the Regency seen in *Que la fête commence* and the portrait of contemporary France that emerges from Tavernier's first feature, *L'horloger de Saint-Paul*. Both works, says Braucourt, depict "societies in which no individual is able to assert himself, to be sure of truth or morality, or simply to comprehend what is going on about him." See Guy Braucourt, "Le glaive et la balance," *Ecran* 36 (May 1975): 61.

26. Winock, *Nationalisme, antisémitisme et fascisme en France*, 435.

27. Sunil Khilnani, *Arguing Revolution* (New Haven: Yale University Press, 1993), 121.

28. "Surely everyone agrees," writes Pierre Nora, "that it was the Revolution that gave the word 'nation' its synergy and energy. It crystallized the word's three meanings: social (a body of citizens equal before the law), legal (constituent power as opposed to constituted power) and historical (a community of men united by continuity, by a common past and future." See Pierre Nora, "Nation," in *A Critical Dictionary of the French Revolution*, 472.

29. As if to illustrate the long reach and continuing resonance of this void, as late as 1990 the editors of a new journal, *La Règle du jeu*, declared that one of their principal aims was to "explore" the emptiness left by the death of the communist dream. "Communism," declared the editors poetically, "was the dream of men before it became their nightmare. It haunted their lives. . . . It was the fixed star at the center of their analyses, their revolts, their disenchantments, their passions. All this means that its failure [is] . . . an immense event that leaves behind it [the] void . . . left by religions that have just died." See "Editorial," *La Règle du jeu*, 1990, 4.

30. "Anyone familiar with modern French history," writes George Ross, "knows the great power which Left ideas and postures have had over the French intelligentsia. From the Dreyfus Affair onwards there had always existed complex connivance between high Parisian intellectuals and provincial networks of *profs* to disseminate universalistic and progressive messages to 'uplift the masses.' " See Ross, introduction to *The Mitterand Experiment: Continuity and Change in Modern France*, 9.

31. Referring to the massive opus on Flaubert which obsessed Sartre toward the close of his career, in 1979 Stanley Hoffmann remarked that "the traditional role of the intellectual—to serve as a self-appointed conscience and guide of the nation, thus to propose ideals and to speak out about its present and its future—has to a considerable extent disappeared. Sartre's last active years as a writer have been spent on his negative identity, called Flaubert." See Hoffmann, *The European Sisyphus: Essays on Europe, 1964–1994*, 201.

32. "In the end," continues Pinto, "no common ground could be found between a newly defensive intelligentsia bent on redefining its *raison d'être* in a historically relativist and critical antitotalitarian light, and a political Left at first inbred with a cultural/political triumphalism, whose identity floundered as it sought to construct a more pragmatic and realistic profile." See Diana Pinto, "The Left, the Intellectuals, and Culture," in *The Mitterand Experiment: Continuity and Change in Modern France*, 217.

33. All citations are taken from articles that were originally published in *Le monde* and later collected in *Socrate et la rose: Les intellectuels face au pouvoir socialiste*, ed. Emile Malet (Neuilly: Editions du Quotidien, 1983), 22, 63, 115.

34. Engelbert, "Le discours historique de Bertrand Tavernier," 114.

35. Ibid.

36. Winock, *Nationalisme, antisémitisme et fascisme en France*, 162.

37. Noting that the "dramatic intensity" of the Dreyfus Affair revealed a new kind of "clash" in French society, Winock writes that "throughout the twentieth century one can observe, if not reproductions of the Dreyfus Affair, at least a series of correspondences with it." Ibid., 158.

38. Marcel Oms, "De la Belle Epoque à la guerre de 14–18," in *L'histoire de France au cinéma*, 171. Oms makes the interesting point that, for obvious ideological reasons, early Soviet cinema offered several films dealing with the Commune.

39. Ibid.

40. Published by Gallimard in 1973, *Moi, Pierre Rivière, ayant égorgé ma mère, ma soeur, et mon frère: Un cas de parricide au XIXe siècle* was translated into English two years later. See *I, Pierre Rivière, having slaughtered my mother, my sister and my brother . . . A Case of Parricide in the Nineteenth Century*, trans. F. Jellinek (New York: Pantheon, 1975).

41. Allio's rejection of conventional film technique is, certainly, one of the reasons that several critics, notably those associated with *Les cahiers du cinéma*, greatly preferred his work to that of Tavernier. Their suspicions of Tavernier may also have stemmed, of course, from the director's long-standing association with *Positif*, a left-wing journal that often took positions opposed to those of *Cahiers*.

42. Michel Foucault, "Présentation," in *Moi, Pierre Rivière*, 12.

43. "Trois cinéastes en quête de l'histoire," 109.

44. Foucault, "Présentation," in *Moi, Pierre Rivière*, 13.

45. "Entretien avec Bertrand Tavernier," *Ecran* 46 (April 19, 1976): 51.

46. Cited by Douin, *Tavernier*, 99.

47. "Le cinéma de Bertrand Tavernier," *Ecran* 62 (October 15, 1977): 24.

48. Referring to a famous criminal dandy of the last century, Tavernier observed that "there was a Rimbaud side to Vacher/Bouvier; but [he was] also savage, self-taught—a bit like Lacenaire." See "Entretien avec Bertrand Tavernier," *Ecran* 46, 51.

49. In an article that bears upon the links between social misery and madness in the last century—and which is included in the published text of *Moi, Pierre Rivière*—J. P. Peter and Jeanne Favret tell of peasants who, after committing terrible crimes, were subsequently appalled by their acts. Suggesting that such deeds were a way for the murderers to symbolically destroy themselves and/or their dreadful existence, the authors describe one case thus: "The wife of a day laborer, in need, and no longer able to bear the cries of her fifteen-month-old son, sticks him in the neck with a cleaver, bleeds him, cuts off a thigh and eats it." See "L'animal, le fou, la mort," in *Moi, Pierre Rivière*, 249.

50. "Le cinéma de Bertrand Tavernier," *Ecran* 62, 24.

51. Remarking that the "passions and dramas" of this complex era fascinated him, the director observed that Bouvier is "active between the death of Van Gogh and the beginnings of Freud. Maurice Barrès is overwhelmed by the execution of the anarchist Emile Henry and writes an unforgottable *récit* about it. Ravachol kills while playing the accordion. The church . . . fights against lay schools. . . . The syndicalist movement develops. At Villeboeuf, an explosion in a mine that had refused to take security measures kills fifty-four children." See Bertrand Tavernier, "Les rapports de la justice avec la folie et l'histoire," *L'avant-scène du cinéma* 170 (1976): 5.

52. For those on the Left, writes Michel Sineux, "Joan, abandoned by the royalty and calumniated by the church, had to be laicized, freed from conservative churchmen, and returned to the people from [whose ranks] she had come." See Sineux, "Temps des cerises, temps sans pitié," 64.

53. Observing that, at this time, the warrior-maiden was seen as the opposite of the Jew, Michel Winock proceeds to point out that whereas Jews were urban, cosmopolitan, and "foreign," Joan came from, belonged to, the very soil of France. She was was thus glorified not only for her military brilliance but for "incarnating the essence of Frenchness." See Michel Winock, "Jeanne d'Arc," in *Les lieux de mémoire*, III.3, 710.

54. On the subject of vagrants in late-nineteenth-century France, see Robert A. Nye, *Crime, Madness and Politics in Modern France: The Medical Concept of National Decline* (Princeton, N.J.: Princeton University Press, 1984), esp. 55–59, 172–77.

55. Matt K. Matsuda, *The Memory of the Modern* (New York: Oxford University Press, 1996), 124.

56. Nye, *Crime, Madness and Politics in Modern France*, 180.

57. Cited by Douin, *Tavernier*, 94.

58. For Joutard's remarks, see "L'histoire au cinéma: Conversation avec René Allio, Marc Ferro, Philippe Joutard, Emmanuel Le Roy Ladurie," *Positif* 189 (January 1977): 10. On that same page, a harsh Emmanuel Le Roy Ladurie calls the tableau which appears at the end of *Le juge et l'assassin* "incomprehensible."

59. Girardet, *Le nationalisme français*, 173–74.

60. Winock, *Nationalisme, anti-sémitisme et fascisme en France*, 208.

61. "Le cinéma de Bertrand Tavernier," *Ecran* 62, 25.

62. "Far from announcing an increase in class warfare in France," observes Michel Winock, "the Paris Commune closes the cycle." See Winock, *Nationalisme, antisémitisme et fascisme en France*, 159.

63. This is not to deny that personal factors may have contributed to the increased darkness of both films. These were difficult years for Tavernier: in the course of the 1980s the director was faced with the collapse of his marriage as well as the illness and death of his father.

64. Cited by Douin, *Tavernier*, 142.

In the course of this same interview, Tavernier noted that even the camera angles of this film—where all is seized from above or below—were meant to further the sensation of tension and menace, of a world out of joint. "I was almost never at eye level," he observed, "I tried to achieve broken, shattered, tilts and framings."

65. "John Ford et les peaux rouges: Entretien avec Bertrand Tavernier," *Positif* 343 (September 1989): 29.

66. Praising the film for its portrayal of a "true Middle Ages," a "tragic" fourteenth century, Le Goff wrote that "all the religious figures are there . . . from the sorceress . . . to the hermit . . . to the impotent curé, to Béatrice . . . and to Cortemart, the great blasphemer who, to better escape from a God whom he denies yet fears, demands that his body be thrown into the sea." See Jacques Le Goff, "Un document d'âme," *Le monde*, November 12, 1987, 11.

67. Along with Retz, the figure of Cortemart also evokes that of Francesco Cenci. The subject of works by Shelley and Antonin Artaud, Cenci was a notoriously debauched and sadistic Roman nobleman of the Renaissance. Like Cortemart, Cenci had a daughter named Beatrice whom he raped and tortured.

68. Laurent Vachaud, "Entretien avec Bertrand Tavernier: 'Ne pas savoir à l'avance qui a tort et qui a raison,' " *Positif* 429 (November 1996): 19.

69. Although Jean-Pierre Jeancolas notes that Conan's behavior is "morally un-justifiable," he sees him, significantly, as an "ambiguous hero." "It is difficult," writes Jeancolas, "to know how to feel about this character. In a Western, someone who kills Indians with their own methods would be a positive hero. In a film about war—but which is obviously a cry against war—Conan presents a trap . . . for us. We find him brave, likable . . . [but] inhuman. . . . He is morally unjustifiable." Jean-Pierre Jeancolas, "*Capitaine Conan*," *Positif* 429 (November 1996): 17–18.

70. Noting that both *La passion Béatrice* and *La vie et rien d'autre* were films about "love," Tavernier went on to underscore the critical difference between these two works. Whereas *La passion Béatrice*, he said, portrayed a love that was "disappointed, repressed, barbarous, and deadly," in *La vie et rien d'autre*, instead, it was the *background* of love that was full of violence and horror. He wanted, he said, to "speak about war while making a film about peace." See "Les colères de Bertrand Tavernier," *Le Figaro*, July 12, 1989, 31.

71. Antoine Prost, "Verdun," in *Les lieux de mémoire*, II.3, 118.

72. On the mnemonic resonance of such monuments, see Antoine Prost, "Les monuments aux morts," in *Les lieux de mémoire*, I.

73. Nicole Lapierre, "Dialectique de la mémoire et de l'oubli," *Communications* 49 (1989): 5. Special issue entitled "La mémoire et l'oubli."

74. Marcel Oms, "La France contemporaine," in *L'histoire de France au cinéma*, 242.

75. Michel Cadé, "La trace et l'écho: Le cinéma français témoin de son temps," *CinémAction* 66 (1993): 33.

76. Jean-Marie Frodin, "*La Guerre sans nom*," *Le monde*, February 20, 1992, 25.

77. Arecco, *Tavernier*, 108.

78. "Entretien avec Bertrand Tavernier and Patrick Rotman," *Le monde*, February 20, 1992, 26.

79. See, for example, George Ross, "The Tragedy of the French Left," *New Left Review* 171 (September–October 1988).

80. "Entretien avec Bertrand Tavernier and Patrick Rotman," 26.

Chapter V
Memory and Its Losses: Troubled Dreams
of Empire

1. Jacques Julliard, "La réussite gaullienne," in *Les idées en France: 1945–1988*, 191.

2. Philip Dine, *Images of the Algerian War: French Fiction and Film, 1954–1992* (Oxford: Clarendon Press, 1994), 8.

3. John Rockwell "Colonial Era of France in Four Films," *New York Times*, July 8, 1992, B3.

4. As Philip Dine points out, the origins of the term *pied-noir* remain obscure: it may refer to the "black feet" of the early settlers who worked in the fields, or to the army boots worn by the first French military occupiers of Algeria. See Dine, *Images of the Algerian War*, 9.

5. Rouän has acknowledged the autobiographical cast of her film in several interviews. See, for example, an interview with Annette Insdorf in *France Magazine*, Winter 1991, 41.

6. Closely associated with this tumultuous period of Vietnam's history, which he has portrayed in novels as well as films, Schoendoerffer was, in fact, among those invited to accompany Mitterand when the French president made a historic state visit to Vietnam in February of 1993.

7. François de la Bretèque, "Le film en costumes: Un bon sujet?" *CinémAction* 65 (1992): 113.

8. Charles-Robert Algeron, "Conclusion," in *La guerre d'Algérie et les français*, ed. Jean-Pierre Rioux (Paris: Fayard, 1990), 623.

An important anthology devoted to the Algerian War, *La guerre d'Algérie et les français* contains several essays that, like Algeron's, examine the divergent memories deposited by France's struggle to retain Algeria.

9. In this respect, as in others, the Algerian War bore a striking resemblance to America's war in Vietnam. In fact, the similarities between these two protracted and ultimately futile struggles are the subject of an extended study by David L. Schalk: *War and the Ivory Tower: Algeria and Vietnam* (New York: Oxford University Press, 1991).

10. Robert Frank, "Les troubles de la mémoire française," in *La guerre d'Algérie et les français*, 607.

11. Underscoring the impossibility of commemorating this war, historian Claude Liazu writes that the Algerian War cannot "find [its] place in our historical vulgate because [it] negates it: defeat, divisiveness, loss of innocence." Claude Liazu, "Le contingent entre silence et discours ancien combattant," in *La guerre d'Algérie et les français*, 515.

12. Stora, *La gangrène et l'oubli*, 209.

13. Benjamin Stora notes that one former settler recalls being called a "dirty *pied-noir*" by French people; another remembers seeing wall graffiti reading "*pied-noir* go home." See ibid., 257–58.

14. Dine, *Images of the Algerian War*, 122.

15. See Stora, *La gangrène et l'oubli*, 270.

16. Alain-Gérard Slama, "La Guerre d'Algérie en littérature ou la comédie des masques," in *La guerre d'Algérie et les français*, 597.

17. The fearful tone of such questions is only exacerbated by the social problems—drugs, crime, high unemployment—that are often associated with the new immigrants, who are frequently desperately poor and confined to troubled ghettos on the outskirts of France's major cities. And to these social problems must be added the threat of terrorist bombings like those carried out in 1995 by Islamic fundamentalists who hoped to force France to cut its ties to the military-backed government in Algeria. Remarking upon the continuing reverberations in France of the Algerian War, in the wake of one attack, *New York Times* commentator Craig Whitney wrote that "there is no escaping history, the French discovered again this week as the second civil war of the century in their former colony of Algeria came home to them with a vengeance." See Craig Whitney, "History's Fetters Entangling France on Algeria," *New York Times*, October 21, 1995, A3.

18. In the national elections of 1997, *Le front national* gained sufficient votes to achieve an equal footing with the parties of the moderate Right.

19. It is telling, for example, that although Algeria was considered a part of France, native inhabitants never enjoyed the same rights and privileges as those of European descent. Indeed, the colonial regime violated one of the very principles of the French Republic insofar as citizenship was accorded as a function of the religious community to which one belonged. See, on this issue, Stora, *La gangrène et l'oubli*, 22.

20. Convinced that France should expel its huge immigrant population, Le Pen even insists that young *Beurs*—who, as the French-born children of *Maghrébin* immigrants, are automatically citizens of France—renounce all ties to their "roots" if they wish not only to be "French" but simply to remain in France.

21. After one of Le Pen's more outrageous statements—"the races," he declared, "are not created "equal"—then prime minister Alain Juppé called the leader of *Le front national* "deeply, almost viscerally racist, anti-Semitic and xenophobic." See Marlise Simons, "French Far Right Thrives on Outrage," *New York Times*, October 2, 1996, A8.

22. Liazu, "Le contingent entre silence et discours ancien combattant," 513.

23. Alain Ruscio, "French Public Opinion and the War in Indochina: 1945–1954," in *War and Society in Twentieth-Century France*," ed. Michael Scriven and Peter Wagstaff (New York: Berg, 1991), 119.

24. Henri Navarre, *L'agonie de l'Indochine* (Paris: Plon, 1956), 320.

25. Philip Cerny, "Non-Terrorism and the Politics of Repressive Tolerance," in *Social Movements and Protest in France*, ed. Philip Cerny (New York: St. Martin's Press, 1982), 101.

26. Cited by Stora, *La gangrène et l'oubli*, 112.

27. Cited in ibid., 91.

28. Despite the fact that *Le crabe-tambour* softened the military discourse, critical reactions to the film testified to its continuing "impossibility." On the Left, especially, reactions seemed ideologically driven. For example, Freddy Buache observed sarcastically that *Le crabe-tambour* represented little more than Schoendoerffer's attempt "to convince himself and his viewers that his fresco is in the same vein as Conrad." Even a more temperate critic like Jacques Siclier, who admitted to finding *Le crabe-tambour* very beautiful—the film did, in fact, win three *César* awards—seemed defensive about his own reactions. Warning against easy political labels, he timidly asked whether Schoendoerffer necessarily had to be considered right-wing. For Philippe de Comes and Michel Marin, there is no question but that certain critics "refuse to recognize the merits of *Le crabe-tambour* because of obscure grudges and susceptibilities that are clearly ideological and totally misplaced."

See Freddy Buache, *Le cinéma français des années '70* (Paris: Hatier, 1990), 196; Jacques Siclier, *Le cinéma français*, vol. 2 (Paris: Ramsay, 1991), 28; Philippe de Comes and Michel Marin, *Le cinéma français: 1960–1985* (Paris: Atlas, 1985), 139.

29. I am grateful to Jim Harmon for this telling observation.

30. Girardet, *Mythes et mythologies politiques*, 105.

31. Pierre Schoendoerffer, *L'adieu au roi* (Paris: Grasset, 1969), 21.

32. Martin Evans, "The French Army and the Algerian War: Crisis of Identity," in *War and Society in Twentieth-Century France*, 153.

33. François de la Bretèque, "L'Indochine au coeur d'une oeuvre: *L'Illiade* et *l'Odyssée* de Pierre Schoendoerffer," *Les cahiers de la cinémathèque* 57 (October 1992): 76.

34. Ibid., 82.

35. Benjamin Stora, "Oran, été 1962," in *Fins d'empire*, ed. Jean-Pierre Rioux (Paris: Plon, 1992), 338.

36. Dine, *Images of the Algerian War*, 146.

37. Nora, *Les français d'Algérie* (Paris: René Julliard, 1961), 93.

In terms of the "denial" analyzed by Nora, it is noteworthy that the deeply censored French television network was careful to deny its viewers any glimpse of Algerian rebels while the war was underway. Thus, as Benjamin Stora observes, the only real images of the war "were broadcast in the United States by Fox Movietone." See Stora, *La gangrène et l'oubli*, 45.

38. Nora, *Les français d'Algérie*, 184.

Some of the most interesting pages in Nora's book concern Albert Camus's *L'étranger*. Set in Algeria, where the writer was born and spent his youth, Camus's novel depicts a *pied-noir* named Merseult who, with no apparent motive, kills an Arab. Questioning the conventional, and implicitly universal, "absurdist" or "existentialist" reading of the novel, Nora suggests that *L'étranger* depicts the specific "psychological relationship" between *pied-noir* and Arab—a relationship that is "not acknowledged and that haunts the Europeans of Algeria." In this sense, one might say that Meursault literally does not "see" the Arab he kills. See *Les français d'Algérie*, 192.

39. For her subjects, writes Roche, this trauma virtually divided their lives in two. "The interviews as a whole," she observes, "clearly bring to light the creation of a 'before' and an 'after' that . . . always function in the same way. . . . 'Before' is strongly valorized and the subject of nostalgia; 'after' is seen pejoratively." See Anne Roche, "La perte et la parole: Témoignages oraux de pieds-noirs," in *La guerre d'Algérie et les français*, 527.

40. Ibid., 532.

41. Nora, *Les français d'Algérie*, 153.

42. Roche, "La perte et la parole," 531.

43. Dine, *Images of the Algerian War*, 165.

44. Siclier, *Le cinéma français* 2:205.

On the same page, Siclier also observes—and this is one more indication of the intensely subjective focus of the film—that the three sisters might well "incarnate three states of the female condition in a Catholic and conservative milieu, in a historical context where certainties waver and traditions crumble."

45. Cited by Stora, *La gangrène et l'oubli*, 288.

46. John Talbott, *The War without a Name: France in Algeria, 1954–1962* (London: Faber and Faber, 1981), 14.

47. In this respect it is interesting to compare the shadowy figure of Gritte's lover in *Outremer* with the fully developed character of the Chinese lover in *L'amant*. Although the past is seen through the eyes of the female protagonist in

both films, in sharp contrast to *Outremer*, *L'amant* presents a male protagonist who has almost as much psychological weight and depth as the woman he loves.

48. Stora, *La gangrène et l'oubli*, 247.

This phenomenon is described by Primo Levi when he observes that "certainly practice keeps memories fresh and alive in the same manner in which a muscle often used remains efficient, but it is also true that a memory evoked too often, and expressed in the form of a story, tends to become fixed in a stereotype, in a form tested by experience, crystallized, perfected, adorned, installing itself in the place of the raw memory and growing at its expense." See Primo Levi, *The Drowned and the Saved*, trans. Raymond Rosenthal (New York: Vintage, 1989), 24.

49. Nora, "Entre mémoire et histoire," in *Les lieux de mémoire* I, xvii.

50. Ibid., xviii.

51. Ibid., xix.

52. Ibid., xxi.

53. Ibid., xxii.

54. Ibid.

55. Ibid., xxii–xxiii.

56. Ibid., xxix.

57. Writing about Holocaust survivors, Sidra DeKoven Ezrahi makes much the same point. "Within survivor communities," she writes, "private memories are subsumed into collective memory which in turn becomes the group's epistemological ground and the imagination's battlefield." See Ezrahi, "The Holocaust and the Shifting Boundaries of Art and History," *History and Memory* 1, no. 2 (Fall–Winter 1989): 77.

58. Nora, "Entre mémoire et histoire," xxx.

59. "The passage from memory to history has given each group the obligation to redefine its identity by the revitalization of its own history. The duty to remember turns each of us into his/her own historian. . . . The psychologization of memory gives everyone the feeling that salvation ultimately depends upon repaying this impossible debt." Ibid., xxix, xxxi.

60. Ibid., xxv.

61. Ibid., xxiv.

62. Ibid., xxxi–xxxii.

63. Girardet, *Mythes et mythologies politiques*, 109.

64. Ibid., 180.

65. Marc Ferro, *L'histoire sous surveillance* (Paris: Calmann-Lévy, 1985), 46.

66. Robert Gildea, *The Past in French History* (New Haven: Yale University Press, 1994), 10.

67. In this context, it is interesting to compare Nora's essay with one written by Stanley Hoffmann a few years earlier: "Fragments Floating in the Here and Now." Although Hoffmann shares Nora's concern that France has lost touch with its past, unlike Nora he attributes this loss less to the changing shape of memory than to the historical traumas France has suffered in recent decades. Like other Western nations, writes Hoffmann, the French "feel, more or less confusedly, that their normal historical development has been interrupted, that their past has been devalued, that their highest achievement—nationality—has plunged them into disaster

followed by impotence, that they have moved from the age of self-determination to that in which the outside world determines their fate." See Hoffmann, "Fragments Floating in the Here and Now," in his *The European Sisyphus*, 189.

68. Pierre Nora, "La mémoire collective," in *La nouvelle histoire*, 399.

Chapter VI
A la recherche du temps perdu: **The Specter of Populism**

1. Raphaël Bassan, "Trois néo-baroques français," *La revue du cinéma* 449 (May 1989): 46–53.

2. René Prédal, *Le cinéma français contemporain* (Paris: Nathan, 1991), 462. Critics for *Les cahiers du cinéma*, in particular, are far more sympathetic to Carax than to Besson or Beineix. This is hardly surprising since Carax once wrote for *Cahiers*.

3. "For these directors who grew up watching television and advertising spots," writes Jean Collet, "and who have made commercials themselves, it is a question of keeping the spectator breathless, of seducing by effects, images, and striking editing." Cited by René Prédal in his *Le cinéma français depuis 1945*, 466.

4. "L'image a bougé: Abécédaire du cinéma français," *Les cahiers du cinéma* 381 (March 1986): 29.

5. "The important thing," writes Bergala, "was less to respect reality (modernism was not a kind of neorealism) than to make it disgorge, cinematographically, its fragment of truth." See Alain Bergala, "Le vrai, le faux, le factice," *Les cahiers du cinéma* 351 (September 1983): 5.

6. For Bergala, the "simple forgetfulness of the principle of reality" does more than mark a new moment in film history. It also means that the very "magic" of cinema is lost. "Despite everything," he writes, "the truth is that the magic of cinema, including the seduction of the false, is fundamentally linked to its ontological realism." See Bergala, "Le vrai, le faux, le factice," 7–8.

7. Ibid., 7.

8. Susan Hayward, "*France avance-détour-retour*: French cinema of the 1980s," in *Contemporary France*, ed. Jolyon Howorth and George Ross (London: Pinter, 1987), 162.

9. Olivier Assayas, "La publicité, point aveugle du cinéma français," *Les cahiers du cinéma* 351 (September 1983): 22.

10. Alain Bergala, "D'une certaine manière," *Les cahiers du cinéma* 370 (April 1985): 14. Bergala proceeds to argue that television encourages this indiscriminate borrowing since it disconnects films "from their origins and robs them of any particular aura."

11. Fredric Jameson, "Postmodernism, or The Cultural Logic of Late Capitalism," *New Left Review* 146 (July–August 1984): 65.

12. Hayward, "*France avance-détour-retour*," 163.

13. Michèle Lagny, Marie-Claire Ropars, and Pierre Sorlin, *Générique des années 30* (Vincennes: Presses Universitaires de Vincennes, 1986), 6.

14. Dudley Andrew, *Mists of Regret: Culture and Sensibility in Classic French Film* (Princeton, N.J.: Princeton University Press, 1995), 90.

15. Cited in ibid., 13.

16. Claude Gauteur and Ginette Vincendeau, *Jean Gabin: Anatomie d'un mythe* (Paris: Nathan, 1993), 141.

17. Ibid.

18. Françoise Cachin, "Le paysage du peintre," in *Les lieux de mémoire* II.1, 435.

19. "It is always the same story," observed critic André Bazin of the personna created by Gabin in these roles, "and one that must inevitably end unhappily, like the story of Oedipus or Phaedra. Gabin is the tragic hero of the contemporary cinema."

See André Bazin, "The Destiny of Jean Gabin," in *Rediscovering French Film*, ed. Mary Lea Bandy (New York: MOMA, 1983), 123.

20. Vincendeau, *Jean Gabin: Anatomie d'un mythe*, 96.

21. Robin Buss, *The French through Their Films* (New York: Ungar, 1988), 125.

22. Vincendeau, *Jean Gabin: Anatomie d'un mythe*, 141; Andrew, *Mists of Regret*, 226.

23. Buss, *The French through Their Films*, 70.

24. Roberto Escobar and Vittorio Giacci, *Il Cinema del Fronte Popolare: Francia 1937–1937* (Milan: Il Formichiere, 1980), 214.

To my mind populist motifs go back further still: made in 1921, Louis Delluc's *Fièvre*, for example, features the kind of seedy port, frequented by down-and-out characters, that Carné would later use in *Quai des brumes*.

25. Ginette Vincendeau, "The Popular Cinema of the Popular Front," in *La vie est à nous!: French Cinema of the Popular Front 1935–1938*, ed. Ginette Vincendeau and Keith Reader (London: BFI, 1986), 96.

In an essay published in this same volume, Keith Reader also emphasizes the enormous resonance—if not the tremendous number—of populist films: in his view, this "narrow canon" of films constitutes "the major cultural component of the Popular Front myth." See Reader, "Renoir's Popular Front Films," in *La vie est à nous*, 40.

26. Marcel Carné, "Quand le cinéma descendra-t-il dans la rue?" in *Cités-Cinés* (Paris: Ramsay, 1987), 309. Originally in *Cinémagazine* 11 (November 1933).

27. Buss, *The French through Their Films*, 58.

28. Goffredo Fofi, "The Cinema of the Popular Front in France (1934–38)," *Screen* 13, no. 4 (1972): 39.

29. André Bazin, "The Disincarnation of Carné," in *Rediscovering French Film*, 131.

30. Pascal Ory, *La belle illusion: Culture et politique sous le signe du Front Populaire* (Paris: Plon, 1994), 463.

31. Christian Amalvi, "Le 14-Juillet," in *Les lieux de mémoire* I, 458.

32. Vincendeau, "The Popular Cinema of the Popular Front," in *La vie est a nous*, 98.

33. Historian Jean-Pierre Rioux points out that this anniversary engendered "no passion at all and virtually no new work." See Rioux, "Twentieth Century Historiography: Clio in a Phyrgian Bonnet," in *Contemporary France*, 208.

34. In 1982, *Diva* was the surprise winner of four *Césars*: for sound, music, photography, and best first film.

35. Fredric Jameson, "*Diva* and French Socialism," in his *Signatures of the Visible* (New York: Routledge, 1990), 56.

36. Ibid., 58.

37. Ibid., 59.

38. Hoffmann also appears to suggest that the dilemma faced by the Socialists— a dilemma that appears unresolvable in Jameson's essay—might well have been handled more successfully by then president Mitterand. In Hoffmann's view, Mitterand "never bothered to try to get the Socialist Party to adjust its ideas . . . and to give up its old Socialist commitments to the expansion of state agencies and to nationalization. The party thus displayed a depressing split between its archaic and verbal radicalism and its resignation to the new status quo emphasizing the importance of efficient management and competitiveness abroad." See Stanley Hoffmann, "The New France?" *New York Review of Books*, July 13, 1995, 50.

39. Written by Jean Aurenche and Henri Jeanson, *Hôtel du Nord* is Carné's only film of the 1930s in which Prévert did not have a hand.

40. Trauner himself constitutes another link between populist films of the 1930s and those of the "cinéma du look." Closely associated with the cinema of Carné, Trauner was also responsible for the sets for *Subway*.

41. Cited by Edward Baron Turk in his *Child of Paradise: Marcel Carné and the Golden Age of French Cinema* (Cambridge: Harvard University Press), 109.

42. Ibid., 109–10.

43. Yann Lardeau, "Le décor et le masque," *Les cahiers du cinéma* 351 (September 1983): 14.

44. Ibid.

45. Jean Baudrillard, *L'échange symbolique et la mort* (Paris: Gallimard, 1976), 83.

46. Guy Austin suggests that, in addition to cinematic echoes from the 1930s, Carax's film also contains passing references to films by Bresson and Truffaut. See Austin, *Contemporary French Cinema*, 134.

47. Designed by Alexandre Trauner, the set of Carné's film features a small bridge spanning what was then a commercial waterway for barges, the Canal St. Martin.

48. "The most melodramatic details," writes René Prédal of Carax's work, "lose all realism and are nothing but the signs of a subjective journey marked, as in a dream, by opaque existences lived by anguished characters." See Prédal, *Le cinéma français depuis 1945*, 464.

49. Terry Eagleton, *Against the Grain: Essays 1975–1985* (London: Verso, 1986), 145.

50. Maurice Agulhon, "Paris: La traversée d'est en ouest," in *Les lieux de mémoire* III.3, 870.

51. "Up until recent times," writes Maurice Agulhon, "everyone knew that in Paris, when the 'Left' took to the streets to demonstrate, it would take place 'from Bastille to République.'" See ibid., 871.

52. On this scene, see Turk, *Child of Paradise*, 133.

53. Amalvi, "Le 14-Juillet," 455.

54. On the links between *Delicatessen* and the "Beineix-Besson-Carax syndrome," see Prédal, *Le cinéma français depuis 1945*, 470.

55. Guy Austin also points out that the villain of the film, a tyrannical "butcher," embodies "the term applied during the Occupation to war criminals such as Klaus Barbie, 'the Butcher of Lyons.' " See Austin, *Contemporary French Cinema*, 137.

56. These observations owe a great deal to an unpublished paper by Carrie Rosenbaum.

57. Bassan, "Trois néo-baroques français," 48.

58. Mongin uses this term in a discussion of another film of the "cinéma du look": Luc Besson's *Le grand bleu* (*The Big Blue*, 1988). Although the protagonist of Besson's film seemingly has everything to live for, he inexplicably commits suicide. See Olivier Mongin, "*Le Grand Bleu* ou le trou noir de nos passions," *Esprit* 158 (January 1990): 84.

59. Bassan, "Trois néo-baroques francais," 47.

60. Jean Baudrillard, *Simulations*, trans. Paul Foss, Paul Patton, and Philip Beitchman (New York: Semiotext(e), 1983), 12.

61. Alain Touraine, Michel Wieviorka, and François Dubet, *Le mouvement ouvrier* (Paris: Fayard, 1984), 10.

62. To find support and comradeship, disaffected young people in particular gravitate toward what French sociologist Michel Maffesoli describes as "tribes." But unlike traditional communities, such "tribes"—which are defined only by a "look," an attitude—have no shared values or aspirations. See Michel Maffesoli, *Le temps des tribus* (Paris: Meridiens Klinsieck, 1988).

63. For those who loved Paris as it once was, and who bemoaned the increasing sterility of the city, this project, in particular, seemed little less than sacrilegious. "To understand and to relive Old Paris," raged Louis Chevalier in *The Assassination of Paris*, "it sufficed to make a tour of les Halles. To grasp and to understand what has happened to Paris it suffices, if one has the stomach for it and no sense of the past, to go and see what has replaced les Halles. . . . The misnamed Forum des Halles has no other purpose than to concentrate in a deep, fetid underground all that Paris has to show and offer as high-class merchandise." See Chevalier, *The Assassination of Paris*, trans. David Jordan (Chicago: Univeristy of Chicago Press, 1994), 260.

For the views of still another vehement critic of the "new" Paris, see André Fermigier, *La bataille de Paris* (Paris: Gallimard, 1991). As a commentator for *Le nouvel observateur* and later *Le monde*, Fermigier railed against the changes that swept over Paris in the 1970s.

64. Buss, *The French through Their Films*, 61.

65. "The juxtaposition of a 'working-class, Republican' Paris next to a 'bourgeois' Paris," writes Maurice Agulhon, "belongs to a historical phase in the midst of disappearing." See Agulhon, "Paris: La traversée d'est en ouest," 899.

66. Michelle Perrot, "Les vies ouvrières," in *Les lieux de mémoire* III.3, 27.

67. Gilles Deleuze, *Logique du sens* (Paris: Minuit, 1969), 302.

68. In 1994, after a bitter fight, France won exclusion of the audiovisual industry from free-trade rules adopted by GATT (the General Agreement on Tariffs and Trade). But a new battle looms: France wants to preserve the European Union regulation that European productions constitute at least half of the movies shown on television. See "Sacré Bleu! French Film Is Confronting Hollywood's Crass Commercialism," *New York Times*, January 8, 1996, C1, 8.

69. "Fleeing a Fallow France for Greener U.S. Pastures," *New York Times*, October 22, H14.

70. Bazin, "The Disincarnation of Carné," 131.

71. Michel Mardore, "Le choix des sujets," *CinémAction* 66 (1993): 131.

72. Alain Tanner, "Des cinéastes d'appartement parisien," *CinémAction* 66 (1993): 148. Originally in *Les cahiers du cinéma* 455–56 (May 1992).

73. Charlie Van Damne, "Du cinéma muet au cinéma mutique?" *CinémAction* 66 (1993): 164.

74. Philippe Madral, "Un cinéma créatif," *CinémAction* 66 (1993): 145.

75. Michel Cadé, "Le cinéma commerciel français," *CinémAction* 66 (1993): 71.

76. See "Sacré Bleu! French Film Is Confronting Hollywood's Crass Commercialism."

77. Hoffmann, "Thoughts on the French Nation Today," 77.

78. François de la Bretèque, "Un cinema de la déférence," *CinémAction* 66 (1993): 23.

Epilogue

1. Winock, *Nationalisme, antisémitisme et fascisme en France*, 103.

2. Pierre Nora, "L'ère de la commemoration," in *Les lieux de mémoire* III.3, 991.

3. Cited by Alain Riding, "Malraux Joins the Greats," *New York Times*, November 25, 1996, C11.

4. Discussing the ways in which the Final Solution affected the very idea of progress, philosopher and social commentator Alain Finkielkraut declares, "In unleashing a limitless cruelty, it implicated progress both in its technical form (the sophistication of a killing machine) and its moral one (the domestication of [psychic] impulses, the subjection of will to law)." See Alain Finkielkraut, *La mémoire vaine: Du crime contre l'humanité* (Paris: Gallimard, 1989), 56.

5. Ferenc Fehér, "The Pyrrhic Victory of Art," in *Postmodern Conditions*, ed. Andrew Milner, Philip Thomson, and Chris Worth (New York: Berg, 1990), 91.

6. Pierre Nora, "La nation-mémoire," in *Les lieux de mémoire* III.3, 654.

Index

Note: Unless otherwise noted, headings refer to things French, e.g., Revolution refers to French Revolution.

Abel, Richard, 16, 197n.37
A bout de souffle, 161–62
Agulhon, Maurice, 179, 186, 223n.51, 224n.65
Algeria, 47, 48, 218n.19
Algerian War, 22, 25, 31, 40, 46, 50, 85, 101, 125, 136–37, 217n.11; censorship of, 49, 219n.37; divergent memories of, 131–35, 217n.6; legacy of, 135–36, 217n.17; and practice of torture, 31, 48–49, 63; and Vietnam War, 125, 134, 217n.9. See also *Crabe-Tambour, Le*; Empire; France: divisions; *Guerre sans nom, La*; military; *Outremer*; *pieds-noirs*; racism
Algeron, Charles Robert, 132
Allio, René, 12, 21–22, 23, 24, 100, 112–13, 116, 198n.52, 214n.41
All the Mornings of the World. See *Tous les matins du monde*
Amalvi, Christian, 168, 180, 181
L'amant, 130, 131, 147, 219n.47
Amants du Pont-Neuf, Les, 11, 29, 30, 159, 163, 169, 173, 174, 177–82, 185, 223n. 46
Andrew, Dudley, 164, 165, 204n.60
Angelo, Yves, 23
Annales school, 10, 19, 20, 23, 25, 102. *See also* history; *l'histoire des mentalités*; *Que la fête commence*
Annaud, Jean-Jacques, 130, 187
L'année dernière à Marienbad, 32, 33, 38, 39, 40, 61, 201n.9, 202nn. 24 and 25
années noires, les, 65, 68, 83, 90, 96
A nous la liberté, 166, 172
anti-Semitism, 51, 52, 55, 70, 86, 88, 92, 93, 135, 204n.50; apologies for, 95–96; 210n.76; and Dreyfus Affair, 110, 117; and Jewish stereotypes, 51, 54–55, 77; renewal of, 84–85, 208nn. 48 and 49. *See also* Blum, Léon; *Chagrin et la pitié, Le*; deportations; *Dernier métro, Le*; Dreyfus Affair; Jews; *Lacombe Lucien*; *Stavisky*; Vichy
Apocalypse Now, 141
Arecco, Sergio, 126, 212n.16

Archives interdites: Les peurs françaises face à l'histoire contemporaine, 26
Arletty, 164
L'assassinat de Marat, 15
Assassination of Paris, The, 224n.63
Assayas, Olivier, 161
L'Atalante, 165, 169, 177, 178, 181
Aubrac, Lucie, 90
Audiard, Jacques, 96
Aurenche, Jean, 100, 211n.6
Au revoir les enfants, 66, 86, 87–89, 90, 91
Austin, Guy, 198n.56, 206n.19, 223n.46, 224n.55
Autour de minuit, 98
Azéma, Jean-Pierre, 75

Barbie, Klaus, 89, 90, 92, 210n.75
Bassan, Raphaël, 159, 184, 185
Bastille Day, 177, 179–80, 181
Baudrillard, Jean, 177, 185
Bazin, André, 38, 168, 187, 222n.19
Béatrice. See *Passion Béatrice, La*
Becker, Jacques, 111
Beineix, Jean-Jacques, 11, 159–60, 161, 163, 169–77 passim, 182, 221n.2
Belle équipe, La, 167, 168, 169
Belmondo, Jean-Paul, 51, 56
Benayoun, Robert, 40, 57
Bergala, Alain, 160, 161, 221nn. 5 and 6, 222n.10
Bernard, Raymond, 17
Besson, Luc, 159–63, 221n.2, 224n.58
Bête humaine, La, 165, 166
Bibliothèque nationale, 41–42
Birnbaum, Pierre, 54, 84, 96, 209n.50
Blanc, Michel, 192, 193
Blanchot, Maurice, 201n.12
Blum, Léon, 52, 204n.50
Bogart, Humphrey, 161
Bonitzer, Pascal, 39, 76
Bonnet, Jean-Claude, 15, 197n.31
Bory, Jean-Louis, 74
Bost, Pierre, 100, 211n.6
Boulevard des Hirondelles, 90

Bousquet, René, 93, 210n.68
Boyer, Charles, 56
Braucourt, Guy, 212n.25
Breathless. See *A bout de souffle*
Bresson, Robert, 21, 22
Bruno, Eduardo, 77
Buache, Freddy, 218n.28
Burch, Noel, 42
Burrin, Philippe, 68
Buss, Robin, 165, 166, 167, 185–86

Cachin, Françoise, 165
Cadé, Michel, 125–26
Cahiers du cinéma, Les, 214n.41, 221n.2
Camisards, Les, 21–22, 23, 100, 113
Camisard War, 21, 198n.53
Camus, Albert, 219n.38
Capdenac, Michel, 79
Capitaine Conan, 98, 100, 122, 123, 216n.69
Carax, Leos, 11, 159, 161, 163, 173, 177–82, 221n.2, 223n.48
Carné, Marcel, 11, 22, 159, 163, 164, 165, 166, 169, 174, 175, 223n.40, 223n.47. *See also* poetic realism; populism
Caro, Marc, 159, 184
Carrière, Jean-Claude, 198n.57
Casque d'Or, 111
Castoriadis, Cornelius, 149
Cayrol, Jean, 32, 34, 46, 200n.6
Cenci, Francesco, 215n.67
censorship, 35, 37, 49, 70, 210n.14, 219n.37
centurions, 141
Cerny, Philippe, 137
Ceux de chez nous, 17
Chabrol, Claude, 66, 86, 90
Chagrin et la pitié, Le, 13, 65, 69–73, 75, 76, 78, 82, 83, 91, 206nn. 6 and 16; and counterlegend of the Occupation, 65, 70–73, 126
Chantons sous l'Occupation, 90
Châtelet, François, 108
Chéreau, Patrice, 23
Chevalier, Louis, 224n.63
Children of Paradise. See *Enfants du paradis, Les*
Chirac, Jacques, 69, 210n.76
cinéma du look, 11, 159–63, 168–84 passim, 186–87, 221n.3
"cinema of quality," 99–100

Clair, René, 11, 159, 163, 165, 166, 167, 169, 172, 180, 183, 184, 187. *See also* populism
Clean Slate. See *Coup de torchon*
Clockmaker, The. See *L'horloger de Saint-Paul*
collaboration, 36, 70, 71, 73, 75, 88, 90. See also *Chagrin et la pitié, Le*; *Lacombe Lucien*; Vichy; Vichy syndrome
Collet, Jean, 221n.3
Colonel Chabert, Le, 23
Combe, Sonia, 26
Comes, Philippe de, 218n.28
Commune, 100, 101, 110–11, 115, 117, 118, 120, 156, 214n.38, 215n.62. See also *Juge et l'assassin, Le*
Communist Party, 7, 28, 20, 78, 107
Coppola, Francis Ford
Corneau, Alain, 23
Costa-Gavras, Constantin, 20
Coup de torchon, 120, 123
Crabe-tambour, Le, 10, 29, 30, 131, 132, 134, 136, 137–42, 150, 151, 155, 156, 158, 218n.28. See also Algerian War; Empire; military
Crime de M. Lange, Le, 100, 128, 166, 167, 169, 172, 182, 185
Cyrano, 23

Daney, Serge, 31
Daybreak. See *Jour se lève, Le*
Day for Night. See *Nuit américaine, La*
De Gaulle, Charles, 3, 13, 18, 27, 106, 190, 206nn. 11 and 19; and Algerian War, 49, 125, 133, 135, 137, 147; and anti-Semitism, 84–85, 208n.48; death of, 78–79; embodies French *grandeur*, 37; and resistancialism, 10, 36–37, 50, 66–68, 71
Deleuze, Gilles, 8, 186; and *gauchiste* mentality, 104, 212n.19; on Resnais's cinema, 31, 33, 41, 202n.26
Delicatessen, 159, 163, 169, 182–84, 224n.55
Demeure, Jacques, 102
Depardieu, Gérard, 176, 177
deportations, 54, 64, 73, 90, 92, 95, 207n.23, 209n.53; of children of Izieu, 89–90, 95; of Vel d'Hiv, 60, 93, 95, 210n.68. *See also* anti-Semitism; *Chagrin et la pitié, Le*; documentaries; *Hotel Terminus*; *Providence*
Dernier métro, Le, 9, 80–83, 87, 89, 91
Dien Bien Phu, 130

Dine, Philip, 8, 130, 134, 144, 216n.4
Diva, 11, 159, 163, 169–73, 175, 177, 180, 183, 184, 185, 222n.34
"*Diva* and French Socialism," 170, 172
documentaries, 90–91, 95
Dosse, François, 4
Drach, Michel, 20
drame algérien, le. *See* Algerian War
Dreyfus Affair, 52, 117, 204n.50; and anti-Semitism, 110, 118; apologies for, 210n.76; and intellectuals, 107, 109, 213n.30; and national divisions, 67, 109–10, 213n.37. *See also* anti-Semitism; *Juge et l'assassin, Le*
Drummer-Crab, The. See Crabe-tambour, Le
Duhamel, Alain, 26
Dumas, Alexandre, 100, 102
Duras, Marguerite, 4, 32, 43, 130, 200n.5
Duvivier, Julien, 165, 168

Eagleton, Terry, 179
Ellis, Jack, 164
Empire, 10, 46, 130–31, 133, 134, 137, 158. See also *Crabe-tambour, Le*; "Entre mémoire et histoire"; military; *Outremer*; pieds-noirs
Enfants du paradis, Les, 164
Enfants du Vel d'Hiv, Les, 90
Enfants gâtés, Les, 100
Engelbert, Manfred, 108–9
"Entre mémoire et histoire," 136, 151–58, 220n.59. *See also* memory; Nora, Pierre; site(s) of memory
Epstein, Anne-Monique, 207n.21
l'épuration. See purges
Erickson, Kai, 32, 200n.7
Escobar, Robert, 166
L'étranger, 219n.38
Evans, Martin, 140
événements, les. See May '68
Ezrahi, Sidra De Koven, 220n.57

Fabre-Luce, Alfred, 70
Faurisson, Robert, 85
Fehér, Ferenc, 191, 192
Femme Nikita, La, 159, 163, 169
Fermigier, André, 224n.63
Ferro, Marc, 11, 12, 72, 157, 196n.17, 207n.21
Film d'Art, 15, 15

Final Solution. *See* Holocaust
Finkielkraut, Alain, 201n.12, 209n.49, 225n.4
First World War. *See* World War I
Fofi, Goffredo, 168
Foucault, Michel, 18, 19, 68, 79, 112, 113, 116. See also *Juge et l'assassin, Le*; marginality; power
Français d'Algérie, Les, 144
France, 25–26; "a certain idea of," 3, 13, 18, 21–22, 24, 46, 106, 136, 151, 156, 190, 207n.20; and cinema, 6–7; divisions, 7, 9, 21, 23, 109–10; *grandeur/gloire* of, 4, 7, 17, 18, 23, 68, 69, 78, 101, 102; national identity, 3–4, 8, 24, 27–29, 135–36, 165, 188–89, 190–93
France raciste, La, 26
Frank, Robert, 133
Friedlander, Saul, 24
Front national, Le, 7, 110, 135, 218nn. 18 and 21. *See also* Le Pen, Jean-Marie; racism

Gabin, Jean, 164, 165, 168, 174, 175, 176, 177; and French identity, 165–66. *See also* populism
Gance, Abel, 17, 123, 166
Gangrène et l'oubli: la mémoire de la Guerre d'Algérie, La, 5
Garçon, François, 3
gauchiste climate, 9, 19–21. See also *Chagrin et la pitié, Le*; May '68; *Que la fête commence*
gauchiste thought, 102, 104, 109, 111, 123, 212n.19. *See also* Foucault, Michel; *Juge et l'assassin, Le*; marginality; power
Générique des années 30, 163
Genette, Gérald, 202n.24
Giacci, Vittorio, 166
Gildea, Robert, 157
Girardet, Raoul, 118; on political myths, 6, 7, 11, 12, 131, 139, 155, 156, 196nn. 14 and 21, 202n.20
Giraudoux, Jean, 56, 58
Godard, Jean-Luc, 49, 99, 112, 161–62, 163
golden age, 26, 135–36; in "Entre mémoire et histoire," 151–53, 155–58; of French cinema, 159, 163–68, 187; myth of, 7, 10, 11, 12, 26, 135–36, 196n.21
Grand bleu, Le, 224n.55
Grande Illusion, La, 126, 128, 166

Grenier, Richard, 81
Grosse fatigue, 192–93
Guernica, 62, 31, 41
Guerre sans nom, La, 101, 123, 125–27, 129, 130, 131, 134
Guibbert, Pierre, 17, 197n.34
Guitry, Sacha, 17, 18, 56, 57, 197n.39

Halimi, André, 90
Harcourt, Peter, 41, 201nn. 8 and 10, 202n.23
Hatot, Georges, 15, 197n.35
Havel, Václav, 29
Hayward, Susan, 162, 207n.31
Henriot, Philippe, 91
Hertzberg, Hendrik, 31
Higgins, Lynn, 8, 35, 45
Hiroshima mon amour, 8, 31, 32, 33, 34, 35, 38, 40, 42–46, 47, 52, 62, 200n.5, 201n.9
Hirsch, Arthur, 18
L'histoire de France au cinéma, 5, 8
Histoire des femmes, 66, 86–87, 90
l'histoire des mentalités, 9, 18, 20, 24, 25. See also *Annales* school; history; *mentalités*
history, 3, 4, 8, 138, 147, 151; acceleration of, 24, 25, 29, 152; after May '68, 18–20, 25; new social, 24, 98
Hoffmann, Stanley, 25, 70, 88, 89, 199n.66, 220–21n.67; on French identity, 28, 188; on intellectuals' role, 107, 213n.31; on Socialists' dilemma, 29, 172, 223n.38
Holocaust, 225n.4; and limits of representation, 34, 43, 201n.12; survivors of, 44, 220n.57; and Vichy complicity in, 35, 64, 93, 94
L'horloger de Saint-Paul, 98, 100, 104, 111, 211n.7, 212n.25
Horseman on the Roof, The. See *Hussard sur le toit, Le*
Hôtel du Nord, 164, 174, 175, 177, 180, 181, 223n.47
Hotel Terminus, 89, 90, 91
Hussard sur le toit, Le, 23
Huston, John, 100

ideology; crisis of, 29, 99, 106–8, 118, 213n.29
Images of the Algerian War: French Fiction and Film, 1954–1992, 8
Indochina, 130, 131, 132, 135, 136, 138, 139. See also *Crabe-tambour, Le*; Empire; military

Indochine, 130, 131
Infantino, Stephen, 183
I, Pierre Rivière, having killed my mother, my sister, and my brother. See *Moi, Pierre Rivière, ayant tué ma mère, ma soeur, et mon frère*
Ishaghpour, Youssef, 53, 58, 62, 63, 202n.25, 203n.38, 204n.58

J'accuse (Gance), 123
J'accuse (Zola), 109
Jameson, Frederic, 162, 170–71, 173, 223n.38
Jeancolas, Jean-Pierre, 69, 70, 216n.69
Jean de Hachette, 17, 22
Jeanne la Pucelle, 122
Je t'aime je t'aime, 33, 39, 201n.9
Jeunet, Jean-Pierre, 159, 184
Jewish memory, 65, 66, 83–85, 90
Jews, 84–86, 95, 209n.52; and Dreyfus Affair, 110, 215,n.53. See also anti-Semitism; *Au revoir les enfants*; deportations; *Lacombe Lucien*; *Stavisky*; Vichy
Joan of Arc, 15, 17, 21, 22, 101, 117, 122, 197n.33, 214n.52, 215n.53
Jour se lève, Le, 165, 166, 167, 168, 174, 187
Joutard, Philippe, 21, 16, 118, 198n.53
Judge and the Assassin, The. See *Juge et l'assassin, Le*
Judt, Tony, 68, 93, 210n.68
Juge et l'assassin, Le, 99, 101, 104, 109–20, 123, 214n.51
Julliard, Jacques, 130
July Fourteenth. See *Quatorze juillet, Le*

Kael, Pauline, 74, 88
Khilnani, Sunil, 106, 107
Kristeva, Julia, 32, 40, 62, 200n.5

Laborie, Pierre, 207n.23
La Bretèque, François de, 132, 141, 189
Lacombe Lucien, 9, 13, 20, 53, 65–66, 73–80, 86, 88, 207nn. 28 and 31
Lancelot du Lac, 20–21
Lang, Jack, 31, 198n.56
Langer, Lawrence, 44
Lanzmann, Claude, 69, 126, 201n.13
Lapierre, Nicole, 125
Lardeau, Yann, 82, 176
Last Metro, The. See *Dernier métro, Le*
Last Year at Marienbad. See *L'année dernière à Marienbad*

Laval, Pierre, 68, 72, 73

Leconte, Patrice, 23

Left, 7, 15, 27, 28, 49, 53, 67, 68, 70, 106, 107, 108, 213nn. 30 and 32, 214n.52; and Commune, 111; and Dreyfus Affair, 110, 117; and Stavisky Affair, 51, 52. See also *Diva*; *Juge et l'assassin, Le*; *Que la fête commence*

legendary narratives. *See* political myth(s)

Le Goff, Jacques, 11, 19, 20, 24, 29, 103, 122, 196n.22, 215n.66

Le Pen, Jean-Marie, 110, 135, 218nn. 20 and 21. See also *Front national, Le*; racism; xenophobia

Le Roy Ladurie, Emmanuel, 118, 215n.58

Let Joy Reign Supreme. See *Que la fête commence*

Levi, Primo, 220n.48

Lévy, Bernard-Henri, 190, 199n.75

Liazu, Claude, 136, 217n.11

lieu(x) de mémoire. *See* site(s) of memory

Lieux de mémoire, Les, 3, 4, 5, 24, 151

Life and Nothing But. See *Vie et rien d'autre, La*

Lover, The. See *L'amant*

Lovers of Pont-Neuf, The. See *Amants du Pont-Neuf, Les*

Lubitsch, Ernst, 56, 57

Lune dans le caniveau, La, 159, 163, 169, 173–77, 182, 185

Madral, Philippe, 188

Maffesoli, Michel, 224n.62

Maghrébin(s), 135, 149, 150, 157, 218n.20

Magretta, William and Joan, 212n.21

Malle, Louis, 9, 13, 20, 65, 66, 75, 76, 78, 80, 81, 86, 87, 88, 89, 207n.28, 208n.35

Malraux, André, 141, 190

Mardore, Michel, 187

marginality, 18, 19, 21, 112, 114, 115–16, 214n.49. *See also* Foucault, Michel; *Juge et l'assassin, Le*; power; *Que la fête commence*

Marin, Michel, 218n.28

Marseillaise, La, 100, 128, 168, 197n.37

Marxism, 28, 29, 108, 127

Matsuda, Matt, 117

May '68, 10, 12, 26, 28, 65, 69, 85, 106, 118, 197n.41, 198n.42, 199n.75; and film, 21–22, 78; and history, 18–19. See also *Chagrin et la pitié, Le*; *gauchiste* climate; *gauchiste* thought; *Que la fête commence*

Méliès, Georges, 15, 111, 122

Mélo, 33

memory, 131, 136; collective, 13, 20, 127–28; in "Entre mémoire et histoire"; institutions of, 41. *See also* site(s) of memory

Mendras, Henri, 25, 26, 106

Ménil, Alain, 201n.9

mentalités, 5, 20, 23, 24, 98, 102, 113, 123. See also *Annales* school; *l'histoire des mentalités*

Mercer, David, 59

Mermet, Gérard, 25

Michelet, Jules, 13, 14, 98, 191

Middle Ages, 21, 22, 98, 101, 122

Milice, 71, 75, 91, 92, 94, 95. *See also* collaboration; *Lacombe Lucien*; Vichy

military, 131, 133, 134, 136–38. See also Algerian War; *Crabe-tambour, Le*; Empire

Million, Le, 163, 167, 172, 174, 182, 183, 184, 185

Miracle des loups, Le, 17

Mitry, Jean, 175

Mitterand, François, 70, 209n.58; and Socialists' dilemma, 28, 29, 172, 223n.38; and Vichy past, 92–93, 94, 95, 210nn. 67 and 68

Moi, Pierre Rivière, ayant tué ma mère, ma soeur, et mon frère, 112, 116

Monaco, James, 53, 55, 58, 203n.33, 204n.61

Mongin, Olivier, 185, 224n.58

Moon in the Gutter, The. See *Lune dans le caniveau, La*

Morgan, Michèle, 163, 174

Mort de Robespierre, La, 15

Mouvement ouvrier, Le, 185

Muriel, 9, 31, 39, 40, 46–50, 60, 62, 63, 134, 201n.9

Muriel ou le temps d'un retour. See *Muriel*

Mythes et mythologies politiques, 6, 139

Napoleon, 15, 17, 21, 101, 197n.34

Napoléon, 17

National Revolution, 72, 75, 93

Navarre, Henri, 136

Nettelbeck, Colin, 82

New Novel, New Wave, New Politics: Fiction and the Representation of History in Postwar France, 8

New Wave, 20, 39, 51, 99, 100, 160, 161, 162, 163

Night and Fog, 8, 31, 32, 33, 34, 35, 37–38, 40, 41, 43, 44, 46, 48, 52, 62
Noiret, Philippe, 99
Nora, Pierre, 3, 4, 6, 7, 8, 10, 11, 13, 24, 25, 50, 136, 192, 195n.8, 213n.28; on contemporary memory, 151–58; on *L'étranger*, 219n.38; on *pied-noir* memory, 144–45, 146
Nuit américaine, La, 80, 81
Nuit et brouillard. See *Night and Fog*
Nye, Robert A., 118

Occupation. *See* Vichy
L'oeil de Vichy, 90
Oms, Marcel, 16, 111, 125, 214n.38
Ophuls, Marcel, 12, 13, 65, 69, 70, 71, 72, 73, 75, 83, 89, 126
d'Orléans, Philippe, 101, 102, 103, 105
Ory, Pascal, 73, 168
Outremer, 10, 29, 30, 131, 132, 136, 142–51, 155, 156, 158, 219n.44; and *L'amant*, 219n.47
Overseas. See *Outremer*

Papon, Maurice, 64, 66, 91, 95, 210n.75
Paris, 14; and Commune, 14, 110–11; and René Clair, 164–65; as site of memory, 177, 179–80; and urban changes, 185–86, 224nn. 63 and 65
Pascal, Christine, 108, 119
Passion Béatrice, La, 100, 101, 120–22, 123, 215nn. 64, 66, and 67, 216n.70
Past in French History, The, 157
patrie, la, 14, 110, 152, 156
patrimoine, 24, 165
Paxton, Robert, 67, 68, 206n.6, 209n.53
Péan, Pierre, 92, 93, 94
Pearls of the Crown. See *Perles de la couronne, Les*
Pépé le Moko, 165
Perceval le Gallois, 22
Perles de la couronne, Les, 17
Perrot, Michelle, 186
Pétain, Marshal Philippe, 49, 68, 71, 72, 82, 92, 93, 94, 206n.19
Petit soldat, Le, 49
Peurs françaises, Les, 26
Pfaff, William, 36
pieds-noirs, 133, 134, 216n.4; and collective memories, 131–32, 144–45, 150–51; and racism, 144–46, 148, 219n.38. *See also* Algerian War; Outremer

Pinto, Diana, 108, 213n.32
places of memory. *See* site(s) of memory
poetic realism, 167, 174–75
Poirot-Delpech, Bertrand, 69
political myth(s), 7, 8, 10, 11, 12, 36, 70, 96, 97, 151, 155, 196n.14, 201n.20; and cinema, 6, 132. *See also* golden age; resistancialism; Revolution; unity
Popular Front, 52, 67, 75, 107, 110, 128, 158, 169, 204n.50; and films of the 1930s, 166–68, 180, 181
populism, 166–68, 180, 185–86, 222nn. 24 and 25
Port of Shadows. See *Quai des brumes, Le*
Positif, 53, 214n.41
power, 18, 19, 21, 104–5, 109, 111, 114, 119, 121, 123. *See also* Foucault, Michel; *Juge et l'assassin, Le*; marginality; *Que la fête commence*
Prédal, René, 20, 31, 77, 159, 178, 200n.4, 206n.16, 223n.48
Prévert, Jacques, 22, 164, 167, 174, 211n.6
Prise du pouvoir de Louis XIV, La, 102, 212n.16
Prost, Antoine, 124
Proust, Marcel, 5, 30, 154
Providence, 9, 33, 59–62, 63, 205n.69
Pryce-Jones, David, 73
purges, 45, 63

Quai des brumes, Le, 163, 165, 167, 168, 174, 185, 187
Quatorze juillet, Le, 180, 181
Que la fête commence, 20, 98, 100, 101–9, 111, 115, 118, 119, 120, 122, 127, 128, 212nn. 16, 18, 21, and 25

racism, 134, 135, 140, 218nn. 19, 20, and 21; and *pieds-noirs*, 144, 145, 148–50
Rappenau, Jean-Paul, 23
Reader, Keith, 198n.42, 222n.25
Regency, 20, 25, 101, 106, 212n.25. See also *Que la fête commence*
Règle du jeu, La, 128
Reine Margot, La, 23
Remontons les Champs-Elysées, 17
Renan, Ernest, 14
Renoir, Jean, 11, 100, 159, 163, 165, 166, 167, 184, 187, 197n.37; and Tavernier, 126, 128

Resistance, 71, 72, 74, 75, 78, 79, 81, 88, 91, 92, 96, 137; myth of (*see* resistancialism)

resistancialism, 9, 10, 36–37, 50, 64, 66–68, 69, 71, 82, 89, 96, 126, 205n.2

Resnais, Alain, 8, 9, 12, 17, 20, 30, 31–40, 41–63 passim, 134, 201n.9, 203nn. 29 and 48

rétro films, 9, 10, 53, 63, 91, 96, 97, 98, 130, 131

rétro phenomenon, 65, 73

Retz, Gilles de, 122, 215n.67

Revolution, 7, 13, 25, 67, 107, 110, 213n.28; commemoration of, 165, 190; and film(s), 17, 21, 100, 101, 118, 128; and Jews, 84, 92; myth of, 10, 30, 120. See also *Juge et l'assassin, Le*; *Que la fête commence*

Ridicule, 23

Right, 7, 15, 27, 50, 67, 70, 107, 128, 171; and Dreyfus Affair, 110, 117; and Stavisky Affair, 51–52, 53, 204n.59; and Vichy, 37, 68, 79

Rioux, Jean-Pierre, 222n.33

Rise to Power of Louis XIV, The. See *Prise du pouvoir de Louis XIV, La*

Rivette, Jacques, 122

Robbe-Grillet, Alain, 32

Roche, Anne, 145, 146, 149, 150, 219n.39

Rohmer, Eric, 22

Ropars-Wuilleumier, Marie-Claire, 49

Rosenzweig, Luc, 94

Ross, George, 199n.77, 213n.30

Rossellini, Roberto, 102

Roth, Michael, 31, 44

Rotman, Patrick, 125, 127

Roüan, Brigitte, 10, 131–32, 142, 143, 147, 217n.5

Roue, La, 166

Rouget de Lisle chantant la Marseillaise, 15

Round Midnight. See *Autour de minuit*

Rousso, Henry, 5, 6, 35, 45, 66, 67, 70, 71, 72, 86, 206n.6, 207n.20; on Jewish memory, 83, 85; on resistancialism, 36, 37, 205n.2; on Vichy syndrome, 64, 206n.7

Royal Affairs of Versailles. See *Si Versailles m'était conté*

Rules of the Game. See *Règle du jeu, La*

Ruscio, Alain, 136

Sacred Union, 16, 46

Sade, Marquis de, 122

St. Bartholomew's Day Massacre, 16, 23

St. Simon, duke of, 102, 105

Samson, Pierre, 53

Sartre, Jean-Paul, 107, 213n.31

Sauvage, Pierre, 90

Schmitt, Jean-Claude, 19

Schoendoerffer, Pierre, 10, 130, 131, 132, 137, 138, 139, 140, 143, 191, 217n.6

Section spéciale, 20

Self-Made Hero, A. See *Un héros très discret*

Semprun, Jorge, 50, 53

Shakespeare, William, 58

Shoah, 69, 126, 201n.13

Shoot the Piano Player. See *Tirez sur le pianiste*

Siclier, Jacques, 148, 218n.28, 219n.44

Sineux, Michel, 105, 214n.52

site(s) of memory, 4, 24, 111, 177, 179–80, 186–87, 192; and cinema, 13, 30, 159. See also *Amants du Pont-Neuf, Les*; Bastille Day; *Bibliothèque nationale*; "Entre mémoire et histoire"; Paris; Tomb of the Unknown Soldier; Verdun; *Vie et rien d'autre, La*

Si Versailles m'était conté, 17

Slama, Alain-Gérard, 135

Socialists, 190; and dilemmas of the 1980s, 28–29, 30, 171–72, 213n.32, 223n.38; "divorce" from intellectuals, 107–8; and Mitterand's past, 93. See also *Diva*; *Juge et l'assassin, Le*

Sorrow and the Pity, The. See *Chagrin et la pitié, Le*

Sous les toits de Paris, 172, 182

Spanish Civil War, 31, 55

Spoiled Children. See *Enfants gâtés, Les*

Stavisky, 9, 20, 33, 40, 50–59, 60, 62

Stavisky, Serge Alexandre, 51, 52, 53, 204n.58

Stavisky Affair, 51–52. See also *Stavisky*

Statues Also Die. See *Statues meurent aussi, Les*

Statues meurent aussi, Les, 35, 40

Stora, Benjamin, 5, 133, 135, 144, 151, 157, 217n.13, 219n.37

Story of a Cheat, The, 56

Story of Women. See *Histoire des femmes*

Subway, 162, 223n.40

Sunday in the Country, A. See *Un dimanche à la campagne*

Talbott, John, 150
Tanner, Alain, 187–88
Tavernier, Bertrand, 5, 10, 12, 20, 29, 98–
    101, 101–29 passim, 130, 134, 191,
    211nn. 3, 5, 6, and 11, 215n.63; and
    counterportrait of French past, 98, 109,
    110, 121, 122, 127
Thirard, Paul-Louis, 53
Third Republic, 14, 57; as "golden age,"
    151, 153, 156; and use of history, 15, 19
Tirez sur le pianiste, 161
Tiso, Ciriaco, 77
Tomb of the Unknown Soldier, 124
Toni, 128, 166
Tournoi, Le, 197n.37
Tous les matins du monde, 23
Toute la mémoire du monde, 33, 40, 41–42,
    50, 203nn. 32 and 33
Touvier, Paul, 91, 92, 94, 95
Trauner, Alexandre, 175, 223nn. 40 and 47
Trotsky, Leon, 53, 54, 55, 204n.58
Truffaut, François, 9, 17, 66, 80, 81, 82, 83,
    90, 99, 161, 163
Turk, Edward Baron, 175

Un dimanche à la campagne, 98, 100
Une jeunesse française: François Mitterand, 92
Ungar, Steven, 204n.60
Un héros très discret, 96–97
unity, myth of, 7, 9, 10, 21, 111, 156; and re-
    sistancialism, 66, 89

Vacher, Joseph, 113, 117
Van Damne, Charlie, 188
Van Gogh, 31
Verdun, 124
Vichy, 5, 6, 8, 9, 31, 34, 69, 90, 107, 110,
    204n.50; and controversies about, 91–94,
    209n.58; internal struggles of, 45, 49, 66–
    67, 71, 82; and Jews, 84–86, 92, 93, 94,
    209n.53; memories of, 35–37, 64–68, 79,
    83, 125, 206nn. 6 and 7; recent attitudes
    toward, 94–97. See also années noires, les;
anti-Semitism; collaboration; deporta-
    tions; Jews; purges
Vichy syndrome, 64, 65, 79, 91, 94, 96–97
Vichy Syndrome: History and Memory in
    France since 1944, The, 36, 64
Vie est à nous, La, 128
Vie et rien d'autre, La, 100, 122, 123–25,
    216n.70
Vierny, Sacha, 204n.61
Vietnam War, 139, 141, 196n.19, 217n.6;
    and Algerian War, 125, 127, 134, 217n.9
Vigo, Jean, 159, 163, 165, 166, 177, 178
Vincendau, Ginette, 164, 166, 168,
    211n.5
Violons du bal, Les, 20
Visiteurs du soir, Les, 22
Voie royale, La, 141

Walk with Love and Death, A, 100
Wargnier, Régis, 130
Weapons of the Spirit, 90
Weber, Eugen, 52, 58, 204n.59
Whitney, Craig, 217n.17
Wieviorka, Michel, 26
Wilkinson, James, 5, 9
Winock, Michel, 15, 16, 27, 52, 106,
    197n.33, 205n.5, 206n.11, 215n.62; on
    contemporary sense of national crisis, 30,
    190; on Dreyfus Affair, 109, 110, 118,
    213n.37, 215n.53
Wood, Nancy, 195n.7
World War I, 16, 27, 36, 100, 123, 124
World War II, 35, 36, 46, 60, 107, 127

xenophobia, 27, 53, 67, 72, 92, 110, 111,
    135, 136

Yanne, Josée, 90

Z, 53
Zecca, Ferdinand, 197n.35
Zimmer, Christian, 79
Zola, Emile, 107, 109, 117, 166